D. H. Lawrence
Future Primitive

D. H. Lawrence

Future Primitive

Dolores LaChapelle

Introduction by Thomas J. Lyon

Volume 5
Philosophy and the Environment

University of North Texas Press
Denton, Texas

10 9 8 7 6 5 4 3 2 1

Requests for permission to reproduce material from this work should be sent to:

Permissions
University of North Texas Press
PO Box 13856
Denton TX 76203

The paper used in this book meets the minimum requirements of the American National Standard for Permanence of Paper for Printed Library Materials, Z39.48-1984. Binding materials have been chosen for durability.

I wish to thank Viking Penguin for permission to reprint two poems by D. H. Lawrence: "Bavarian Gentians" by D. H. Lawrence, "Manifesto," from *The Complete Poems of D. H. Lawrence* by D. H. Lawrence, edited by V. de Sola Pinto & F. W. Roberts. Copyright © 1964, 1971 by Angelo Ravagli and C. M. Weekley, Executors of the Estate of Frieda Lawrence Ravagli. Used by Permission of Viking Penguin, a division of Penguin Books USA Inc.

Library of Congress Cataloging-in-publication Data

LaChapelle, Dolores
D. H. Lawrence : future primitive / by Dolores LaChapelle ; introduction by Thomas J. Lyon.
p.   cm. — (Philosophy and the environment series ; no. 5)
Includes bibliographical references.
ISBN 1-57441-007-5
1. Lawrence, D. H. (David Herbert), 1885–1930—Knowledge—Natural history. 2. Environmental protection—Great Britain—History. 3. Environmental protection in literature. 4. Human ecology in literature. 5. Primitivism in literature. 6. Landscape in literature. 7. Nature in literature. I. Title. II. Series: Philosophy and the environment series ; v. 5.
PR6023.A93Z6396   1996   95–51087
823' .912—dc20   CIP

Cover design by Amy Layton

"Here, on this little ranch under the Rocky Mountains, a big pine tree rises like a guardian spirit in front of the cabin where we live . . . I have become conscious of the tree, and of its interpenetration into my life. . . . I am conscious that it helps to change me, vitally. . . .

Of course, if I like to cut myself off, and say it is all bunk, a tree is merely so much lumber not yet sawn, then in a great measure I shall be cut off. So much depends on one's attitude. One can shut many, many doors of receptivity in oneself; or one can open many doors that are shut.

I prefer to open my doors to the coming of the tree. Its raw earth-power and its raw sky-power, its resinous erectness and resistance, its sharpness of hissing needles and relentlessness of roots, all that goes to the primitive savageness of a pine tree, goes also to the strength of man.

Give me of your power, then, oh tree! And I will give you of mine."

—D. H. Lawrence in "Pan in America"

Contents

Preface

"Central between the flash of day and the black of night. . . . The mystery of the evening-star brilliant in silence and distance between the downward-surging plunge of the sun and the vast, hollow seething of inpouring night. The magnificence of the watchful morning-star, that watches between the night and the day, the gleaming clue to the two opposites." I thrilled to these words of D. H. Lawrence when I found them just as I was completing the manuscript for my first book, *Earth Festivals*. This was the lyrical description I needed for the powerful planet Venus, the Morning Star which stands between the darkness of night and the light of day and only appears in full glory when night and day are in a balanced relationship.

Some months after finding this brief passage I read the book it came from, *The Plumed Serpent*, with its underlying theme best expressed by the heroine, Kate: "No! It's not a helpless, panic reversal. It is conscious, carefully chosen. We must go back to pick up old threads. We must take up the old broken impulse that will connect us with the mystery of the cosmos again, now we are at the end of our tether."

I wondered how this lower class Englishman, son of a coal-miner, could know such things way back in the 1920s. Curious, I read everything Lawrence wrote and found many gems which I have used in rituals in natural settings throughout the years and passed on to others all over the country. Through the years, when I spoke of Lawrence during lectures or workshops, people would ask me to categorize his work, but none of the usual academic labels seemed to fit. They have tried to confine Lawrence within literary genres such as: a Georgian poet, an imagist, a vitalist, a follower of the French symbolistes, a romantic or a transcendentalist.

Browsing in an old issue of *CoEvolution Quarterly*, I found "Future Primitive," the name of an article by the internationally renowned ecologist and biogeographer, Raymond Dasmann, senior ecologist at the International Union for the Conservation of Nature at Morges, Switzerland. The article was a paper given at a conference in New

Zealand and first printed in the British journal, *The Ecologist*. It was erudite and scholarly but Dasmann's conclusion encompassed all that and much more when he stated: "I cannot see much hope for the future of either parks or people, unless some of the old sense of belonging to the natural world, of being a part of nature, and not hostile to it is restored. In an article prepared for *Planet Drum*, Jerry Gorsline and Linn House have made this comparison," and he quotes a large section from it beginning with: "We have been awakened to the richness and complexity of the primitive mind which merges sanctity, food, life and death—where culture is integrated and employs for its cognition a body of metaphor drawn from and structured in relation to that ecosystem." This is precisely what D. H. Lawrence lived and wrote about so long ago and now I had a name for it. Toward the end of his speech, Dasmann said: "I would propose that the answer for nature conservation in the South Pacific as elsewhere, will be found to lie in the direction of "Future Primitive."[1]

Foremost throughout Lawrence's entire life was his intense relationship with nature. Two other basic influences on him were tuberculosis and the mining culture where he grew up. In reading biographies of Lawrence I found that most of the authors had no real understanding of either of these factors; while my own life had provided me with living insight into their effects on Lawrence. In 1925 (Lawrence died in 1930) my father, then an enlisted man in the U.S. Army, was diagnosed as having tuberculosis and shipped back from the Phillipines to Fitzsimmons General Hospital, located in Denver, Colorado, because high altitude was considered helpful in treating the disease. In those days there were no drugs to cure TB. Some of my father's close friends were also former patients. Because I grew up among these men I felt it amusing to read the accounts of some literary critics as to how tuberculosis affected Lawrence. My father and his friends were not the querulous, angry, fearful men which these critics claim tuberculosis produces. Rather, they were full of life, too full of emotion and laughter to allow them to recover easily through the only means then available—total bed rest. Many of them were released from the hospital with seriously damaged lungs. I remember how they turned aside to spit blood into the tobacco tins, which most of them carried for that purpose. But then they turned back to the conversation, just as full of life as ever. In some accounts of Lawrence's life there is horrified mention of his spitting up blood; however this was an accepted occurrence in the daily life of those afflicted with tuberculosis. Much later in my life I spent a winter in Davos, Switzerland, where my husband was doing research at the Swiss Avalanche Institute. Countries such as England and the Netherlands had TB sanitariums there because of the high altitude. Any time of the day that I walked by these buildings I heard the laughter of patients from their rooms or from the sun porches. Of course they had bad days, too, but generally, the major problem that tuberculosis patients have is intense living.

Living in the last "hard rock mining town" in Colorado—Silverton—has helped me understand Lawrence's mining town background and his father's life among his "mates." There is something of that miner's "tribal life" to this day in Silverton. It's the intensity of life and death underground which bonds the men together.

Lawrence's simple, work-filled life seems to provide little foundation for the scandal-oriented stories and the vituperation which surrounds his name. But, as his friend Richard Adlington explained, Lawrence had offended the leading intellectuals of England and they never forgave him.

Aldous Huxley was Lawrence's closest friend during the latter part of his life. During an interview on the BBC in 1961, Huxley told about how fascinating Lawrence's reactions to nature were and how it was always "a great pleasure to go for a walk with Lawrence. The way he perceived the world—so intense, and exciting."[2] Huxley continued by quoting Vernon Lee, who said that Lawrence "sees more than a human being ought to see."[3]

Perhaps the worst sin of all in the eyes of the intellectual leaders of England was that Lawrence took nature seriously. The same theme runs through all his work from his very first novel, *The White Peacock*, to the last line in his final book, *Apocalypse*. Always it is nature. He said this over and over again—in letters and essays—and no one understood him. In his work on Hardy, never published until after his death, he asks the question: "What is the real hero of Hardy's book, *Return of the Native*?" He answers that it is Egdon Heath itself, the "primitive, primal earth. . . . Here is the deep, black source from whence all these little contents of lives are drawn."[4] Always, Lawrence sought to elaborate on possible ways to regain the wholeness with the earth that our modern industrial culture was losing. This is not going back; it is living as a "future primitive," now. In his poem, "Reach Out," Lawrence addresses the men of the "old ways" in these words: "I have come back to you, for I never left you."[5]

Life in all its aspects and life to its fullest was what mattered most to Lawrence. Adlington wrote: "Of all human beings I have known, he was by far the most continuously and vividly alive and receptive."[6] Lawrence's great commandment was "Thou shalt acknowledge the wonder."[7]

In a recent issue of the *Environmental Review*, Del Janik explains that "Lawrence was a revolutionary writer. His novels are filled with contempt for modern industrial civilization and permeated by a desire to change it. . . . In his later works he offered hints toward a restructuring of human society based on a recognition that man is not, after all, the measure of the universe. That his name has been invoked and his ideas have been echoed so often by writers who came to share his post-humanistic philosophy, from William Carlos Williams . . . to Gary Snyder, is evidence that Lawrence stood at the beginning of the development of a new environmental consciousness in literature."[8]

I share with you not only what Lawrence found in his life-long relationship to the earth but also tell of the incredible villification and persecution which came to him from those who, for whatever religious, political, economic or intellectual reasons, feared the "old ways" of harmonious and balanced living on the earth.

Dolores LaChapelle
Way of the Mountain Learning Center
Silverton, Colorado

D. H. Lawrence, Dolores LaChapelle, and the Wholeness of Things

Another book on D. H. Lawrence? He is already "the most frequently studied English novelist of the twentieth century," in the 1984 assessment of scholar Alastair Niven. A veritable industry, including an academic journal addressed solely to his work, has grown up around Lawrence's ideas, his way of writing, his life. Why should we pay attention to what Dolores LaChapelle has to say about him? She is not, professionally speaking, a literary critic or biographer, and furthermore doesn't put herself forward as a Lawrence specialist, in the academic sense. But she has met Lawrence, so I believe, on his home ground, and has seen that ground clearly because of her own experience. She reads him familiarly. Working from a critical viewpoint broader than what we have come to expect, in our specialized time, from literary professionals, she nevertheless offers a sharply focused supposition of her subject's inward life. She has something new to say about Lawrence. The newness, though, is not so much in detail added but in a power to make us rethink the entire way we have looked at Lawrence, or literature in general—or perhaps the very world. LaChapelle's starting point is not that of the Western philosophical majority. She simply does not accept the dualistic and "objective" intellectual assumptions that drive the world-dominant industrial society, the assumptions so neatly codified by René Descartes in the early seventeenth century: "I think, therefore I am." To LaChapelle, this is a fragment talking, not a whole human being. She begins from a post-Cartesian position, and so, she says, did Lawrence. Her study, built on close reading and a rangy intuition, sets forth the evidence that in order to understand Lawrence well and truly, one must step with him beyond the tamed, modern mentality.

Dolores LaChapelle is a self-taught scholar with a strong sensitivity to natural surroundings. What most of us distantly call "the environment," she feels as the constant shaper of her life and thoughts. In 1957, as she writes in her recent book, *Deep Powder Snow* (Durango, CO: Kivaki Books, 1993), she began spending summers at the edge of a glacier in the Olympic Mountains of Washington, in a high camp set up by glaciologists. She was the camp cook but had time to roam and to read. Among the books she brought to camp was George Seidel's *Martin Heidegger and the Pre-Socratics*.

> When I began reading it, I discovered that the sections Seidel found most difficult in Heidegger's thinking, I found the clearest. Seidel had a Christian orientation, and it seemed to me that his difficulties came from trying to fit Heidegger into a Christian system. Since I was in a location far from either the academic or the Christian world, I was much closer to Being and saw more clearly what Heidegger was attempting in his thinking. Heidegger himself, during his quest for Being, spent a great deal of time at Todtnauberg, his retreat on a mountain. (p. 44)

The key is place. A wild place is most effective, and best of all, according to LaChapelle, is a wild *mountain* place. We absorb not specific ideas so much as capacity, scope, depth. When nature is the reference, the daily ambience, and when we are actively in contact with nature, moving and working thus with Being, we think differently. In her published remarks on Heidegger, Jung, Nietzsche, and any number of other contemplators of the human condition, including D. H. Lawrence, LaChapelle's method is essentially thus: live close to the mountain, to Being, and then when you pick up another's book, listen for the authentic note. Look closely to see if the writer has truly been there, *been someplace*. A place is a particular, touchable manifestation of the totality.

The standard, then, is health (wholeness)—perceived by a vulnerable, discovering, seeing mind. Real knowledge comes from this ultimate source, and is inherently physical, emotional, moral, intellectual, and spiritual. All of these, and all at once. Disembodied, dualistic knowledge is a kind of lie. "For us to be in the world validly," LaChapelle writes, "it's not laid out for us like a straight road, but is shown forth by the relationship discovered anew at every step as we move along our path in the world and among the others of the fourfold: the earth, the sky, and the gods."

According to some of his acquaintances, D. H. Lawrence could be quarrelsome, mercurial, ungrateful, and peremptory. Others have described him as gentle and understanding, cooperative and hard-working. With this Lawrence of the differing personal descriptions— the social Lawrence, that is—Dolores LaChapelle has small concern. She is drawn instead to the Lawrence of the moment of pure perception, the Lawrence who listened to his body and his intuition, the Lawrence whose best seeing transcended the social self and the calculating mentality. This is the Lawrence who wrote the books that have moved us. This man could see the passing daily reality under the sign of the eternal, certainly, but unlike many in the Western mystical tradition, had no wish for a bodiless, purely "spiritual" bliss. He was as located and as engaged as Henry David Thoreau, and he delighted, as Thoreau did, in the materiality of life. "He always took a big part in domestic work, infusing into it a special relish, and illuminating with a superrational quality the most menial thing," wrote a friend, Rosalind Thornycroft Popham. His intense connectedness and passionate response to things in turn seemed to elevate life for many of those around him: Achsah Barlow Brewster, a longtime friend, wrote simply that "Springtime seemed much more springtime because he was there." The detail and physicality of his writing, the amazingly strong sense of reality and presence, flow from the center, the connection. Otherwise we wouldn't be reading him still. In social life, like all of us, he may have seemed this or that. But the essence lies deeper, and Lawrence's genius lay in his ability to communicate essence. The ash tree outside the Morels' home, in *Sons and Lovers*, moving in the wind as the living being it is, doesn't just awaken *ideas* of childhood, family, fleeting and tender life—as movingly described by Lawrence, the tree takes us into these realities in their original oneness, into the very event of perception.

Dolores LaChapelle's own located life generates her insights into Lawrence. Again and again, in *Earth Wisdom* and in *Sacred Land Sacred* xvi

Sex, Rapture of the Deep (her major books before this one), it is place that guides, place that reveals. The place where one dwells is the concrete reality, coming before all talk of philosophy, before all ideas, before thinking itself. It is place, felt in this manner, that allows LaChapelle into Lawrence's world. And it is this participation that most decisively distinguishes her from the academicians. As did Lawrence (and Thoreau, again), she grieves over the loss of place brought about by the economics of the industrial growth society. The world in which a mountain stood wild and had its full being was trembling with sacred potential: a human being could realize that mountain, could transcend the limited sense of self through whose perceptual filters the mountain had seemed likewise separate and alone. Such a possibility of transcendence animated the old world and the old way, and was kept alive by the traditions of thousands of human generations. The modern way, without a second thought, puts a microwave tower on top of the mountain. This is the fatal mark of the human ego, and it destroys the deeper life of place, a very serious loss. Perhaps it is the greatest loss possible. In 1926, less than four years before his death, Lawrence revisited his home country in Nottinghamshire:

> This countryside is dead: or so inert, it is as good as dead. The old sheep-bridge where I used to swing as a boy is now an iron affair. The brook where we caught minnows now runs on a concrete bed. The old sheep-dip, the dipping-hole, as we called it, where we bathed, has somehow disappeared, so has the mill-dam and the little water-fall. It's all a concrete arrangement now, like a sewer. ("Autobiographical Fragment," in Edward D. McDonald, editor, *Phoenix: The Posthumous Papers of D. H. Lawrence*. London: William Heinemann, 1961. p. 822.)

Lawrence began his most famous novel, *Lady Chatterley's Lover*, within a few weeks of this visit. As Alastair Niven has pointed out, "*Lady Chatterley's Lover* is a cry of lamentation for disappearing England." It is also, of course, one of the great affirmations of human sexuality. The genius of Dolores LaChapelle, so I believe, is to see that the place-dimension and the sex-dimension go together profoundly. Awakened natures like Whitman's, or Lawrence's, or LaChapelle's, see in sexual love primary evidence for the coherence of existence. We are exactly what we are, biologically and spiritually, and first of all we are *here*. The cool, distanced Cartesian mind is not here; it sees life in fragments, therefore abuses place and sex, and the other animals, and indeed all of once-sacred life, with the self-same mechanical indifference. It was that mechanical indifference that drove Lawrence wild. As he was about place, he was in the highest sense passionate about sex. "Sex for him was the sacred symbol of life," wrote Franz Schoenberner. Lawrence's earnest depiction of sex is the very antithesis of pornography. In this area, LaChapelle's background in Taoist studies may have helped give her insight. But her findings are not to be seen, I think, as an application of a paradigm. Taoism, after all, is simply another manifestation of the tradition of wholeness. Lawrence was not a Taoist, or any other kind of -ist, and LaChapelle is similarly non-programmatic. What they both work from, and wish from the heart to preserve somehow, is the birthright continuity of our species with the living, real world.

Much has been written recently about "eco-criticism," the application of ecological principles to literary texts. Most fundamentally, it would seem, an eco-critic should see the world relationally, should start from a perception analogous to the systems theory of ecologists. Without this basic shift in mentality, a transcendence of the dualistic way of seeing most of us carry through life, eco-criticism will be a mechanical, surface thing, destined to join other critical movements in the academic landfills. To see, as here, a writer fearlessly take a stand in literal place, declare herself with emotional sincerity, join another writer at his essence, and then argue for the natural as a revivable human ideal, is exhilarating. It makes me, for one, believe again that literature, and criticism as well, might be redeeming.

Thomas J. Lyon
Logan, Utah

"Future Primitive"

As I walk over the hill I'm paying attention to the trees and the ground. The river comes into view and suddenly I'm stunned by the realization that I am not the same person who started the walk! I am transformed by a ceremony residing in the land itself. The place dictates the mandate for human activities there and that mandate can be perceived directly through a ceremony that lives in the woods like an almost tangible creature. I am transformed, transfixed. . . . We have been awakened to the richness and complexity of the primitive mind which merges sanctity, food, life and death—where culture is integrated with nature at the level of the *particular ecosystem* and employs for its cognition a body of metaphor drawn from and structured in relation to the ecosystem. We have found therein a mode of thinking parallel to modern science but operating at the entirely different level of sensible intuition; a tradition that prepared the ground for the Neolithic revolution; a science of the *concrete*, where nature is the model for culture because the mind has been nourished and weaned on nature; a logic that recognizes soil fertility, the magic of animals, the continuum of mind between species. Successful culture is a semi-permeable membrane between man and nature. We are witnessing North America's post-industrial phase right now, during which human society strives to remain predominant over nature. No mere extrapolation from present to future seems possible. We are in transition from one condition of symbiotic balance—the primitive—to another which we call the *future primitive* . . . a condition having the attributes of a mature ecosystem: stable, diverse, in symbiotic balance again . . . a community of beings joined by rim and basin, air and watershed, food chains—ceremonies. . . . We will be informed by earthworms and plankton. We will study that authority which resides in place and act out our lives accordingly. There is no separate existence.

—Jeremiah Gorsline and Freeman House

(First published as one of the pieces in *Planet Drum*'s Bundle #3 "North Pacific Rim Alive," 1974. *Planet Drum* originally put out bundles rather than books. Planet Drum Foundation, Box 31251, San Francisco, CA 94131)

1

Growing Up Near Sherwood Forest

Beside the path lies the old quarry, part of it very old and deep
and filled in with oak trees and guelder-rose and tangles of briars
. . . . In the soft, still afternoon I found the quarry not very much
changed. The red berries shone quietly on the briars. And in this
still, warm, secret place of the earth I felt my old childish longing
to pass through a gate, into a deeper, sunnier, more silent world.[1]
—D. H. Lawrence, after his last visit to his home town in
1927, three years before his death.

D. H. Lawrence's grandfather was a tailor who came from the
south of England into Nottinghamshire in the middle of the
nineteenth century to make the heavy pit clothes which the men
wore when working underground in the Brinsley mine. His home
was a small cottage in an old quarry-bed near the mine-pit.

A mile from the quarry was the town of Eastwood, where the
company built housing for the miners.[2] Here, in Eastwood, Lawrence
was born in 1885. The town is only a mile from the Erewash, the
stream which divides Nottinghamshire from Derbyshire. This is the
country of Sherwood Forest, the site in medieval times of the
legendary Robin Hood and still earlier, in the pre-Roman era, of the
Druids.[3] Lawrence and his young friends "with permission" could
enter the woods and climb up the long hill "under the splendid oak

1

and ash, elm and beech and alder, to Robin Hood's Well and Maid Marian's Dancing Green."[4]

But the quarry itself was young Lawrence's secret childhood place.[5] Each year the "briars" growing there furnished him with the first luscious blackberries of the season which he took proudly home to his mother. Later he wrote that these blackberries had given him "the joy of finding something, the joy of accepting something straight from the hand of Nature, and the joy of contributing to the family exchequer." He "scoured the coppices and wood and old quarries, so long as a blackberry was to be found . . . he could not bear to go home to his mother empty. That, he felt, would disappoint her, and he would have died rather."[6]

The first poems he ever wrote were named for the flowers which grew in the quarry: "Campions" and "Guelder Roses." In "Guelder Roses" he contrasts the dreamy beauty and purity of the guelder roses, gone at the end of the spring day, with the "glow of immortal fruit/Heavy nodding clusters of crimson red" which come, not from the "stems of virginity," but from the life-loving, careless briars. Even in "Campions," he refers to the guelder roses as "too chaste and pure."[7] Very near the end of his life, in his last novel, *Lady Chatterley's Lover*, Lawrence wrote again of guelder roses. They are growing round the keeper's hut. When Connie Chatterley arrives at the hut and sees the guelder roses, the red oaks, and the tangle of bramble, she muses that perhaps this was one of the few "unravished places" left in the whole world.

When Lawrence left England after the war, he traveled and lived on many different continents until finally, near the end of his life, he returned for a brief visit to his native countryside. Disgusted and revolted both by the ugliness imposed on the land by the enlarged modern mines and by the grimy brick houses of the sooty towns, he once again took the old foot path up to the quarry. Seeing it again, he wrote: "I felt as I had always felt, there was something there." Hearing a sudden rock fall, he found that it exposed a vug of quartz within the rock, glittering in the sun. It fascinated him and he had to climb into the tiny cave which he found to be warm, "as if the shiny rock were warm and alive, and it seemed to me there was a strange perfume, of rock, of living rock like hard, bright flesh, faintly perfumed with phlox." He felt safe, and wrote that "the world doesn't exist for me." In a reverie, a different world appeared to him. Later, he wrote down this dream fantasy, but it was not published until 1936, some years after his death.[9]

When he was a child, he heard the legend that the little caves in the quarry rock were "everlasting wells," similar to the wells at Matlock. At the time he thought it meant that whatever was put into the cave—an apple or a flower—would not die but would be everlasting. When he grew up and went to Matlock, he saw that the dripping water deposited a stony crust on everything and thus petrified it. He then realized that the object was no longer truly alive but, in spite of this, the original childish idea of "everlasting" life in such a place stayed with him throughout his life. It became part of the dream fantasy, "An Autobiographical Fragment," in which he wrote that he fell asleep and then came awake very, very slowly, finding it difficult to regain full consciousness. In this half-conscious state, he found that he was still at the quarry but he was being helped up and out by two men who had found him. When he looked out he saw only gentle rolling park-like hills with clumps of trees and no sign of human habitation; yet it was all well cared for. The men led him to their town of soft yellow stone. There were no sharp edges; it was all curves. Long ago Eastwood had seemed like this to him when the afternoon light was glowing on it and he had wished it were the golden city of Jerusalem. There was a great stillness and yet a feeling of closeness with everyone and everything within the town in his dream fantasy. The people were either beautifully naked like "berries on a bush" or clothed in soft flowing short mantles.

In Lawrence's dream fantasy he looked from the town over a different Sherwood Forest: it had once again become the enormous dense forest it had been in the Druid times. The sun was just touching the tops of the trees and the people all gathered, dancing softly and moving intricately. "The thing happened by instinct, like the wheeling and flashing of a school of fish or of a flock of birds dipping and spreading in the sky." They were ritually dancing the sun down. Once it was down, they all left. He was fed and clothed with "an instinctive calmness and dignity everywhere, in every moment." But when he is brought before the leader he finds that it is the year 2927, and he had gone to sleep in October, 1927. Although he is frightened at first, the leader explains that he went to sleep in a chrysalis womb of the earth and woke up like a butterfly. When he asks how long he will live, the leader asks him why should he measure it, since "life is not a clock." Just at this point the written fragment ends.

Although this "Autobiographical Fragment" was written very late in Lawrence's life, the rocks of that old quarry still moved him, deep within the unconscious depths of his being. Lawrence fully realized that the power of his writing came directly from his unconscious; therefore he never wanted to analyze these "dark gods" within. He left that to others, such as C. G. Jung, whose ideas he heard discussed but whom he steadfastly refused to read. As a matter of fact, Jung had a remarkably similar, deeply-felt experience among rocks when he was very young. Because Jung spent his life mapping the unconscious, and particularly the effects of early childhood experiences, it is useful to take a look at his experience with rocks because it sheds further light on Lawrence's development.

From the time Jung was seven years old until he was nine, he played in some small caves between the large blocks of stone making up an old wall which surrounded the family garden. There was a particular rock which protruded from the slope just in front of this wall. Here, Jung often sat alone, playing an imaginary game where sometimes he became the rock and other times the rock became him. Thirty years later, now a married man with children of his own and a successful career, he returned to his childhood home and stood on that slope. Immediately, he was a child again and his life in Zurich seemed alien and far away: "For the world of my childhood in which I had just become absorbed was *eternal* and I had been wrenched away from it. . . . The pull of that other world was so strong that I had to tear myself violently from the spot in order not to lose hold."[10] Lawrence wrote in very much the same way when he returned to the rock cavern of his childhood. As mentioned above, he noted that he felt safe and apart from the influences of "the world."

Lawrence began writing full time in 1912 when he began his

novel, *The Sisters*. At about the same time C. G. Jung was undergoing
the ordeal of his first explorations of the unconscious. Jung went
through a long period of turmoil during which he had a series of
dreams which he was afraid to explore because he feared that he
might "become a prey to the fantasies." Finally, in December, 1913,
he overcame these fears and plunged into the attempt to understand
the unconscious. This led to the most trying times in his life. Only
toward the end of the first World War, when he began spontaneously
drawing mandalas, was he able to bring order out of the chaos and
begin to "understand that the goal of psychic development is the
self." Not until 1928 was the issue totally resolved for him with the
arrival of Richard Wilhelm's manuscript about the Taoist classic, *The
Secret of the Golden Flower*. This manuscript from China gave Jung
"undreamed-of confirmation" of ideas. Thus ended his long
isolation.[11] Later in his work, stone became for Jung the symbol of
the complete "Self," thus he built his rock Tower at Bollingen.

 Although Lawrence's fiction came from these same unconscious
depths that Jung had been probing, Lawrence was more interested
in how the unconscious forces worked out in the lives of his
characters than in analyzing these depths. Intuitively, he knew that
the analytical method could kill the very thing it analyzed.

 Returning to the influence the rock quarry had on Lawrence, it
turns out that not only did it deeply influence his childhood, but
this influence continued into his adult work as a writer. Lawrence
explained that in one part of the quarry it was always sunny, warm
and dry with light-colored stone, and in the old, deep part it was
always dark with poisonous nightshade growing. But one had to
crawl into the dark part to get inside the little caves. Some literary
critics attribute Lawrence's continued interest in the polarities of
the day-world and the night-world to his father's daily return from
the dark mine into the ordinary world. But here in the old quarry, as
a child, Lawrence would have *directly* experienced the simultaneous
lure and fear of the dark and the sudden return to the bright sunny
world as he climbed back out of the caves.

 This basic polarity in Lawrence extended to his relationships with
his parents: his father standing for the darkness and vitality of the

unconscious life and his mother for the brightness of the "mental" life. Generally it is assumed that Lawrence loved his mother and, because of her influence, hated his father. In reality it was much more complex. Ada, Lawrence's younger sister, wrote: "We used to wonder that mother and father, so utterly unsuitable to each other, would be married." She remembers, however, that her father was a handsome man with wavy black hair and a large beard which he never shaved and that he had "a very melodious voice." Her parents met at a party in Nottinghamshire and her mother had been attracted by his "graceful dancing," his gallant manner and his overflowing humor and good spirits. He, in turn, was interested in the "quiet, reserved and ladylike girl." And Ada goes on to say that there might not have been so much misery in their childhood had her mother been more tolerant, but she was from such a strict and Puritanical background that almost everything the father did went against her deepest feelings. In other words, although Lydia, the mother, married John Arthur for his vitality, she did her best to destroy that quality in him. As the children grew older, they shut him out of their lives because Lydia wanted it that way.[12]

Ford Madox Ford was the editor of the *English Review*, where Lawrence's work was first published. Ford, who met Lawrence's father once, realized that Lawrence "shrank from" his father but commented, "I think he was wrong. His father was by no means commonplace. He certainly drank . . . or no, he got drunk at times. But he exercised a good deal of influence over his mates in the mine and he was very ingenious with tools . . . evidence of a creative gift." In fact, Ford attributed Lawrence's "natural sense of form . . . that was perhaps his most singular characteristic" to the influence of his father. "His father was obviously not a dancing master and minor craftsman for nothing."[13]

Much later, in an article entitled "Enslaved by Civilization," Lawrence wrote that his father's generation of miners "was still wild." His father had been part of the last generation of Englishmen who escaped compulsory schooling. He had never been to a real school, only to a "dame's school," where the teacher had only succeeded in making him able to write his name. His feelings had escaped the teacher's "clutches entirely" as well as those of his mother.[14] At the age of ten Lawrence's father went to work in the coal pit. In their free time he and his friends spent most of their time outdoors, poaching rabbits and hunting mushrooms. He knew the names of all the local birds and animals.[15]

An old Eastwood miner, interviewed in 1955, had very little to say about D. H. Lawrence: "But his father, now there was a man. Full of life and friendliness. They still talk about him in Eastwood. He could dance, too, till his legs broke to bits." The old man's opinion of Lawrence's mother, however, was quite different: "She thought that much of herself. But she was nothing."[16]

Lawrence's mother was "town-bred" and spoke the "King's English." Never in her life would she condescend to speak the local dialect. Naturally her husband spoke this dialect and the children, too, when she couldn't hear them.[17] Lydia was "small and slight in figure, her brown hair sprinkled with gray, brushed straight back from a broad brow; clear blue eyes . . . a delicately shaped nose . . . and a sure carriage." She loved to read and often discussed religion and philosophy with the local minister.[18] Before she was twenty she had published some poetry in a local magazine.[19] She died of cancer in 1910, just as Lawrence's first book, *The White Peacock*, was being published.

Although it is generally assumed that young Lawrence hated his father, actually, his feelings were much more complex. At the Chambers farm one afternoon, he was trying to teach the children how to dance. May, Jessie Chambers' older sister, wrote that Lawrence was counting out the waltz for them but it simply wasn't working right. The next week he came back and said that he had been wrong and showed them the correct way. When May asked him who told him how to count right, "reddening, he admitted it was his father, and having broken the ice and allowed his father to have any good points, he talked a lot about Mr. Lawrence's knowledge of dancing. It was easy to see he was proud of him as an authority on dancing."[20] May wrote of another revealing incident. Lawrence and the Chambers children had found some mushrooms and were quarreling over who should have them. Lawrence finally said, "Well, if you want to know, I want them for my father's tea." May was very surprised and told him that he didn't seem to hate him as much as he pretended to. Lawrence replied: "I have to hate him for Mother's sake." Lawrence further explained that he wanted to take his father the mushrooms because "he loves wild things you find."[21]

Later in his life Lawrence came to appreciate his father more. Achsah Brewster writes of an incident that occurred when the Lawrences were staying with them in Ceylon, before they traveled on to Taos. They were sitting on the verandah watching a workman arrange a screen. The workman "was alert; with sure, graceful movement and fine head; his dark eyes flashing; his features regular. . . . Lawrence pensively watched him, announcing that he resembled his father—the same clean-cut and exuberant spirit, a true pagan. He added that he had not done justice to his father in *Sons and Lovers* and felt like rewriting it. When children, they had accepted the dictum of their mother that their father was a drunkard, therefore was contemptible, but that as Lawrence had grown older he had come to see him in a different light; to see his unquenchable fire and relish for living." Brewster went on to explain that Lawrence told them that he now put the blame on his mother for her self-righteousness and "invulnerable Christian virtue." Lawrence remembered how his mother would gather the children together to wait for the father's return from a night out with his friends. The children would "sit quaking" as she told "blacker and blacker" stories of his shortcomings. When the father finally arrived, she would lash out at him for his drunkenness and make the children agree with her that he was no good as a father. but their father would only try to reassure the frightened children and say: "Never mind, my duckies, you needna be afraid of me. I'll do ye na harm." Lawrence told Brewster that he couldn't forgive his mother for that.[22]

Only two years before his death, Lawrence admitted to Rhys Davies that he respected his father much more now and wished that he had not written of him "in such a bitterly hostile way" in *Sons and Lovers*. Davies said that Lawrence could see that his father, in those early years, had the old "male spirit of England, pre-puritan, he was natural and unruined deep in himself."[23]

Lawrence's health was precarious from the time he was born and, after he almost died from a bronchitis attack when he was only two weeks old, his mother became even more worried that he would not live very long.[24] Although his fragile health precluded his playing the rougher games with boys, he had many friends during all the years he was growing up. Ada remarked that he "had a genius for inventing games indoors" and that everyone wanted to dance with him. His movements were so light."[25] Emily, his older sister, tells of how they dressed up to play charades and of how they often sang with friends at their house.[26] Whether he was at home or at the Chambers' farm house, Lawrence was the organizer and instigator for the entire group.

Lawrence's real love was the unspoiled countryside still extending in all directions around Eastwood. With the encouragement of both parents, he learned to be an alert observer— to search for the first flowers of spring and for the hidden mushrooms. He wrote later of "hunting through the wet grass for the white-skinned, wonderful naked bodies crouched secretly in the green."[27] At a very early age he began to learn the names of the plants and animals, thus further sharpening his observation. Wherever Lawrence went in later life he immediately began to learn the names of the plants in the vicinity. Years later, an old friend, William Edward Hopkin wrote: "It was a delight to go rambling with him. How he acquired his knowledge I never knew. He seemed to be one of those rare persons that receive direct revelation from some source."[28]

The roaming freedom of his early childhood was cut short by schools. "I shall never forget the anguish with which I wept, the first day, I was captured. I was roped in."[29] Although learning came easily to him, he resented being cut off from the life of the woods and, whenever possible, he would simply fail to show up at school. Mabel Collishaw, a long-ago schoolmate of Lawrence, tells of how Bertie would talk her into going with him to the flower-filled meadows instead of school. There he would talk to the flowers and she would tell him that he was "dotty" for doing that. Often he would encourage her to make up poems with him; each one contributing a line. He once wrote a poem for her when they were about eleven years old: "We sit in a lovely meadow / my sweetheart and me / And we are oh so happy / Mid the flowers, birds, and the bees." The last time she saw him they were both twenty and "chanced to meet near the quarry—a fitting place, for there as children we had shared so many joys and sorrows. . . . hand in hand we had sat quietly watching the hundreds of rabbits playing."[30]

In 1901 Lawrence and his mother first went to visit the Chambers family at the Haggs. Immediately upon arriving there Lawrence asked May to show him the woods. He said he would go by himself, but admitted, "only I'm afraid the keepers would turn me back." At first she refused but later, when he mentioned how careful he had been not to step on any of the violets along the path, she told him she would show him "the most secret spot in the wood. And in the rich glow of late afternoon we entered the shadows of the great oaks, and followed a narrow path to the heart of the wood." There she stopped a moment to carefully sniff the air to be sure there was no tobacco smoke and then led him into a tiny clearing. In front of them was a small hut made of saplings, still covered with their bark. She told him it was the keeper's hut. That is why she had first made sure there was no tobacco smoke in the air.[31] This is the first mention of the game-keeper, a figure who later appeared in several of Lawrence's novels.

Jessie Chambers tells of a time when she and Lawrence together with her brothers and his sister accidentally wandered into a private portion of the woods. They found a spot "like fairyland—a stream flowing between smooth green banks starred with primroses, which are rare in our woods. We were enchanted." Suddenly a "burly, red-haired keeper" rushed through the trees, angrily waving a stick, and shouted that we were on private property." He took their names and forced them to leave.[32] In both these written records of two different occasions when Lawrence had penetrated into the most hidden, enchanting part of the woods, he found either the keeper's hut or the keeper himself guarding the woods. It is no wonder that, for him, gamekeepers came to stand for a different kind of human being—one who stood for the freedom of wilderness against the intrusion of the common, industrialized working-class life of Lawrence's neighbors.

A further insight comes from a passage in *Sons and Lovers*. Young Paul Morel is trying to get a job so he goes to the library to look at the ads in the newspapers. He stands, looking out the window, musing: "Already he was a prisoner of industrialism." He sees the sunflowers below the window, the valley full of corn shining in the sun and the distant woods "dark and fascinating. His heart went down. He was being taken into bondage. His freedom in the beloved home valley was going now."[33]

Lawrence's "beloved home valley" provides the clue to the origin of his unique genius. Adult genius has its roots in the child's relationship with the natural world; however, it is not surprising that this has been overlooked in Lawrence's case because documentary proof of this crucial factor in genius was not available until 1977 when Edith Cobb's book, *The Ecology of Imagination in Childhood*, was finally published. Summarizing the material from her collection of the biographies of three hundred creative thinkers since the sixteenth century, she found that there was a particular time in early childhood when each was awakened to the existence of some potential, aroused by a particular experience of self and nature, and that the cause of this awakening was "an acute sensory response to the natural world."[34]

An awareness of "timeless, spaceless, total bliss occupied me," is the way poet Kenneth Rexroth explained what happened to him when he was five years old and encountered a load of new-mown hay. He goes on to say that this bliss seemed to him to be his "normal and natural life which was going on all the time and [his] sudden acute consciousness of it only a matter of attention."[35] At about the same age, C. S. Lewis had a similar experience when he saw a flowering currant bush and an enormous bliss came over him. "It had taken only a moment of time; and in a certain sense everything else that had ever happened to me was insignificant in comparison."[36]

Combining information from this collection of biographies, together with her thirty years of research, Cobb writes that "there is a special period, the little-understood, prepubertal, halcyon, middle age of childhood, approximately from five or six to eleven or twelve ... when the natural world is experienced in some highly evocative way, producing in the child a sense of some profound continuity with natural processes." The child seems to experience both "an awareness of his own unique separateness and identity, and also a continuity, a renewal of relationship with nature as process." She notes that this original childhood experience may be "extended through memory into a lifelong renewal of the early power to learn and to evolve."[37] This is the source of the ever-fresh joy in new discovery which people of genius, such as Lawrence, exhibit continuously throughout their lives.

Cobb defines genius as "an evolutionary phenomenon, at biocultural levels, beginning with the natural genius of childhood and the *spirit of place*."[38] In fact, as she explains, the term *genius*, in its earlier usage, "referred most frequently to the spirit of place, *genius loci*, which we can now interpret to mean a living ecological relationship between an observer and an environment, a person and a place."[39]

Lawrence had a further advantage in his encounters with nature; because of his father's influence he had learned the names of plants and where they grew. Paul Shepard, author of *The Tender Carnivore and the Sacred Game*, claims that because of the inherited nervous system of the hunter-gatherer, collecting and learning the names of plants and animals is more important than any other learning activity for the child. Taxonomic training "establishes a framework into which the accumulated encounters with non-human can be fitted in an orderly way, making possible mature confrontations with the new and unknown."[40]

Both of Lawrence's parents had shared in his love of nature to some extent; so also did Jessie Chambers, the next deep relationship in his life. In addition, she shared the world of books and ideas with him and was the only one of his friends who encouraged him to be a writer. His earliest pieces were written for her and often dedicated to her, and she was the one who sent off his writing to *The English Review*, where it was first published.[41] In *Sons and Lovers*, a passage illuminates this aspect of their relationship. When Paul (Lawrence) finished writing something, he always wanted to take it to Miriam (Jessie). "Then he was stimulated into knowledge of the work he had produced unconsciously. In contact with Miriam he gained insight; his vision went deeper. From his mother he drew the life-warmth, the strength to produce; Miriam urged this warmth into intensity like a white light."[42] What he did for her is mirrored in another passage from *Sons and Lovers*. Miriam wanted to show him a particular wild-rose bush which she had found. She was excited by its beauty but "till he had seen it, she felt it had not come into her soul. Only he could make it her own, immortal." As they approached it she got very anxious and tense and passionately looked forward to showing him the flowers. "They were going to have a communion together—something that thrilled her, something holy."[43] Miriam almost worshipped him, but "half the time he grieved for her, half the time he hated her." He appreciated that she brought out the best in him and in his writing, but he felt that he "could not stay with her because she did not take the rest of him."[44] So he turned to others for sexual passion.

Lawrence went into teacher training and was a "pupil-teacher" at Ilkeston in Derbyshire, where he had to control a large class of collier's boys. He later called it "savage teaching." Then in 1902, the Education Act centralizing teacher training made it necessary for Lawrence and the other young teachers of the area to travel three days a week to Ilkeston. Usually they went in by train in the morning and walked the three miles back through the fields in the afternoon. The group included Franky and Grit Cooper, two young women who lived next door to the Lawrence house at Lynn Croft; his sister, Ada; Jessie Chambers; her brother Alan; Louise Burrows; Richard Pogmore; George Neville and a couple of other friends. They called themselves the "Pagans."[45]

Lawrence didn't care much for the headmaster he had to work under but he was happy among the Pagans as they all traveled together between Ilkeston and home. He was the leader on the hikes they took together on their holidays. Ada reports that "nothing escaped Lawrence's attention . . . however deep in conversation he might be. He was the first to see a baby rabbit or cock-pheasant, the first primrose."[46] George Neville later wrote that on holidays they "always tramped, tramped, many times the livelong day, and at least one day in every holiday we contrived to spend tramping in the Derbyshire dales. . . . I think we gathered, pressed and mounted specimens of every plant, shrub and tree to be found for miles around."[47] Again, Lawrence found the joy of living and learning with others in nature. His friends' enthusiasm whenever he spotted new plants and animals increased his powers of perception.

He helped in the hay fields where he worked with the father and sons of the Chambers' family. His sister and other friends of "the Pagans" would often bring a picnic lunch and join them in the field. After the lunch was finished the picnic often turned into dancing or games before they went back to work. Forty years later, David, Jessie's younger brother, still remembered the fun they had. And Jessie's father told her mother, "Work goes like fun when Bert's there, it's no trouble at all to keep them going."[48]

Lawrence was willing to help with whatever job needed doing. He would help Jessie's mother by getting the water for the boiler and making up the fires. Jessie tells of the time when there was a basket of pickling onions which stood outside the back door for weeks, waiting for someone to get the time to peel them. "They suddenly disappeared, and mother said that Bert had peeled them; he just sat down and did them without saying a word to anyone. No task seemed dull or monotonous to him. He brought such vitality to the doing that he transformed it into something creative."[49]

Of all the people who knew Lawrence, Aldous Huxley was perhaps the one who most clearly defined his rare ability to approach everything with such total awareness that it became a creative experience. In 1952, on the twenty-second anniversary of Lawrence's death, a taped discussion was held in the library of the University of California at Los Angeles. M. Ewing, the moderator, asked Huxley: "What sort of gifts would you say he had?"

"He was a great passer of examinations," Huxley answered. Then he went on to say:

He read very widely; he could pick up extraordinarily quickly out of anything that he read, all the significant facts. And I think—in a sense— because of that—he had a certain contempt for those capacities. I mean they came, in a way, too easily for him and he didn't take very much interest in them. But he was not interested in the life of the intellectual as such, precisely because he could have been a great intellectual. He had something else which was obviously the core of his whole genius, which was this immediate sensitivity to the world at large. He had this capacity for being, so to speak, naked in the presence of what is actually present in the world. And I think one can trace that throughout his writings as a persistent theme. . . . And this was essentially the basis of his life and was his greatest gift, I think: this capacity to be aware of the universe in all its levels, from the inanimate and the animal and the vegetable through the human, right up to something beyond. I think he was more aware on every level than anyone I've ever known.

When Ewing asked whether this feeling may have come from inspirations from any particular book which Lawrence read, Huxley answered: "He was born, I'm convinced, with this awareness." He went on to say that literary influences are only "important inasmuch as they canalize and direct a thing. But I don't think they evoke it actually very much or create it."[50]

Lawrence was certainly born with this awareness but so is every human child. To develop this awareness, however, the child must be enabled to interact freely with the "spirit of place" within his own immediate natural surroundings. This, Lawrence was able to do, not only because he was encouraged by both parents to become aware of natural things such as flowers, mushrooms, and blackberries, but also because there were still remnants of Sherwood Forest near his town of Eastwood. What is most unusual about

Lawrence is not that he was born with such awareness but that he continued throughout his life to develop ever greater awareness. It all began in his beloved home countryside. How much he suffered when he had to leave that countryside to teach school in Croydon is shown in his first novel, *The White Peacock*. Cyril, a character based on Lawrence himself, has gone to teach in a suburb of London:

> The spirit of that wild little slope to the hill would come upon me, and there in the suburb of London I would walk wrapped in the sense of a small wet place in the valley of Nethermere. A strange voice within me arose and called for the hill path; again I could feel the wood waiting for me, calling and calling, and I crying for the wood, yet the space of many miles was between us. Since I left the valley of home I have not much feared any other loss. The hills of Nethermere had been my walls, and the sky of Nethermere my roof overhead. It seemed almost as if, at home, I might lift my hand to the ceiling of the valley, and touch my own beloved sky . . . whose stars were constant to me, born when I was born, whose sun had been all my father to me. But now the skies were strange over my head, and Orion walked past me unnoticing, he who night after night had stood over the woods to spend with me a wonderful hour . . . when does the night throw open her vastness for me, and send me the stars for company? There is no night in a city.[51]

2

"More than a human being ought to see"—The Spirit of Place

Local ecosystems speak to you if you know how to listen but you've got to listen well in one place, first. . . . Then you can go to other places and the earth will continue to speak to you.[1]
—Gary Snyder

During the summer of 1909 Lawrence spent some time on the Isle of Wight and was flooded with the beauty of sun and sand and flowers which he found there. In his second novel, *The Trespasser*, nineteen of the thirty-one chapters are concerned with the island's beauty, intimately intertwined with the love affair of Siegmund and Helena: sky, earth, sea and love are inseparable.

Both Helena and Siegmund are overcome by the peace and the stillness. Siegmund had always thought of himself as an outcast; but, out walking one night, he realizes, "How can one be outcast in one's own night, and the moon always naked to us. Whatever I have or haven't from now on, the darkness is a sort of mother, and the moon a sister, and the stars children, and sometimes the sea is a brother and there's a family in one house, you see." Helena seemed to connect him with all things "as if she were the nerve through which he received intelligence of the sun, and wind, and sea, and of the moon and the darkness."[2]

Down on the shore the next day, Siegmund feels the warm sand. Pouring it over himself, he is smooth; and later, washing it off in the sea he feels fresh, "as if he had washed away all the years of soilure in this morning's sea and sun and sand. It was the purification. Siegmund became again a happy priest of the sun."[3] This scene becomes a kind of initiation ritual in which Lawrence expresses his deep feelings for the island, which he had come to love still more in sharing these feelings with a woman. At this time in his life he and Helen Corke, another teacher at Croydon, were close friends. Helen wrote of the two of them wandering "our weekends over the Surrey Hills, gathering primroses or blackberries in season, but always the herb philosophy."[4]

Lawrence, on a family holiday with his mother and sister, spent only two weeks on the Isle of Wight; but later that year, gazing out at the Isle as he wandered the Surrey Hills with Helen, she told him of the tragic suicide of her lover, which occurred just after they had returned from five days on the Isle. Later she showed Lawrence the entries in her diary, written during that time, and within three months Lawrence had the first draft of *The Trespasser* completed.[5]

In March 1912 Lawrence met Frieda Weekley. Two months later they left together for Europe where they spent an idyllic time in the mountains of the Bavarian Tyrol, traveled through Europe and lived for a few months in Italy. Eventually they returned to England and were married on the 13th of July, 1914. They had hoped to leave England again but the outbreak of the war prevented any further travel. After a series of temporary rooms in or near London, they finally moved to Cornwall where they lived for two years. Here Lawrence was once again able to establish roots. "It is very fine here, foxgloves everywhere between the rocks and ferns. There is some magic in the country. It gives me a strange satisfaction."[6] While in Cornwall he wrote his *Studies in Classic American Literature,* with its introductory essay, "The Spirit of Place": "Every continent has its own great spirit of place. Every people is polarized in some particular locality, which is home, the homeland. Different places on the face of the earth have different vital effluence, different vibration, different chemical exhalation, different polarity with different stars: call it what you like. But the spirit of place is a great reality." He points out that places can die as Rome did and as England seemed to him to be doing. He warns that "Men are less free than they imagine." They are not free, he says, when they are breaking loose in aimless wandering or escaping to "some wild west. Men are free when they are in a living homeland . . . free when they are obeying some deep, inward voice of religious belief. Obeying from within. Men are free when they belong to a living, organic, *believing* community, active in fulfilling some unfulfilled, perhaps unrealized purpose."[7]

Lawrence produced beautifully written, deep studies of many of the places where he traveled or lived. In 1922 the Lawrences stayed for only three months in Australia; yet even in this short space of time "it was as if through a sixth sense something came to him of the country itself, of the place itself."[8] Here in Australia he wrote of "heaven and earth so new as if no man had ever breathed in it, no foot ever trodden on it. . . . The great weight of the spirit that lies so heavily on Europe doesn't exist here. . . . It is interesting—a new experience. . . . Yet the weird, unawakened country is wonderful."[9] W. Siebenhaar, who lived most of his life in Australia, wrote that it was a "wonder that in so short a space of time, and at so unpropitious a stage of the year, Lawrence succeeded in obtaining an estimate of the magic of the scene."[10] They left Australia to travel on to Taos, their final destination. The revelation which the landscape of Taos and Mexico offered to Lawrence is explored in Chapter 5.

During the last years of his life, the Lawrences lived in the Villa Mirenda above Florence. Walter Wilkinson, an English puppet-master who lived near them, wrote that Lawrence "seems to have lived always against an immense landscape." This was true in Cornwall, in Australia, in New Mexico and Mexico and in the Italian lakes and mountains. It was equally true of the Villa Mirenda. Wilkinson writes that, as one climbed up the road toward the villa there came into sight the "wide flat view over the plain of the Arno, away to Monte Morello and the peaks of the Apennines."[11] Lawrence wrote one of his last books, *Lady Chatterley's Lover*, sitting in the woods near the villa. Even though he was very ill he could still write joyously of the nightingale which "sings with a ringing, punching vividness and a pristine assertiveness that makes a mere man sit down and consider."[12]

Lawrence's incredible ability to see "more than a human being ought to see"[13] continually surprised and amazed his friends. In fact even those who personally disliked Lawrence paid tribute to this aspect of the man.

Ford Madox Ford, the rather proper Edwardian editor of the *English Review*, who first published Lawrence, wrote at length of his first meeting with the author. Ford wrote that Lawrence just walked in, unannounced, and began telling him how much he didn't like his office. Eventually, Lawrence mentioned that the *English Review* was planning to publish his short story, "Odour of Chrysanthemums." Ford states, "That cleared the matter up, but I don't know that it made Lawrence himself any less disturbing." Ford goes on to say that whenever he opens one of Lawrence's books or "merely resume[s] reading one of his novels, I have had a feeling of disturbance—not so much as if something odd was going to happen to me but as if I myself might be going to do something eccentric." He further explains that some of Lawrence's followers would say that this disturbance "is caused by my coming in contact with his as-it-were dryad nature. As if it were the sort of disturbing emotion caused in manufacturers or bankers by seeing, in a deep woodland, the God Pan—or Priapus—peeping round beside the trunk of an ancient oak."

When Ford went for a walk with Lawrence in the Gardens or the park he saw a "new side of Lawrence that was not father-mother derived—that was pure D. H. It was his passionate—as it were an almost super-sex-passionate—delight in the openings of flowers and leaves." He says that he and Lawrence would be talking of literature when Lawrence, who had been "drawing wisdom from a distinguished, rather portly Editor, would become a half-mad, woodland creature," kneeling down to the flower to gently touch it. Ford found Lawrence's writings on nature entirely different from other English novelists. When Lawrence writes of nature these passages "run like fire through his books and are exciting—because of the life that comes into his writing . . . you have the sense that there really was to him a side that was supernatural . . . in tune with deep woodlands, which are queer places." They parted when Lawrence brought him the first half of the manuscript of *The Trespasser* and Ford called it a "thoroughly bad hybrid book."[14]

Even though Cecil Gray, the Scottish composer who lived near the Lawrences in Cornwall, actively disliked Lawrence; he could write that where Lawrence "realized himself completely, was in the world of nature . . . and with trees." Gray states, "In all literature there is little, if anything, to compare with the extraordinary depth and delicacy of Lawrence's perceptions of Nature in all its forms and manifestations. He was a faun, a child of Pan, a satyr (and he even looked the part). That was the essential Lawrence; there he was truly great."[15]

Maurice Lesemann gives us the most penetrating insight of all: "The exultation . . . so predominant in the early love poems and in the clear lyricism of *The Trespasser*, still appears—most freely now in his feeling for places, his whole sense of a town or a mountain." Lesemann then goes on to say that these matters do not really concern Lawrence much. What he is really concerned with is "certain human relationships and with certain visions which he has had for the future. He is concerned with finding a philosophy which shall show him a rhythm running through the inconsistent truths of experience. But these others—for which alone many people read him—these come almost unconsidered out of the casual, daily abundance of his mind."[16] Lesemann shows that the ordinary, daily observations of Lawrence typify the very kind of writing which is usually most rare. Here is where Lawrence approached the primitive's "direct engagement with nature." The anthropologist Stanley Diamond writes that among primitives "the sense of reality is heightened to the point where it sometimes seems to 'blaze'. It is at this point that the experiences of primitive and mystic converge, for mysticism is no more than reality, perceived at its ultimate subjective pitch."[17]

Those who knew Lawrence best—his wife, Frieda and his friends—provide even more specific insights into his remarkable powers of perception. Frieda explains: "All those that went for a walk with him remember what an experience it was. It seemed all he saw out of doors he saw for the first time, and he noticed everything, every first flower in the spring, every color, every smell. We would gather pounds of early dandelions and make them into beer. All the wild strawberries and raspberries we gathered in their turn."[18]

The English writer Norman Douglas insists that "the prevalent conception of Lawrence as a misanthrope is wrong. He was a man of naturally blithe disposition, full of childlike curiosity. The core of his mind was unsophisticated. He touched upon the common things of earth with tenderness and grace. . . . There was something elemental in him, something of the *Erdgeist*."[19]

To Franz Schoenberner, the German writer and editor who met Lawrence in September of 1927, he seemed like "a sick faun who out of sheer friendliness had left his mysterious woods, adapting himself for some hours in manner and appearance to the usual human pattern; but one felt him likely to disappear at any moment with a light caper over the tea table and through the window, to return to the company of other goat-footed half gods. . . . Only a few people whom I have met have given me this feeling of their living in a sphere of pure essentiality where everything and everyone assumes a new and higher substance."[20]

Two of Lawrence's oldest friends were the Honorable Herbert Asquith and his wife, Lady Cynthia. Asquith wrote that Lawrence "sometimes called to mind the idea of a faun, receptive and alert to every sound of the fields and woods; there was something spritelike, electric, elemental, in the spirit which moved this slight sensitive form . . . his power of vision was as sensitive as his power of utterance and he could see heaven in the tint of a sheet of sand."[21] Lady Cynthia noted "the astonishing acuteness of his senses. . . . Yet to some degree . . . he enabled you temporarily to share that intensified existence; for his faculty for communicating to others something of his own perceptiveness made a walk with him a wonderfully enhanced experience. In fact it made me feel that hitherto I had to all intents and purposes walked the earth with my eyes blindfolded and my ears plugged."[22]

Because Lawrence's perceptions were clear he innately

understood that the sun and the moon are the primary pacemakers of all biological rhythms; thus, for him, neither the sun nor moon nor any other natural entity ever became merely a symbol. Lawrence is not a symbolist as many Lawrence scholars such as Harry T. Moore and Professor William Tindall affirm when they try to align him with the *correspondence* tradition established by Baudelaire. Another Lawrence scholar, Mark Spilka, however, makes this distinction clear when he explains that "the French symbolists were searching for the spiritual infinite, and Lawrence was not: his symbols operate at a different level of language than theirs, and for different ends; they are not suggestive evocations of timeless spiritual reality, but material and focal expressions of those vague but powerful forces of nature which occur, quite patently, in time."[23] For example, in Lawrence's novel *The Rainbow*, Ursula and Skrebensky spend the night together out on the downs at midsummer and, as the dawn comes they stand together high up on "an earth-work of the stone-age men" waiting for the sun. They see a faint touch of rose on the eastern skyline, "and then yellow, pale, new-created yellow, the whole quivering and poising momentarily over the fountain on the sky's rim." The scene continues:

> The rose hovered and quivered, fused to flame, to a transient red, while the yellow urged out in great waves, thrown from the ever-increasing fountain, great waves of yellow flinging into the sky, scattering its spray over the darkness, which became bluer and bluer, paler, till soon it would itself be a radiance, which had been darkness.
>
> The sun was coming. There was a quivering, a powerful terrifying swim of molten light. Then the molten source itself surged forth, revealing itself. The sun was in the sky, too powerful to look at.[24]

In this one passage Lawrence combined the power of a particular place, the downs, which had been recognized by humans at least since the Megalithic Age when the stone monuments were placed there; the ancient recognition of the sun at the summer solstice (mid-summer day) and the living relationship between two lovers and the rising sun. In the hectic days during the First World War, this kind of writing seemed poetic nonsense, of no real importance as mankind girded itself for a great battle. Lawrence, however, knew that whatever he was feeling his way toward was far more fundamental than this war, which was merely a final stage in the anti-life process of modern industrial civilization. Lawrence could only follow his instincts, as he did not have access to the decades of research in anthropology, psychology and related disciplines which have taken place since his death.

It is now recognized that, probably since the race began, human beings have stood in just such a worshipful attitude as did Ursula waiting for the sun. C. G. Jung, when he visited the natives living near Mt. Elgon in Africa, witnessed the ceremony in which they waited for the sun to rise and then, as it rose, spit into their hands and held their hands palm upward toward the sun. An elder of the tribe told Jung that "this was the true religion of all peoples, that all . . . tribes from as far as the eye could see from the mountains and endlessly further, worshipped *adhísta*, that is, the sun at the moment of rising. Only then was the sun *mungu*, God." Jung points out that the other spirit was *ayík*, the dark spirit of evil, danger and fear. The tribal ceremony of a gift of their own spittle was an offering of their living soul. Jung goes on to say that the important moment is when "with the typical suddenness of the tropics, the first ray of light shoots forth like an arrow and night passes into life-filled light."

Jung reports that during the time he spent near Mt. Elgon, each day he went out just before sunrise, when the growing light of the sun and the cry of the bell bird ringing round the horizon caused him to feel as if he were "inside a temple. It was the most sacred hour of the day." Near his spot was a high cliff inhabited by big baboons. "Every morning they sat quietly, almost motionless, on the ridge of the cliff facing the sun, whereas throughout the rest of the day they ranged noisily through the forest, screeching and chattering. Like me, they seemed to be waiting for the sunrise. They reminded me of the great baboons of the temple of Abu Simbel in

Egypt, which perform the gesture of adoration. They tell the same story: for untold ages men have worshipped the great god who redeems the world by rising out of the darkness as a *radiant light* in the heavens. . . . The *moment* in which light comes *is* God." Jung refers to the ancient Egyptian concept of Horus and Set and states: "Here, evidently, was a primordial African experience that had flowed down to the coasts of the Mediterranean along with the sacred waters of the Nile: *adhísta*, the rising sun, the principle of light, like Horus; *ayík*, the principle of darkness."[25]

Jung later found this same approach to the sun among the Taos Indians. He talked on the roof with Ochwiay Biano (whose name means Mountain Lake) as they sat waiting for the sun to rise. As it moved higher into the sky, Biano said, "Is not he who moves there our father? . . . Nothing can be done without the sun." He further informed Jung that the Taos people performed their religious dances "not only for ourselves but for the Americans also . . . for the whole world."[26]

The Hopi Indians also affirm that their religious rituals are ceremonies which are necessary for the good of the whole world. Frank Waters tells of the personal relationship between John Lansa, an old Hopi, and the sun:

> He would stand in the open doorway facing east, barefooted and stripped to the waist. The first deep yellow to appear in the sky was sun pollen. Four times he would scrape it off the horizon with his cupped hand and put it in his mouth. This fed his body. As the sun began to rise, he breathed deeply four times to cleanse his heart and his insides. The four times he spread the first rays of the sun over himself from head to feet, clothing himself in its power.[27]

Before Jung left the Taos Pueblo, Ochwiay Biano said to him: "After all, we are a people who live on the roof of the world; we are the sons of Father Sun, and with our religion we daily help our father to go across the sky. We do this not only for ourselves, but for the whole world. If we were to cease practicing our religion, in ten years the sun would no longer rise. Then it would be night forever."[28]

More than fifty years later, in 1974, Loloma, the Hopi artist and jewelry maker said: "The sun is becoming darker. Every day there is less light." He went on to tell Stan Steiner of how he had been asked to go to a Convocation of Indian Scholars at Princeton University. There, everyone made long, academic speeches about the problems of the Indian people and the future of America; but they ignored the true problem. "I stood up. And all I had to say were seven words: In the East, there is no sun!" And he sat down.[29]

Although it is obvious that the sun is responsible for all life and warmth on the earth, we are now beginning to find out that our reaction to the sun goes still deeper. After twenty years of research, Maki Takata of Toho University in Tokyo, proved the correlation between the flocculation of blood serum and sunspots. He developed the "Takata reaction," which involves the chemical testing of albumin in blood serum, by analyzing the propensity for albumin to curdle into small lumps. If little reagent is needed to cause flocculation, the index is high; when much reagent is needed the index is low. "In males this index was supposedly constant, while in females it varied depending on the menstrual cycle." This factor made Takata's reaction a basic analytical tool for gynecologists.

In January 1938, each hospital which used Takata's reaction found that the index of flocculation had suddenly begun to rise in both sexes. That year there had been a sudden increase in solar activity after years of relative inaction. For the next twenty years Takata worked to gather data until the effect of the sunspots was proved. He further discovered that, while the flocculation index was very low towards the end of the night there was a sudden rise at dawn. "The curve begins a few minutes before sunrise, as if the blood somehow 'foresees' the appearance of the sun." Experiments during eclipses and at 30,000 feet in an airplane confirmed this relationship between the blood and the sun. Takata himself concisely concluded: "Man is a living sun-dial."[30]

Surprisingly, Lawrence points to a relationship between the blood and the sun in his short story "Sun," in which a woman moved into a life-giving relationship to the sun. Lawrence writes that she is not merely taking sun-baths, but that something inside her "unfolded." He adds: "By some mysterious power inside her, deeper than her known consciousness and will, she was put into connection with the sun, and the stream flowed of itself, from her womb."[31]

In the last book Lawrence wrote before he died, the *Apocalypse*, he tried to show that humans can "re-establish the living organic connection, with the cosmos, the sun and earth"—a two-way communication between human beings and the cosmos. His final sentence in the book was: "Start with the sun and the rest will slowly, slowly happen."[32]

While many of Lawrence's friends and all of his critics found it difficult enough to sympathize with his "sun worship," they found it impossible to tolerate his reaction to the full moon.

Jessie Chambers writes of the first time she went with the Lawrence family to the seaside. It was during the summer before Lawrence entered college. She and Lawrence went for a walk along the beach to wait for the moon-rise. She says that "gradually some dark power seemed to take possession of Lawrence, and when the final beauty of the moonrise broke upon us, something seemed to explode inside him . . . his words were wild, and he appeared to be in great distress of mind, and possibly also of body." She realized somehow that he felt she was to blame for his distress and bitterly blamed her. When she protested, he then blamed himself passionately. She writes that this happened two more times on successive occasions on the annual holiday with the Lawrences. The third time was the most intense experience. Lawrence leapt from one moon-drenched boulder to another "until I could have doubted whether he was indeed a human being. I was really frightened then . . . deep in my soul." To her he seemed "dehumanized."[33]

Something of what was going on in Lawrence becomes clear from what he wrote in this passage from *Sons and Lovers*. Paul Morel (Lawrence) and Miriam (Jessie) are on a holiday at the ocean. The sound of the sea is on one side of them, and on the other, the silent sandy shore, as they walk back through a gap in the sand dunes. "Suddenly he started. The whole of his blood seemed to burst into flame, and he could scarcely breathe. An enormous orange moon was staring at them from the rim of the sand-hills." He stood staring, his heart beating heavily, "the muscles of his arm contracted." Half-afraid, Miriam asks him what is wrong, feeling that it must be a religious state. He knows that she is unaware of the "flashes in his blood." He did not fully know himself what was the matter. They were so young, "their intimacy so abstract, he did not know he wanted to crush her on to his breast to ease the ache there."[34]

In *The Trespasser*, when Helena and Siegmund are first together on the Isle of Wight they are blissfully happy, walking beneath the moon which has come out from the "cloud pack" and is "radiant behind the fine veil of mist," which creates a large glowing halo around the moon. The lane they are following turns toward the moon and it seemed as if they "would walk through a large Moorish arch of horse-shoe shape, the enormous white halo opening in front of them. They walked on, keeping their faces to the moon, smiling with wonder and a little rapture."[35]

Throughout *The Rainbow* there are numerous scenes between man and woman beneath the full moon. In those passages where the man is able to enter fully with body and mind into the situation, they are both fulfilled. Such a scene is the serene, full-moon scene at the harvest where Will and Anna come together: "A large gold moon hung heavily to the gray horizon, trees hovered tall, standing back in the dusk, waiting." They walk through a gate into the open field where some of the sheaves of oats have been left lying on the ground by the reapers, while still others are standing in shocks. "They did not want to turn back, yet whither were they to go, towards the moon? For they were separate, single. 'We will put up some sheaves,' said Anna. So they could remain there in the broad, open place." And the rhythm of working in nature takes over. The tresses of the oats hiss like a fountain as each alternately stacks the oats. "There was only the moving to and fro in the moonlight, engrossed, the swinging in the silence, that was marked only by the splash of the sheaves, and silence, and a splash of sheaves." And they move ever nearer as they go down the rows until at last they meet and he takes her in his arms "sweet and fresh" with the night air and the grain.

"And the whole rhythm of him beat into his kisses . . . they stood there folded, suspended in the night."[36] This is one of the few moonlight scenes Lawrence ever wrote in which all the elements are in balance; there is no "sex in the head" but a great flowing together of the moon, the ripe sheaves of oats, male, female and the standing, waiting trees.

In contrast, there are the famous moonlight scenes of Ursula and Skrebensky in *The Rainbow*, which take place a generation later and appear toward the end of the book. Ursula hates houses, and beds even more, so she refuses to love him inside. They spend the midsummer night running naked on the downs, and in the end: "He served her. She took him." But her eyes were open to the stars. Much later Ursula is describing how she felt then and her friend replies, "Then you don't love him." Ursula explains that there is something not in him which some other men have: "A jolly, reckless passionateness that you see—a man who could really let go—." She and Skrebensky are invited to spend the weekend on the coast with a tennis-golf-motorcar party and here Skrebensky is more "sure of himself."

Out walking in the dunes one night, coming up to the crest of a sand dune, suddenly: "There was a great whiteness confronting her, the moon was incandescent as a round furnace door, out of which came the high blast of moonlight . . . a dazzling, terrifying glare of white light." Skrebensky "felt his chest laid bare, where the secret was hidden . . . fusing down to nothingness." But Ursula cried out with the wonder and plunged into the moonlight while he stood behind, "a shadow ever dissolving." Eventually she "clinched hold of him; and his body was powerless in her grip." He wanted to go to a dark hollow, but she led him out to the open slope under the moon, where "the struggle for consummation was terrible . . . till it was agony to his soul." When it was over she lay with eyes open, rigid, looking at the moon with slow tears running down her cheeks. He ran away from these tears. For Ursula, there was now no moon or sea. "She trailed her dead body to the house, to her room, where she lay down inert." In the morning she returned to the superficial life but soon packed her bags to leave. Skrebensky went to her room to ask if she was done with him. She replied, "We have done with each other." When he wonders what it was that he did wrong she admitted that she doesn't know exactly, but that it was all a failure. Then, when he asks if it was his fault, she replies "You couldn't—" but she is unable to continue, so they part.[37] He is relieved when she leaves, and thinks that life is simpler without her, but he cannot stand the nights. In this moonlight scene between Ursula and Skrebensky, Lawrence is saying, the male and female were not in complete body / mind balance with one another; neither was the male in balance with the moon; thus both man and woman were unfulfilled.

It seems that what Lawrence is trying to say in many of his novels is that the full moon when seen alone is beautiful and moving, but when two view it together, both must fully enter into the experience, with both body and mind. It then becomes a joyous, serene, powerful, life-filled ritual; but if either person cannot be fully present because of interference from the conscious mind, then it becomes a negative thing, a tragedy.

In an early poem, "Tarantella," written before 1910, Lawrence told of a man sitting "like a shade" on a rock while the poetic persona dances:

What can I do but dance alone,
Dance to the sliding sea and the moon,
For the moon on my breast and the air on my limbs
and the foam on my feet?

For surely this earnest man has none
Of the night in his soul, and none of the tune
Of the waters within him; only the world's old wisdom to bleat.[38]

Since Paleolithic times, humans have been influenced by the moon. Alexander Marshack has shown that nicks cut into some reindeer bones and mammoth ivory in the Upper Paleolithic period represent notations of lunar sequences.[39] In many different cultures the moon has been linked to the same constellation of Natural events—rain together with plant and animal fertility. Primitive cultures, acknowledging the effects of the moon, held rituals at the new moon or the full moon. The famous Swiss physician, Paracelsus (1493–1541), claimed that the insane grew worse at the dark of the moon; while, in eighteenth century England, a distinction was made between "insane," which meant those people hopelessly psychotic, and "lunatic," those with temporary mental trouble occurring only at the full moon.[40]

Recent scientific studies of the possible mechanism behind these influences of the moon have shown that phases of the moon bring about modulations in the earth's electric and magnetic fields. Dr. Leonard J. Ravitz of the Virginia Department of Health and Education has measured the differences in electric potential between the head and the chest of mental patients. These differences changed from day to day, following a cyclical pattern even in normal subjects. According to Dr. Ravitz, these cycles "paralleled seasonal and lunar changes." Mental patients are affected more intensely than are normal people because the differences in potential are markedly greater for them. Ravitz found that, because of the moon's effect on the ratio of terrestrial electromagnetic forces, it could precipitate disorders in persons whose mental balance was precarious or who were unusually sensitive.[41]

The fact that the full moon has been linked with tuberculosis deaths provides still another source of information when considering the influence of the full moon on Lawrence. Perhaps all his life, certainly for a large part of it, Lawrence battled tuberculosis. Recently, Dr. William Petersen of Chicago found that deaths caused by tuberculosis were most frequent from eleven to seven days before the full moon.[42]

Still more compelling evidence of the lunar phases—because more common—is the effect on bleeders, patients who require unusual methods to stop the bleeding while on the operating table or who must be returned to the operating room to stop the bleeding. A Florida surgeon reports that his records of more than a thousand cases show a great preponderance of bleeders near the time of the full moon and only an insignificant number at the new moon.[43]

Conscious as he was of the moon's effects on his own life,

Lawrence was very interested in others who were similarly influenced. In talking with Rhys Davies, the Welsh novelist who lived near him in France for a few months early in 1929, Lawrence said, "What the Celts have to learn and cherish in themselves is the sense of mysterious magic that is born with them . . . the dark magic that comes with the night especially, when the moon is due, so that they start and quiver, seeing her rise over their hills, and get her magic into their blood."[44]

Lawrence hoped to free people from the deadening effects of the industrial age through his writings; but his critics thought he was merely exaggerating his own "peculiar" feelings in nature. In the last few decades, however, with more research into depth psychology as well as the physical structures of the brain/mind, it is becoming obvious that Lawrence was uniquely able to feel the "old ways" despite all the cricitism. In a recent study of the aboriginal inhabitants of Europe, *Well of Remembrance*, psychotherapist Ralph Metzner explores early Celt and Germanic tribes and their relationship to each aspect of nature. He explains that he is exploring the "animistic-shamanistic worldview of the aboriginal inhabitants of Europe. In that worldview, as reflected in mythology, all of nature is animated by spiritual intelligences, and one can communicate with these. . . . Thus, we can hope to find traces of the Earth-respecting wisdom that we have long forgotten."

"In terms of the metaphor system known as Jungian psychology," according to Metzner, "it is said that gods are *archetypes*, basic ideational patterns that have a life of their own in the collective unconscious of the human species. Such primordial images appear in the dreams and visions of individuals and are manifest in the mythology and art of a culture. When they do appear in dreams or visionary states, they emerge out of the unconscious and into conscious awareness. When they no longer appear and we no longer feel inspired or moved by them, the patterns of knowledge embodied in mythic images can be said to have sunk down into the collective unconscious and become dormant. The gods, we might say, are 'sleeping'."[45]

Because of the unique events of Lawrence's childhood, he never lost contact with the deep levels of his unconscious and often was able to access inherent mythic roots and Earth-honoring wisdom through his writing. Although life would have been simpler for him had he accepted the standards for successful writers and intellectuals of his day—which demanded total negation of what was called "peasant wisdom"—he refused to cut himself off from the effects of the sun and moon and other aspects of nature which have influenced humans for hundreds of thousands of years. He retained this direct contact with nature throughout his life.

During the last year of his life, in 1929, he was working on his *Apocalypse,* writing of the moon's connection with the "nervous consciousness" and "our watery bodies" (blood):

> And we have lost the moon, the cool, bright ever-varying moon. It is she who would caress our nerves, smooth them with the silky hand of her glowing, soothe them into serenity again with her cool presence. For the moon is the mistress and mother of our watery bodies, the pale body of our nervous consciousness and our moist flesh. Oh, the moon could soothe us and heal us like a cool great Artemis between her arms. But we have lost her, in our stupidity we ignore her, and angry she stares down on us and whips us with nervous whips.[46]

One of the reasons Lawrence disliked cities was because, as he put it in *The White Peacock,* "there is no night in a city." He needed the stars because he oriented and stabilized himself by them. After his long ocean voyage from Australia, the long train ride to New Mexico, he had a final uneasy meeting with Mabel Luhan. They stopped to eat before driving on to Taos. Mabel wrote later, "As we made our way out into the dark road where the motor waited, he exclaimed: 'Oh! Look how low the stars hang in the southern sky!' . . . It was the first simple, untroubled notice he had taken of anything since [he] had left the train."[47] In the midst of all this dislocation and unfamiliarity Lawrence had looked to the stars for his bearings.

Because he had never before been in such a low latitude in the Northern hemisphere, he was surprised to see those southern constellations hanging in the sky. The sight of Venus in the sky was important to Lawrence all his life and he mentions it in many of his novels; but, since this planet is one of the central facets of his *Plumed Serpent*, it will be discussed in connection with that novel.

In all of nature, Lawrence's most intimate relationships were with trees. In front of the Lawrence house on Walker Street, where he lived as a child, was a great ash tree. His sister Ada wrote of the fun they had playing around it, "although the moaning wind through its branches seared us as we lay in bed in the winter."[48] Later, after Lawrence got pneumonia and almost died, he was sick for a long time but eagerly looked forward to being well enough to go back to visit the Chambers family at the Haggs. In early spring Jessie's father brought him out to the farm in the milk-flat although he was still very white and thin. Her parents told him to be sure to come up whenever he liked. "Come up through the Warren, Bert," her father said. "You want to get the smell o' them pine trees into your lungs. They're reckoned to be good for weak chests, aren't they? Take deep breaths and get your lungs full of the scent."[49] It may be that not only did Lawrence love trees in themselves but also they actually helped heal him. He was certainly sensitive to the influence of negative ions, which are most plentiful near trees and do facilitate healing.

In his writing Lawrence began to refer directly to the influence of trees after he and Frieda left relatively treeless Cornwall where the sea is the dominant feature. Back in Chapel Farm Cottage near London, he was lying in bed, sick, looking out at the firs and pines, writing to Cecil Gray, "and I think of looking out of the Tregerthen window at the sea. . . . And I no longer want the sea, the space, the abstraction. There is something living and rather splendid about trees. They stand up so proud, and are alive."[50] In a later letter to Gray he tells of a gypsy camp down a sandy lane under some pine trees. "I find here one is soothed with trees. I never knew how soothing trees are—many trees, and patches of open sunlight, and tree-presences—it is almost like having another being."[51]

Lawrence wrote most of his novels and short stories sitting out under a tree in one part of the world or another. In Lawrence's lifetime, sitting under a tree to write was considered so odd that numerous people remarked about it. From the many books written about Lawrence I have been able to gather together a list of the various trees in his life together with the works he wrote under each of them. (See Appendix.) Here I will mention only a few of the more important trees in Lawrence's life.

Frieda wrote: "At Ebersteinburg . . . I would find him leaning against a big pine tree."[52] Here, at the edge of the Black Forest in Germany, Lawrence was writing *Fantasia of the Unconscious*:

> Today only trees, and leaves, and vegetable presences. Huge, straight fir-trees. . . . Their magnificent, strong, round bodies! It almost seems I can hear the slow, powerful sap drumming in their trunks . . . the powerful sap-scented blood roaring up the great columns. . . . I come so well to understand tree-worship. All the old Aryans worshipped the trees. My ancestors.
>
> This towering creature that never had a face. Here am I between his toes like a pea-bug, and him noiselessly overreaching me, and I feel his great blood-jet surging . . . he turns two ways: he thrusts himself tremendously down to the middle earth . . . and he turns himself about in high air; whereas we have eyes on one side of our head only, and only grow upwards.
>
> Plunging himself down into the black humus, with a root's gushing zest, where we can only rot dead; and his tips in high air, where we can only look up to. So vast and powerful and exultant in his two directions. . . .
>
> He towers, and I sit and feel safe. I like to feel him towering round me, I used to be afraid. I used to fear their rushing black lust. But now I like it. I

worship it . . . they are my only shelter and strength.

One of the few places that my soul will haunt, when I am dead, will be this. Among the trees here near Ebersteinburg, where I have been alone and written this book. I can't leave these trees. They have taken some of my soul.[53]

Here, in this passage written among the fir trees, Lawrence mirrors the deep relationship between tree and human, so ancient that it goes back to the pre-human. "The bush apes ancestral to man gradually worked farther from the forest . . . out of the gloaming and into the radiance of the open day, though not without some enduring nostalgia," the human ecologist, Paul Shepard explains. We still feel vulnerable in the open. Along with this vulnerability, "we have an affinity for shade, trees, the nebulous glimmering of the forest interior, the tracery of branches against homogeneous surfaces, climbing, the dizzy childlike joy of looking down from a height . . . are all part of the woody past. Restfulness to the eyes and temperament, unspoken mythological and psychical attachments, remain part of the forest's contribution to the human personality."[54]

Trees have been our "greatest natural benefactors." Crops from trees, fruits and nuts were the basis of Neolithic culture. The cosmic tree connecting the earth with the heavens became a mythological symbol in a great variety of cultures throughout the world. In Greece the first rituals were held in sacred groves of trees; then, as the trees were destroyed by cutting and overgrazing, they were replaced by stone columns. Still later, stone columns became part of the temples, but their tops were carved with the stylized leaves and branches of the original trees.[55]

Far from Ebersteinburg, across the Atlantic, in Mexico, Lawrence spent the summer of 1923 working on a novel. Witter Bynner says that Lawrence went every morning "to a willow tree on the waterfront at the end of the street and wrote."[56] In the novel *The Plumed Serpent*, Lawrence writes of this tree as he tells of his heroine, Kate, sitting "for hours on the shore, under a green willow tree that hung its curtains of pale-green fronds, on the beach."[57]

Lady Chatterley's Lover was written in a "little wood of umbrella pines" near Florence. Mark Schorer described these woods: "They are deep and cool, the umbrella pines old and tall, with straight, thick trunks, and high above, their curious spread of branches . . . here, in this most Italian wood, he imagined his English forest on the estate of Clifford Chatterley."[58]

Pine trees were special favorites of Lawrence throughout his life, but he was especially fond of the great pine in front of his house on the Kiowa ranch in New Mexico. He describes this tree in his short story, "St. Mawr":

> Her cabin faced the slow down-slope of the clearing, the alfalfa field: her long, low cabin, crouching under the great pine-tree that threw up its trunk sheer in front of the house, in the yard. That pine-tree was the guardian of the place. But a bristling, almost demonish guardian, from the far-off crude ages of the world. Its great pillar of pale, flaky-ribbed copper rose there in strange callous indifference, and the grim permanence, which is in pine-trees. A passionless, non-phallic column, rising in the shadows of the pre-sexual world, before the hot-blooded ithyphallic column ever erected itself. A cold blossomless, resinous sap surging and oozing gum, from that pallid brownish bark. And the wind hissing in the needles, like a vast nest of serpents.[59]

Brett described when this great tree was hit by lightning during a hail storm: "The thunder is terrible, the lightning one continuous blaze. An extra loud crash makes us jump out of our skins." It had struck the tree leaving a "great white scar [which] twists and turns down the trunk." Lawrence says, "It is doomed. It has to die."[60] But it didn't: it is still there today with the scar, not quite as noticeable after all these years, but still twisting down the tree. Lawrence did not write under this tree by the cabin, but instead farther up in the woods. Brett would usually have to climb up looking for him because he was so far away he would not hear when he was called for lunch. She would find him "sitting as usual, leaning against a tree, in a deep dream, abstracted, in the world of the story [he was] writing."[61] Joseph Foster, another resident of Taos, who occasionally visited the Lawrences at Kiowa, wrote: "He went off into the wood each morning and came back each noon with a large sheaf of manuscript. . . . He sits down to lunch with Frieda and the Brett and reads the pages he has just written under the tree."[62] Later, Brett types the stories: "Woman Who Rode Away" and "St. Mawr."[63]

Years later, still homesick for the ranch, Lawrence sat sipping wine with Giovanni, the old man at Villa Mirenda, his home near Florence. It was the feast of St. Catherine's day and they were watching the moon over the Mediterranean. Lawrence's eyes followed the track of the moon along the water, leading toward the southwest, and thought of the ranch—how it must look in the moonlight, everything shut up and no one there. "Only the big pine tree in front of the house, standing still and unconcerned, alive. Perhaps when I have a *Weh* at all, my *Heimweh* is for the tree in front of the house, the overshadowing tree whose green top one never looks at. . . . It is so near. One goes out of the door, and the tree-trunk is there, like a guardian angel."[64]

In 1930, only a month before Lawrence died, Earl Brewster was talking with him about their joint plan to have Lawrence stay with the Brewsters in the spring and live in a tent "under a great pine-tree near our house."[65]

Earlier, I referred briefly to the negative ions from vegetation promoting healing. From many references in Lawrence's writing it is clear that he was sensitive to the effects of positive and negative ions. For instance, when he was in Mexico trying to decide whether to rejoin Frieda in Europe or stay in Mexico, he became even more difficult to be with; but, finally, Merrild wrote that: "Lawrence is more human again. At present, he excuses himself on the ground that the air is so changeable that it makes him 'crazy' once in a while. A poor excuse."[66] However, at this same time Lawrence wrote to his friend Koteliansky that there had been many thunder showers "but the sky is blue and bright again."[67]

"Weather sensitive" people are depressed by the preponderance of positive ions in the atmosphere before the onset of thunder showers; thus it is quite likely that Lawrence was truly affected by the "changeable air." This sensitivity to positive ions enabled Lawrence to write a remarkable description of the disturbing effect of the atmosphere before a storm on Mercury Hill near Baden-Baden in Germany: "The hot sun burned overhead, and all was in steam. . . . There was not a breath of wind. . . . There was nothing to do. . . . Even we do not trouble to wander and pick the fat, blue bilberries. . . . out of the universal semi-consciousness of the afternoon arouses a bristling uneasiness. There is a great blackness rising up in the western sky and a thunder storm can be seen rapidly approaching."[68]

Lawrence wrote *Sea and Sardinia* while he was living in Sicily. Each day from his window he watched the moods of Mt. Etna on the horizon. He refers to the volcano as "that wicked witch, resting her thick white snow under heaven, and slowly, slowly rolling her orange-colored smoke . . . sometimes, verily, one can feel a new current of her demon magnetism seize one's living tissue and change the peaceful life of one's active cells. She makes a storm in the living plasm and a new adjustment. And sometimes it is like a madness."[69] And in a letter from Villa Mirenda near Florence he wrote, "I shall be glad when this stupid and muddled winter is at last over. The weather is still very heavy and overcast, sirocco, not nice. It feels as if an earthquake were brewing somewhere."[70]

In each of these passages Lawrence is describing the effects of positive ions; although the fact that ions affected human consciousness was unknown in his time. However, peasants in the Alpine regions had long known about the depressing effects of the "bad wind"—the *Foehn*—on themselves and their animals. For years "civilized" people tried to ignore such effects. The first modern scientific study of the effects of ions on health did not take place until some years after Lawrence's death in 1930. These studies took place in Russia because for many years people had traveled to the "electrical resorts" along the Black Sea for their health. It was found that these healing resorts had a preponderance of negative ions. Only recently has there been any general knowledge in America of the effects of negative versus positive ions on health. The Central Laboratory of Ionization in the Soviet Union claims that in 85% of the cases studied, numerous illnesses can be successfully treated with negative ions. Negative ions make people feel better and promote healing, while positive ions cause headaches, general depression and lethargy; furthermore they contribute to disease—especially that of the throat and lungs. Negative ions are present in moving water, on the tops of high mountains and near vegetation, especially trees. The Soviet researcher Chizhevskii reports that a forest, with its millions of leaves, gives off many more negative ions than does grass.[71] The ion balance of the atmosphere is also affected by an approaching storm front. The negatively-charged cloud base induces a positive charge on the earth's surface. Once the storm arrives, the usual ion balance returns and people feel better.[72]

Lawrence described the feeling he got before a storm as "thunder gathering . . . and making one's whole body feel dislocated."[73] The fact that positive ions are present in a much higher ratio than normal in cities probably further contributed to Lawrence's dislike of cities.

Winds which bring a preponderance of positive ions include the Santa Ana in California, the chinook of the Rocky Mountains, the sirocco, Italy's "father of depression," southern France's mistral, or Israel's sharav. "Typical symptoms, for instance of what the Central Europeans call 'foehn psychosis' include physical weakness, irritability, headaches, anxiety, insomnia, nightmare, nausea, apathy, depression, and a tendency to quarrel."[74] The artist Van Gogh cut off his ear during one mistral wind and committed suicide during another.

A high positive ion concentration depresses serotonin levels. Serotonin is one of several neurotransmitters, a biochemical that plays a very active part in the function of some parts of the brain and nervous system. Its actions relate to levels of pain sensation, emotional states and other nervous-system functions.[75]

As mentioned above, trees produce a preponderance of negative ions, thus making "weather sensitive" people, such as Lawrence, feel better; thus he would naturally gravitate to sitting under a nearby tree to write.

The remarkable clarity of perception which Lawrence showed for the atmospheric conditions around him extended to all the other beings in nature which he encountered. Graham Hough, in his book *The Dark Sun*, explains that in his nature poetry, Lawrence "makes an energetic and intuitive attempt to penetrate the being of natural objects, to show what they are in themselves, not how they can sustain our moral nature. Or it presents encounters between man and the non-human. . . . Of course it is radically subjective; who can know what it is to be pomegranate or a kangaroo. . . . But it has little to do with common human subjectivity; it is more an attempt to put common human subjectivity in its place by showing the myriad of queer, separate, non-human existences around it."[76] Hough goes on to say that the poems in Lawrence's *Birds, Beasts and Flowers* "express a uniqueness of life, not expressed anywhere else in his works or anywhere in anyone else's."[77]

Lawrence tried to show the "otherness" of non-human nature rather than reducing it to its anthropomorphic aspects, the usual method of most English poetry since the Romantic movement which began towards the end of the eighteenth century. Writing sarcastically about Wordsworth trying to fuse the primrose into a "Williamish" oneness with himself, Lawrence said: "He didn't leave it with a soul of its own. It had to have his soul. And nature had to be sweet and pure, Williamish. Sweet-Williamish at that! Anthropomorphised! Anthropomorphism, that allows nothing to call its soul its own, save anthropos. . . ."[78] The corollary of anthropomorphism is that: "The earth exists to be exploited, and is exploited." Lawrence made this statement in his review of the *Gifts of Fortune* by H. M. Tomlinson. He reported that the book was not an ordinary travel book because Tomlinson succeeded in conveying the "strangeness and beauty of life." Lawrence continued, "Once be disillusioned with the man-made world and you still see the magic, the beauty, the delicate realness of all the other life."[79] This is the secret of the continued freshness in Lawrence's writing throughout his life. In a letter to Dr. Trigant Burrow he wrote that the human mind now wants everything "ready-made." He, on the contrary, considers the sun and the rest of the cosmos to be alive and "not ready-made at all." People are "too dead, and too conceited. *Man is the measure of the universe.* Let him be it: idiotic foot-rule which even then is *nothing.* In my opinion, one can never *know*: and never—never *understand.*"[80] This very ability which Lawrence had—to *know* that he doesn't know—allowed him to see more into non-human life than anyone else around him. Rhys Davies wrote of Lawrence: "This power of entering the soul of non-human things is the characteristic I remember most clearly."[81]

Two examples of this "power" of Lawrence—his insight into fish and snakes—stand out. I choose these in particular out of a myriad other possible examples because it is relatively easy for people to care and attempt to understand fellow mammals or even birds, but fish and snakes are another matter.

While in Germany Lawrence caught a fish at Zell-am-See. Later, in a poem about the experience, Lawrence records that he unhooked its mouth, and saw the fish's "horror-tilted eye,"

> And felt him beat in my hand, with his mucous, leaping
> life-throb
> And my heart accused itself
> Thinking: *I am not the measure of creation.*
> *This is beyond me, this fish.*
> *His God stands outside my God.*

Toward the end of the poem he admits that he doesn't *know*; he only wonders—that he cannot know—that the other, the non-human has a value separate from him and cannot be merely used by him with impunity.[82]

Later, in Taomina, Sicily, where Lawrence and Frieda lived for a year, he came one day with his pitcher to get the water. Of the experience, he writes that he "must wait, must stand and wait" because "someone," the snake, was there before him. Lawrence's exquisite sense of living relatedness to all beings is shown here: he neither tried to instantly frighten it away or to kill it. The snake "softly drank through its straight gums" and lifted his head and looked at him as cattle do, and then stooped and drank some more. But he was golden brown, not black, and in Sicily golden snakes are venomous, so part of Lawrence said he should kill the snake. He confesses how much he liked him. "How glad I was he had come like a guest in quiet, to drink at my water-trough / And depart peaceful, pacified and thankless. . . ." Lawrence felt honored but torn with conflict. When the snake had drunk enough: "And lifted his head, dreamily, as one who has drunken . . . And looked around like a god, unseeing, into the air," he turned and climbed up into a hole in the rock wall. Then a sort of horror came over Lawrence as the snake crawled into the "horrid black hole" and he threw a log at the snake. It didn't hit him; instead he vanished into the hole. Lawrence immediately regretted what he had done; he despised both himself and the "voices of accursed human education." The poem ends with: "And so, I missed my chance with one of the lords of life."[83]

Truly, in many cultures snakes are "lords of life." "People are both repelled and fascinated by snakes, even when they have never seen one in nature," reports the Nobel Prize winning biologist, Edward O. Wilson. "In most cultures the serpent is the dominant wild animal of mythical and religious symbolism. Manhattanites dream of them with the same frequency as Zulus." This fascination with snakes comes from our deep evolutionary past. Poisonous snakes have been an important cause of mortality almost everywhere, and alertness to their presence can save lives. Wilson explains: "For humans beings, in a larger metaphorical sense, the mythic, transformed serpent has come to possess both constructive, and destructive power." The serpent is a god for many different cultures from China to the Americas.[84]

In New Mexico, Mabel Luhan took Lawrence to see the Hopi Snake Dance. He was enchanted with these snakes: "their clean, slim length of snake nudity, their beauty, like soft, quiescent lightning." They had been washed and anointed by the snake priests for nine days before the dance; and Lawrence remarked on the "spirit of man soothing and seeking and making interchange with the spirit of the snakes. For the snakes are more rudimentary, nearer to the great convulsive powers."[85]

Lawrence was equally sensitive in his perception of plants. He had studied botany at one time and was an avid collector of specimens when he was young. Writing of a walking trip with Frieda and Lawrence over the Alps to Italy, David Garnett recalls: "Every few yards, Lawrence or I would find some new flower . . . to add to my herbarium, which was enriched in three days by nearly two hundred Alpine species. Lawrence was interested in botany and loved flowers, which at that time played a large part in his symbolism and personal mythology."[86] Lawrence's feeling for flowers is shown in a passage from one of his earlier novels, *The Lost Girl*. The heroine sees an entire bank covered with lavender crocuses: "she felt like going down on her knees and bending her forehead to the earth in an oriental submission, they were so royal, so lovely, so supreme."[87]

In the essay "Flowery Tuscany," following the cycle of wildflowers in the spring, Lawrence wrote of the blue grape-hyacinth, which lasts as long as two months because only a few buds open at a time, beginning from the lower stem and continuing on up to the top. In the early spring the stalk is a "compact tower of night-blue clearing to dawn. . . . If we were tiny as fairies, and lived only a summer, how lovely these great trees of bells should be to us, towers of night and dawn-blue globes. They would rise above us thick and succulent, and the purple globes would push the blue ones up, with white sparks of ripples, and we should see a god in them." Then, combining his love of flowers with mythology, he says that they are the flowers of the "many-breasted Artemis" and that the Cybele of Ephesus "with her clustered breasts was like a grape-hyacinth."[88]

Only two months before his death Lawrence walked with his friend Ghiselin for about a mile along the shore of the Mediterranean until they came to the mouth of a small creek. Sitting down to watch the waves, they began talking about symbols. Lawrence told him: "A flower is the most perfect expression of life," and went on to explain that total individuality lay hidden in the bud and came forth in the blossoming of the individual. He referred to the lotus which came up out of the mud and bloomed so beautifully in the air; but Lawrence emphasized that the lotus blossom could not exist without the "oozing mud" underneath.[89]

Thoughout this chapter I have traced the intensity of Lawrence's relationship to each of the natural beings which he encountered during his lifetime. I have also documented the adverse reactions of other people to his relationships. Intense feelings toward nature were not only considered aberrant in Lawrence's lifetime but have also been considered so in all the decades since. Some beginnings of understanding came after Rachel Carson's book, but not until Edward O. Wilson gave us the word *"biophilia"* did it become intellectually respectable to talk or write about such matters. "Biophilia," according to Wilson is "the innately emotional affiliation of human beings to other living organisms." Our evolutionary history gives us this affinity for life.[90]

In the modern Industrial Growth Society, humans clearcut forests, pour toxic wastes into rivers, and exterminate species due to the forces of greed and fear engendered in such a culture; but such behavior is not innate in human beings.

Lawrence's sensitivity to his surroundings led him to feel deeply the destruction of nature around him while many others took it for granted as part of progress.

Biophilia has become an important component of the new discipline of ecopsychology, founded in 1994 and based on the work of Theodore Roszak, James Hillman and others. Walter Christie, Assistant Chief of Psychiatry at the Maine Medical Center, has developed an ecopsychological technique called "soul tracking" which "explores relationships that are neither wholly in the person [n]or in the environment. Soul tracking is based on the premise that our deepest psychology is most vividly revealed as we engage the natural world." Christie explains that they use many methods to experience resonance and intimacy with a natural place. "These include the use of a 'body fit' in a rock crevice or around a tree." Christie reports that such practices " balance our relationship with nature and reveal just what we need to know at any moment of life. . . . Such techniques of biophilia have the power to compel us deeper in our psyches for traces of the mysteries that make all life coherent."[91]

Like a true primitive, Lawrence sat between the toes of the tree in the Black Forest while writing: "Here am I between his toes like a pea-bug, and him noiselessly overreaching me." Throughout Lawrence's work one can find such examples of his "body fit" to nature around him.

It is important for both humans and the earth that psychology is recognizing the need for affinity to all life. As Wilson says: "Only in the last moment of human history has the delusion arisen that people can flourish apart from the rest of the living world. Primitives struggled to understand the most relevant parts, aware that the right responses gave life and fulfillment, the wrong ones sickness, hunger and death."[92] In the few generations since we have become industrialized, the psyche has not lost that; but it has been deeply hidden in order to conform to modern society.

For Lawrence the rainbow became the symbol of the many interrelationships between earth and sky and human; thus it provides the lyrical ending to *The Rainbow*, the novel he began after he met Frieda. Ursula, the heroine, is finally recovering her health after much mental and physical suffering. She is newly aware of the "stiffened bodies of the colliers" and the ugly houses "advancing over the hills, a dry, brittle, terrible corruption spreading over the face of the land, and she was sick with a nausea so deep. . . ." Suddenly she sees a rainbow forming itself in the blowing clouds.

> The arc bended and strengthened itself till it arched indomitable, making great architecture of light and color and the space of heaven, its pedestals luminous in the corruption of new houses on the low hill, its arch the top of heaven. . . . And the rainbow stood *on the earth*. . . . She saw in the rainbow the earth's new architecture, the old brittle corruption of houses and factories swept away, *the world built up in a living fabric of Truth, fitting to the over-arching heaven.*[93]

3

Weaving Together Male and Female within the Whole of Nature

In the concluding paragraph of his novel, *The Rainbow*, Lawrence wrote of the rainbow as being grounded on the earth: it "stood on the earth . . . fitting to the overarching heaven." In the context of the novel this phrase sums up the truth that he was working toward—not one system, the totally material earth and the other system, the totally spiritual heaven—but both earth and heaven, integral parts of one unified whole system. This glimpse of the unified whole was not possible for him until he met Frieda in March of 1912 and they fell in love in the total way which can only come to two people who have glimpsed the same truth but cannot quite comprehend it.

Only two months later, in May of 1912, he and Frieda left England for the Continent and just a year after their original meeting in March, Lawrence began the novel he first called *The Sisters* and later, *The Rainbow*. He wrote and re-wrote the entire book with, in Frieda's words, "his whole struggling soul." When his editor Edward Garnett sent back the first draft with a letter rejecting it, Lawrence replied: "I felt it insulted rather the thing I *wanted* to say: not me, nor what I had said, but that which I was trying to say, and had failed in. . . . All the time, underneath, there is something deep evolving itself out in me. And it is hard to express a new thing, in sincerity."[1] So hard, in fact, that Lawrence spent the rest of his life trying to find the words to communicate this "new thing."

In the final draft of *The Rainbow,* through the events in Ursula's life, Lawrence shows that if one gets in touch with one's deepest sexual nature it opens up awareness to the greater whole of nature; thus a fulfilling human society could be built in harmony with the greater cosmos. Three stunning blows came almost immediately to destroy this hope. To fully explain the effect of these blows I must recapitulate some of the circumstances surrounding the writing of the novel.

When Lawrence began to work on the novel in March of 1913, he and Frieda were living in Irschenhausen in the Bavarian countryside not too far from Munich. They had a little wooden house among fir trees on the edge of a meadow filled with primulas and gentians. Most of the second draft of the novel was written midst flowering fruit trees near the blue sea in the seaside town of Lerici in Italy. He finished it in May. Frieda's divorce from her first husband was final in May, and since she had received a "saner letter" from him she hoped to see her children again, so in June she and Lawrence returned to England.

Lawrence and Frieda were married in London on July 13, 1914. While in London Lawrence signed a contract with Methuen for the book and got an advance payment.

On the last day of July Lawrence set off on a walking tour of the English Lake District with three other men. Lewis had accompanied Lawrence in his walk across Switzerland. A man named Horne was also along and brought his friend from the Law Bureau, Samuel Koteliansky, who became Lawrence's lifelong friend. Days of walking in the lovely Lake District brought out the singing, the humor and the stories which Lawrence referred to often in later life. All of this suddenly ended when they came to the little town of Barrow-in-Furness, where Lewis lived, and found that war had been declared. The shock was so great that Lawrence wrote later, in January of 1915: "The War finished me: it was the spear through the side of all sorrows and hopes." He refers to the Lake District tour: "It seems like another life—we were happy—four men . . . since then I swear, my soul lay in the tomb—not dead, but with a flat stone over it, a corpse, become corpse-cold."[2]

Upon returning to London after leaving the Lake District, Lawrence received a second blow. Methuen thought *The Rainbow* was unpublishable because of "flagrant love passages." He could not bring himself to work on it again until November of 1914 and then only because he was convinced that if people could see the book they would realize the madness of their present life and change. After a further revision from March to May of 1915, the novel was finally published on September 30th. Reviewers termed it a "monotonous wilderness of phallicism" and filled with "viciousness and suggestiveness." The Director of Public Prosecution began proceedings against it and eventually the 1,011 remaining copies were burned.[3]

Meanwhile in December of 1914 Lawrence met Lady Ottoline Morrell. In late January she brought Bertrand Russell to meet him and the two men found much they could share during their talk; however when Lawrence went to the University to meet the others of the Cambridge group, the third blow fell for him when he saw the prevalent homosexuality there. Lawrence described this experience as "one of the crises of my life. It sent me mad with misery and hostility and rage."[4]

These three blows, following directly upon his glimpse of the fullness of life during the time he was working on the first draft of *The Rainbow* in Bavaria and Italy, led to Lawrence's lifelong efforts to probe the deeper dimensions of the problems of modern industrial civilization. In this chapter I will look into some of the sexual aspects of his life and work because, as Lawrence correctly grasped, the problem of sexuality in its larger dimensions, is at the heart of modern industrial civilization's destruction of humanity and nature. In later chapters I will consider the intellectual and the religious aspects of this destruction.

According to the oversimplified view of many critics and friends of Lawrence, the primary factor in his sexual life was his relationship with his mother, which first exacerbated his relationship with Jessie, and later led to homosexual feelings and his problems with Frieda. This could have been true had he remained bonded to his mother;

but, due to the experiences of his early childhood as related in the first chapter, he managed successfully to make the transition into the next stage—to use Joseph C. Pearce's terminology—bonding with the earth.[5] Actually, more important than the "mother problem" was the dichotomous feeling generated in him by the strong personalities of both his father and his mother. Ostensibly, as a child he followed his mother's way; but actually, the deepest parts of him did not disown his father (as his mother demanded) but instead were a reflection of his father and, in fact, contributed to his essential genius.

At first, Lawrence's older brother, Ernest, was "the pride" of his mother's heart and she concentrated all her hopes on him.[6] It was not until after Ernest left home to work in the city and, later, died of pneumonia, that she turned all her energy to Lawrence. Therefore, during the most impressionable years of his life, he and his father were closer than has been generally recognized. Jessie Chambers's brother, J. D., in his 1964 introduction to her book, quotes a Mr. Taylor, a classmate of Lawrence's at school. Taylor reports that he had often seen Pa Lawrence arriving "home merry with Ada and Bert hanging round his neck like a pair of cherries. There seemed no hatred there." J. D. then goes on to say that "Lawrence shared with his father an irrepressible gaiety and zest for life; but these inestimable gifts could only be enjoyed at the cost of a sense of treason towards his mother."[7]

Just here is the crux of Lawrence's central problem, which he spent the rest of his life writing about and learning to understand. He happened to be born into a situation which was a microcosm of the larger world. His father, as has been noted, was the last generation of Englishmen not to have been "broken" by schooling. His mother was from a slightly higher class—town educated and part of the "European genteel tradition" which included idealism, Christianity and a split between mind and body. Lawrence's father was part of what could be termed a "tribal culture," the pit miners, who had close physical ties with one another and were not yet part of an efficient modern industry. In their time off they lived close to nature— poaching game and wandering with their dogs. In his later years Lawrence said, "I would write a different *Sons and Lovers* now; my mother was wrong, and I thought she was absolutely right."[8]

It is true that Lawrence's mother did all she could to end the relationship between him and Jessie Chambers; however, this was only one aspect of that tormented relationship. The other aspect underlies the scene from *Sons and Lovers* where Paul Morel (Lawrence) and Miriam (Jessie) have their first sexual encounter. Paul and Miriam have been out gathering cherries and he is delighted with her softness and tenderness. He has torn his sleeve on the tree branch and she touches the rip near his shoulder, saying that she will mend it. He is aroused and wants to stay out even though they know it will rain. They move under the trees. He stands against a pine tree trunk and takes her in his arms. "She relinquished herself to him, but it was a sacrifice in which she felt something of horror." Later it begins to rain and the pine smell is strong in the darkness. Paul lies with his head on the dead pine needles, listening to the rain with a very heavy heart. "Now he realized that she had not been with him all the time, that her soul had stood apart, in a sort of horror. He was physically at rest, but no more."[9]

Lawrence often wrote brief poems immediately after an experience and then later worked the situation into a novel or short story. A first draft of a poem which he had written about this time in his life further explains this scene under the pine tree. In the poem, titled "Lightning," a man hears a woman's heart pounding against his. She feels sweet against him so that he doesn't care that the "black night hid her from me, blotted out every speck," But then, "When the lightning flew across her face / And I saw her for the flaring space / Of a second . . . inert with dread, wilted in fear of my kiss." Hearing the thunder and feeling the rain, "Almost I hated her, she was so good / Hated myself, and the place, and my blood / which burned with rage. . . ."[10]

In Lawrence's short story "The Witch `a la Mode," the hero has come back after having been gone a long while, and is now engaged to another. His old friend Winifred says she missed him very much . . ."you snatch things from the Kobolds for me." "Exactly," he said in a biting tone. "Exactly! That's what you want me for, I am to be your crystal, your 'genius.' My length of blood and bone you don't care a rap for. Ah, yes you like me for a crystal-glass, to see things into: to hold up to the light."[11]

The strained friendship between Chambers and Lawrence went on for about ten years. The torment he went through in these years is clear from a few verses in Part IV of a long poem titled "Manifesto," written some years later when he lived in Cornwall with Frieda. He writes of the fierceness of hunger for food and warmth for the body and the hunger for knowledge. "But then came another hunger/ very deep, and ravening." This hunger is more frightening even than that for food; it is "The hunger for the woman." He says that at first he thought it was for any woman, indiscriminately; but finally a woman fed that hunger and he discovered that what many women could not give, (including Jessie Chambers) he found in one, Frieda.

> She stood before me like riches that were mine,
> Even then, in the dark, I was tortured, ravening, unfree,
> Ashamed, and shameful, and vicious,
> A man is so terrified of strong hunger;
> and this terror is the root of all cruelty.

Frieda loved him and was ready for him but he was so "mad with voracious desire" that he almost couldn't accept her. But then,

> When a man is rich, he loses at last the hunger fear.
> I lost at last the fierceness that fears it will starve.
> I could put my face at last between her breasts
> and know that they were given forever
> that I should never starve. . . .

He goes on to say that peace and fulfillment comes from this,

> It is our ratification,
> our heaven, as a matter of fact.
> Immortality, the heaven, is only a projection of this strange but
>   actual fulfillment,
> here in the flesh.[12]

And for all this, he has only one woman to thank, "not mankind, for mankind would have prevented me." Lawrence realized that in some deep way woman, sex, and nature were connected. In *Sons and Lovers*, in the first love scene between Paul Morel and Clara Dawes, a divorced woman (partly modeled on Frieda), they have made love by a canal. When their consciousness returns he writes: "They had met, and included in their meeting the thrust of the manifold grass stems, the cry of the peewit, the wheel of the stars . . . to know the tremendous living flood which carried them always." This great power could "identify them altogether with itself." Knowing they were only small things in the "tremendous heave that lifted every grass blade . . . and every living thing, then why fret about themselves?"[13]

This same effect is portrayed in a short story, "Love Among the Haystacks." Maurice, the younger brother, has stayed alone for the first time at the hayfield and is going to meet Paula there. He is washing up in a stone basin and as he dries himself he feels as if he is not alone. "The flowers, the meadow-sweet particularly haunted him. . . . Things never had looked so personal and full of beauty, he had never known the wonder in himself before."[14] This basic theme, (as given in the sections from "Manifesto," and as noted in the two passages above), contains the germ of much of what Lawrence tried to express in a great deal of his writing, culminating in the "tenderness" of *Lady Chatterley's Lover*.

Lawrence met Frieda (then Frieda Weekley), when he went to tea at the home of Professor Weekley, who had taught one of Lawrence's classes at Nottingham University. According to Frieda's daughter by this marriage, Barbara, her father had once told her mother: "I have got a genius in my evening class."[15]

Lawrence and Frieda were instantly attracted to one another. Soon after they first met she wanted him to spend the night with her. He refused; instead he proposed that they go away together.

In her book, *Not I But the Wind*, Frieda writes that she was surprised that Lawrence could have loved her at first sight because she was thirty-one and had three children. She adds, "I had just met a remarkable disciple of Freud and was full of undigested theories.

This friend did a lot for me." She says that she had been living a conventional life but that this friend "awakened the consciousness of my own proper self."[16]

Because Frieda does not mention his name, his identity remained unknown until 1974 when Martin Green's book, *The Von Richthofen Sisters*, was published. This "remarkable disciple of Freud," Otto Gross, proves to be an important factor in understanding Frieda when Lawrence met her. In addition, what Gross stood for so influenced Frieda that, in turn, he had considerable (though indirect) influence on Lawrence's writing. Furthermore, Gross's ideas proved to be the underlying cause of many of the quarrels between Lawrence and Frieda through the years. Gross was the leading proponent of "the erotic movement," which held that love outside marriage was the only way in which modern man could be linked with "the natural fountain of all." Both Frieda and Else, her sister, were swept along by this movement for some time. In Bavaria, and especially in Munich, this rebellion against the heavy patriarchal culture of Germany, idealized "the woman" in the role of the Magna Mater, who religiously took many lovers and bore many children "without submitting to a husband/father/master."[17]

In the sisterly rivalry between Frieda and Else, Else chose the academic route, becoming one of only four women matriculating at Heidelberg in 1900. Frieda chose the other way to fight patriarchy, by renouncing all work competition with men. In exalting the gaiety and spontaneous living of "womanhood," she so completely suppressed her intellect that many people thought she was stupid. Gross gave her the recognition and acknowledgment which she needed for this role. He declared that Frieda Weekley had "removed the shadow of Freud from his path."[18]

Otto Gross was trained as a doctor and specialized in neurology and psychiatry. In a letter which Freud wrote to Jung in February of 1908, he said that Gross and Jung, himself, were the only ones among all his followers who had "original minds." Freud later repudiated Gross, as he had become too dangerous for Freud's reputation through his sexual libertarianism and his cocaine addiction.[19] (Freud himself had used and recommended cocaine for a brief time, before he knew it was addictive.) In *The Von Richthofen Sisters,* Martin Green states that practically nothing has been written *about* Gross except under the disguise of a character in novels. The only thing in all of Lawrence's works which can be inferred directly to represent Gross is a scene in *Twilight in Italy.* At first glance it seems to be just a passing incident occurring while Lawrence was walking alone through Switzerland to Italy. He meets some anarchists and in an emotion-laden passage refers to the leader as having a new spirit, "strange and pure and slightly frightening . . . a true star-like spirit." But Lawrence goes on to say that he could not "confirm him in his utterance." Green suggests that, since Gross was teaching and practicing anarchism in Switzerland at that time, thus breaking the law, Lawrence may have been referring to him. Although Lawrence was attracted to his ideas, he clearly saw the danger in Gross's way of life; but, at the same time, he somewhat resented being "Frieda's safe option." Gross was later arrested and confined to an insane asylum.[20]

There is considerable evidence that both Frieda and Else were, at different times, Gross's lovers. In this sense, Frieda triumphed over Else because Frieda "had been named the woman of the future" by Gross. "You are exquisite, Beloved . . . so marvelously new—a wonderfully pure soul in you, one kept pure by a genius for *insisting upon yourself,*" Gross wrote. Frieda thus came to Lawrence with a strong, sure sense of her own value. In fact, when she left with Lawrence, she sent her letters from Gross (dated in 1907 and 1908) to her former husband, Weekley, in order to explain her action and show him the true Frieda. By "woman of the future" Gross meant that she was an example of how people would be in the future when they were no longer damaged by all the conditions he fought against. "I know it was through *you,*" Gross wrote, "the only person who *today* has stayed free of chastity as a moral code and Christianity and Democracy and those heaps of nonsense." He then goes on to ask: "How have you been able to keep the curse and the dirt of two gloomy millenia from your soul with your laughter and love?"[21]

Frieda and Gross had spent time together in Amsterdam for a conference. In his letters to her afterward, he asks that she bring her children with her when next coming to Europe so she will not have to return to England.[22] Having her children with her was very important to Frieda; not only because she loved them, but also because they were an important aspect of the Magna Mater image. This contributed to her devastation when her husband kept them, and also accounts for Lawrence's short temper at her sorrow.

The idea of the Goddess or the Magna Mater (Great Mother in Latin) was not new to Lawrence. He had read Jane Harrison's *Ancient Art and Ritual* in 1913. In her work, Harrison documented the importance of the earlier Goddess culture which was supplanted by later patriarchal gods.

Despite the complexities of the Frieda/Lawrence relationship, it is generally agreed by their closest friends that she was the best wife for him. "From the first," Lady Cynthia Asquith wrote, "I very much liked Frieda. Exuberant, warm, burgeoning, she radiated health, strength and generosity of nature." Lady Cynthia says that she totally agreed with Richard Aldington when he wrote, "Whoever thinks he was not in love with Frieda is crazy."[23]

Two Danish artists, Knud Merrild and Kai Gótzsche, spent a winter with the Lawrences in New Mexico. They lived in adjoining cabins and they were together almost every day. Years later Merrild wrote of the time when he and Lawrence were traveling in Mexico. Frieda had gone back to Europe and Lawrence was in deep conflict concerning her. Merrild writes that in the last letter he got from them, Lawrence had rejoined Frieda in Europe and "they were again united, and I was glad to get Frieda's warm greetings. . . . She was so real, genuine and human. I often wondered how she could bear it all. More than once I remember her saying, 'It is not so easy to live with a genius.' Don't I know it, hadn't I seen it? But she did it, did it to the end. She was the anchor to which Lawrence could fasten his stormy ship."[24] Frieda's daughter, Barbara Weekley Barr, who spent some time with the Lawrences when she was grown, admits that their relationship had always been an enigma to her, until Maria Huxley described it as "a great passion." Huxley continued: "Frieda is silly. She is like a child, but Lawrence likes her because she is a child."[25]

Harry T. Moore, in his biography of Lawrence, writes that Frieda "could range in a moment from sophisticated poise to childish eagerness. Physically, she was a magnificent blonde tall animal, with high cheekbones and greenish 'Tartar' eyes flecked with brown."[26] Dorothy Brett, who spent considerable time with the Lawrences at their Kiowa ranch in New Mexico, wrote in a similar vein of Frieda's emotional gamut: "One day she stands, arms akimbo, eyes wild, mouth a long, tight slit; her close-fitting bodice, pleated, full skirts all arrogant and belligerent. The next, she is a big, warm, bounding creature, eyes blue and free, mouth a broad grin, bodice and skirt colorful and glowing: rough, hearty, and undoubtedly handsome."[27]

That Lawrence and Frieda fought outrageously did not mean they did not love one another. In 1951, years after Lawrence's death, Frieda wrote: "When I think of him, there was a splendor, a magnificence about him that I cannot possibly connect with failure. It is just absurd to call Lawrence a sexual weakling, anything but: with his intensity. You don't know how a man like he was, could give himself, body and soul."[28] Lawrence's relief at being rescued by her from his sexual morass was put into his famous poem, "Song of a Man Who Is Loved," where he says his home is "between her breasts" and in the last verse he says that he hopes he will spend eternity "with my face down buried between her breasts. . . ."[29]

Frieda came to the marriage knowing nothing about housework because her childhood was spent in a home with servants. In their daily life together, Lawrence did most of the household chores. Although eventually Frieda learned to wash and cook from Lawrence, she disliked housework while, according to Ghiselin, Lawrence "excel[led] in it."[30] Throughout his life Lawrence helped with whatever work needed doing. As a youth he helped with harvesting in the fields. In New Mexico he chopped his own wood, milked the cow and did all the other necessary chores for living in a mountain environment. His unique attitude toward work is documented by a table in Josephine Miles's book, *Eras and Modes in English Poetry*, which contains the major words used by two hundred poets from the year 1310 to modern times. A major word by Miles's definition is one that is used ten or more times in a passage of 1000 lines. Lawrence is the only poet, among twenty five poets born since 1850 to use the word, "work" with this frequency, and he used it both as a noun and as a verb.[31]

In his daily life Lawrence made little distinction between work and play. He enjoyed baking bread and cooking so much he generally made these activities into celebrations. This aspect of his life, so puzzling to intellectual friends, was merely one of the ways in which he lived as a true primitive.[32] "The primitive work group," according to the anthropologist, Stanley Diamond, "is multifunctional; labor is, of course, utilitarian but it is also sacred—a sport, a dance, a celebration, a thing in itself."[33]

Frieda was totally unlike Lawrence's mother; actually, she had many of his father's qualities. It is unlikely that Lawrence could ever have had a satisfactory sexual relationship with a woman who was in any way "mental" or "spiritual" such as his mother or Jessie Chambers. He once compared Jessie's "will" with his mother's. All his life he wrote against "sex in the head," although he himself was guilty of exactly this "willed" sex at least once, late in his life, with Brett in Ravello. He had been fighting bitterly with Frieda and had gone south to join the Brewsters. Eventually, when he and Brett ended up in adjoining rooms in Ravello, Lawrence entered Brett's room, saying, "I do not believe in a relationship unless there is a physical relationship as well." Brett was afraid that she wouldn't do the right thing and, naturally, it was a failure. The following night, the same thing happened when Lawrence said, "Let's try it again." She writes that all the love she had for him was frustrated by her fear of not being adequate. Brett had never revealed this to anyone until forty years later when she showed a diary and a few typed pages to John Manchester, who helped her with part of the 1974 edition of her book. Manchester writes, "Fortunately, I believe I was able to explain the psychological problems Lawrence might have been having and that she was not to blame herself." Manchester further says that Brett told him that Frieda "was the only woman who could *make* him feel like a *man*."[34]

Frieda's spontaneous, unwilled sexuality attracted him and freed him from all his doubts. As Martin Green explained, Frieda had fled the intellectual world of her sister, Else, to "espouse the world of peasants and primitive cultures, where even men live in the female mode of being."[35] She had "kept the curse and the dirt of two gloomy millennia" from her soul and freed Lawrence from that "genteel tradition" so that he could love fully.

Lawrence obviously recognized in Frieda some of the best qualities of his father. Especially toward the end of his life, Lawrence spoke often of how he had changed his opinion of his father, recognizing, as mentioned earlier in this book, that his father had possessed a great deal of the old gay male spirit of England; pre-Puritan, he was natural and unruined deep in himself.[36]

A. L. Rowse noted in 1952 in his book, *The English Past*, how "relentlessly the wife [Lawrence's mother] made him [Lawrence's father] pay for his failure to come up to her expectations of him. The irony of it is that his part in his son's genius goes unrecognized—and yet one sees that his was the artist's temperament, not hers, that the instinctual sense of life that made the creative strain come through him, the miner living his underground life of the senses, primitive and animal, shut out from the family, forgotten. Yet his was the dance, the ecstasy, the escape into dream. . . . D. H. had his father's cleverness with his hands, forever making things, the father unrecognized; the prophet, the uncompromising, relentless spirit of the mother."[37]

During the course of his life with Frieda there was a basic conflict within Lawrence. When he was happy and secure and well, he valued Frieda's life-affirming qualities. But when he was unsure, either in a social situation or because of his writing, or ill health; then his mother's values surfaced—her Puritanism, her "genteel tradition," her expectations, her emphasis on "will"—and then he hated Frieda with all the smoldering hatred which his mother had instilled in him for his father. This would explain why it was possible for Lawrence and Frieda to make up so easily after brutal fights. He could lash out in utter hatred when operating from an insecure position, but as soon as the immediate impasse was over, his wholeness of body/mind understanding immediately acknowledged Frieda's position as more correct than his. All those who lived near the Lawrences for some time, particularly Mabel

Luhan, Dorothy Brett and the two Danish painters, were surprised by the quickness and ease of their reconciliations.

Whenever Frieda wanted to taunt him, according to Brett, she would hang a cigarette out of the corner of her mouth and leer up at him through the smoke, thereby shocking his Puritan sensibilities. Other times she would mock him with, "If only you were a gentleman; if only you were well-bred, like me—an aristocrat instead of a lower-class man!"[38] The latter maneuver hit hard at his lower-class insecurities. The most notorious fight occurred when Frieda broke a plate over Lawrence's head. In a letter to Lawrence's biographer, Harry T. Moore, in January of 1955, she wrote that she only once broke a plate in a fight with Lawrence, "When Lawrence told me women had no souls and couldn't love!"[39]

Long after Lawrence was dead, in 1952, a young graduate student, Dorothy Mitchell, said to Frieda: "I was wondering what you think, or whether you agree totally with the position he gives to women."

"In a way he seemed to bully one and yet he never really bullied one," Frieda answered. "The more I was myself, the self I was meant to be, the better he liked me."[40]

Contrary to the commonly held opinion that Lawrence put women down, he actually acknowledged their absolutely indispensable role in human life as few other men have ever done. Early on he wrote, "It is hopeless for me to try to do anything without I have a woman at the back of me. . . . the woman keeps me in direct communication with the unknown."[41] What he meant here is more clearly explained in a letter written in March, 1915, to Lady Ottoline Morrell. He tells her: "you should have the pride of your own intrinsic self" and that she should not limit herself to the usual roles of wife or mother. Then he goes on to point out, "Primarily, you belong to a special type . . . like Cassandra in Greece, and some of the great women saints. They were the great media of truth, of the deepest truth. . . ." He goes on to say that the earth needs this prophetess type of woman, and that she should not trust merely her brain or her will but that "faculty for receiving the hidden waves that come from the depths of life, and for transferring them to the unreceptive world."[42] This is Lawrence's clearest explanation of what he means by the "power" of women. This is one aspect of the "power" which was generally recognized by primitives—the idea that woman naturally had the power and did not have to fast or sing all night to get it. In a peyote ceremony described in 1967, at dawn after the men have spent all night singing and working to get the power, the roadman greets the head woman, who comes to the door bringing the water and food of the earth. He gives her a tobacco cigarette and says, "Welcome, you who have the power."[43]

In two of his most important short stories, "The Woman Who Rode Away" and "St. Mawr," Lawrence's character the White woman makes a symbolic journey back to the point where humanity lost its way by choosing only the mental-spiritual over whole body / mind consciousness. In the first story the woman dies to further the "other" consciousness. In the second, the woman finds the possibility of continuing when she says, "This place is sacred," as she once again gets in touch with the earth itself.[44]

"Marriage is the great puzzle of our day. It is our sphinx riddle. Solve it or be torn to bits, is the decree," Lawrence told Danish painter Knud Merrild.[45] In a number of places Lawrence hints at a totally different approach to marriage than was considered normal. In his fiction the best instance is in *Kangaroo*, where he is writing of the relationship between the Australian couple, Jack and Victoria. "So long as she did not betray what was between her and him, as husband and wife, she could do as she liked with the rest of herself. And he could, quite rightly, trust her to be faithful to that indefinable relation which subsisted between them as man and wife. He didn't pretend and didn't want to occupy the whole field of her consciousness."[46] *Kangaroo* was written while Lawrence and Frieda were living totally alone without any friends whatsoever. Large parts of the book have to do with marital battles. In the introduction to Dorothy Brett's book on Lawrence, Manchester quotes from Brett's unpublished autobiography: ". . . in Australia, alone with Frieda, he was so bored he decided that he would never do that again, he must have someone else he cared for with them."[47]

It is clear that occasionally, in Lawrence and Frieda's life together, one or the other was either involved in a sexual relationship with another person or wanted such an arrangement. Paul Delany, in *D. H. Lawrence's Nightmare*, about Lawrence's years in wartime Britain, mentions that Frieda had at least three casual affairs in the first year that Lawrence and she were together. He mentions at least twice when Lawrence may possibly have had an affair of very brief duration, but the evidence is not conclusive.[48] In 1923 when Frieda went back to Europe and Lawrence went to Mexico, she and Middleton Murry became very close. When she visited her family in Germany, Murry went with her and she proposed that they have an affair. He was torn with conflict but eventually refused her because he believed it would have been disloyal to Lawrence.[49] When Lawrence came back to England briefly, he was unhappy with the "chumminess" of Murry and Frieda.

The plan then was for all four, Brett, Murry, Lawrence and Frieda to return together to New Mexico, according to Manchester. Frieda said it was Koteliansky's idea that they all go "so Murry could sleep with her while Lawrence was with Brett."[50] At the last minute Murry did not go and in a letter of July, 1953, he wrote to Frieda that it had been "because Brett was going, too."[51] Lawrence and Brett's affair had ended years before and Brett had not been happy about that. Finally, after Lawrence's death, when Murry went to visit his grave in Venice, he and Frieda became lovers. And it was of this time that he later wrote, "It was from you I learned what a woman's tenderness could be."[52]

Frieda later married Angelo Ravagli, whom she and Lawrence had met when they rented the Villa Bernarda in Spotorno, Italy. The peasant, Giovanni, who looked after the villa had informed them that it belonged to a "Tenente dei Bersaglieri in Savona," a lieutenant in the "Bersaglieri," an elite corps of the Italian Army. Meanwhile they were staying at a little inn and when sent for, Lawrence went to talk to the lieutenant. Returning, he told Frieda, "You must come and look at him, he is so smart."

"So I went and found a figure in uniform with gay plumes and blue sash, as it was the Queen's birthday," Frieda explains.[53] They saw Ravagli often because he did some necessary repairs for them and also began taking English lessons from Lawrence. In fact, he did such good work that Lawrence remarked to Frieda that "he would be useful to have at the Kiowa ranch."[54] Later, Frieda seems to have spent some time with him when she went to close up the Villa and Lawrence impatiently waited for her before they could go over to Port Cros.

Lawrence, as described by Kenneth Rexroth, was "one of those individuals . . . who gave off an unbelievable charge of radar. If you were sitting in a room and he came in behind you the whole place reverberated as if enormous dynamo poles had been put against either wall."[55] Many women besieged him and he sometimes told Frieda she was to keep them away from him. Idella Purnell Stone, who started a poetry magazine in Guadalajara in 1923, tells of sitting in a hotel on Lake Chapala in Mexico when Lawrence came in suddenly, "looking pale and pursued" and sat down by Frieda saying to her, ". . .protect me from these wretched women!"[56] Brett's account is the only published account of any attempted sexual relationship by Lawrence after his marriage; however, Mabel Luhan's archives, which she designated in her will could not be opened until the year 2000, may furnish more information.[57]

In a number of his works Lawrence calls for a new kind of relation between the sexes, even a new kind of marriage. In *Women in Love* he has Birkin criticize stuffy and exclusive marriage, "the world all in couples, each couple in its own little house, watching its own little interests, and stewing in its own little privacy." Yet, at other times Lawrence seemed a vigorous defender of marriage. When he and Frieda first left England for Europe, Lawrence wrote to Edward Garnett from Italy in 1912 that they would stay there until the divorce was consummated and then be married. "Frieda says she's not keen on marrying me—but I want some peace. I want to be able to look ahead and see some rest and security somewhere."[58] What was behind this was Lawrence's fear of the power of Gross and his ideas on "the erotic movement." Not only was he concerned about the possibility that Frieda might again see Gross, but even more, he was concerned with the basic underlying theme of the movement that the woman in the Magna Mater role should take many lovers and bear their children "without submitting to a husband." In November, 1918, several years after he and Frieda were married, he wrote to Katherine Mansfield: "In a way, Frieda is the devouring mother. It is awfully hard, once the sex relation has gone this way, to recover. If we don't recover, we die. But Frieda says I am antediluvian in my positive attitude."[59] Here Frieda was remaining true to Otto Gross' doctrine and Lawrence was fighting it. This conflict continued and was an underlying factor in Lawrence's uncharacteristic defense of Christian marraige. Uncharacteristic in that, not only had Frieda divorced to marry him, but many of his friends were divorced. Once, while visiting Mabel in Taos, they were all sitting in Ida Rauh's house, when Lawrence began "passionately declaiming against divorce." Ida remarked, "Isn't that funny, coming from you." Lawrence, surprised, asked her, "Why?" Ida laughed and said: "Well, you are staying in the house of one divorcee; you are visiting another; and you are married to another."[60]

A fairly common situation in Lawrence's fiction was a love affair in which one member of the couple was a woman married to someone else. In *Lady Chatterley's Lover*, Connie Chatterley, a married woman, leaves her husband to go off with Mellors, the game-keeper. The beautiful relationship between Mellors and Connie was based on Lawrence and Frieda's relationship at its best. Yet, in an essay written well after the book was finished, "Apropos of *Lady Chatterley's Lover*," Lawrence is ostensibly defending Christian marriage when he writes that the Church is "established upon the element of *union in mankind*" and marriage is the fundamental connecting link.

In this same essay, at a deeper level, Lawrence intuitively linked religion and sex in some very beautiful passages. "Sex is the great unifier. In its big slower vibration it is the warmth of heart which makes people happy together, in togetherness." He calls for a renewal of marriage "set again in relationship to the rhythmic cosmos." He goes on to point out: "The Early Christians tried to kill the old pagan rhythm of cosmic ritual, and to some extent succeeded. . . . They wanted to kill the festivals of the year."[61]

Tribal culture integrally linked sex, religion and the rhythms of the cosmos. Lawrence had sensed this, of course, as shown in his writing on the Indians and later on the Etruscans, but in his time there was not yet sufficient research to support his intuitions. Now, decades later, the facts are much clearer.

"Cultural man has been on Earth for some two million years: for over 99 percent of this period he has lived as a hunter-gatherer. Only in the last 10,000 years has man begun to domesticate plants and animals. . . ."[62] Ten thousand years is only four hundred human generations, "too few to allow for any notable genetic change. . . . We and our ancestors are the same people," according to Carleton Coon, a highly revered older anthropologist. He went on to say that, since the same physiological and psychological structure makes up our behavior patterns right now, it is to the hunting cultures we must turn to learn how "nature intended us to live."[63] Because this matter of the "old ways"' is fundamental in understanding what Lawrence was working toward, I will go into it further here. It is important to remember that, in a sense, Lawrence was raised in a hunting/gathering atmosphere. His father and his father's mates poached deer on the Lord's estates; furthermore, both of his parents rewarded him for the berries and mushrooms he brought home to them. Lawrence retained the alert senses of a hunter all his life, allowing him to "see more than a human being ought to see."

Although Carleton Coon states the premise most graphically, other anthropologists had been feeling their way toward similar conclusions; the breakthrough came in 1966 when a conference on "Man the Hunter" was held in Chicago, at which experts from many fields compared their information and found that primitive men, far from living a "nasty, brutish" life, had incredible leisure, spending much of their time in dancing and singing and in ritual.[64]

Paul Shepard, in his *The Tender Carnivore and the Sacred Game*, explains the price we paid when we left this more valid way of life. The human body is not made for long, heavy physical labor such as farming and other mechanized work. In hunting societies, strenuous effort was followed by much leisure. He points out that men and women are equally valuable in a hunting culture—the women for gathering; the men for hunting. Without either of these food sources the tribe dies. The technology is every bit as complex and ingenious and sophisticated as ours and much more efficient from the point of view of the earth itself.[65] "South African and Australian aborigines are able to support a person on 1/75 to 1/100 of what it takes to support an American. . . . [H]unters and gatherers are 75 to 100 times more efficient than we are."[66] In *Stone Age Economics*, Marshall Sahlins points out that the upper Paleolithic culture was the "original affluent society," each individual working an average of only fifteen hours a week.[67]

Throughout the human era on earth no tribal group ever volunteered to change its culture. A tribal group, living in a particular ecosystem, was aware of the limits—you don't destroy all the game; you don't destroy the soil or you don't survive. The other type of culture, biosphere culture, began with early civilizations and imperial states. Gary Snyder succinctly explains that these cultures "spread their economic system out far enough that they can afford to wreck one ecosystem, and keep moving on. Well, that's Rome, that's Babylon,"[68] and every imperialistic culture since then. Industrial England was merely a further extension of the biosphere type of culture.

Throughout his life Lawrence wrote of the damage that the ever-growing industrial process inflicted on the countryside with the destruction of the forests, the fouling of the waters and and the accompanying destruction of the human spirit. In his time few understood his rage against what they felt was progress. Better than anyone else, Lawrence clearly grasped the connection between the destruction of nature and the ever-growing human insensitivity and desperation. Only recently has this correlation become so obvious that David Whyte, a modern bard, is able to write: "Lose your primary entanglements with agonizing beauties of the natural world and you need tremendous lashings of power and money to make up for it. The soul, hungry for belonging, will eat up the whole world if it is bereft of its primary marriage with the trees, sky, and ocean with which it has co-evolved and over millions of years come to love."[69]

To Lawrence it seemed that the restrictions imposed by narrow Christian teachings on the developing young person was at the heart of the process of alienation from nature without—and true human nature within.

At the crucial time of life when the young person must make the difficult transition to adulthood, the basic physical need of the young organism for sexual activity was surrounded by so many restrictions and difficulties, that to survive the young person was forced to limit his or her awareness and sensitivity. In Lawrence's youth, when he was "starving for sex," an older woman, Alice Dax, helped him. Hopkin once inadvertently heard Mrs. Dax tell his own wife: "Sallie, I gave Bert sex, I had to. . . . I took him upstairs and gave him sex. He came downstairs and finished the poem." And though she fell deeply in love with Lawrence, she did not try to hold him but gave him up for his own good. After his death, Alice Dax wrote to Frieda in 1935, that she thought Frieda had been the right one for him.[70]

Lawrence's unusual compassion for the married man in such cases is shown both in his personal life (in his attempts to write to Professor Weekley, Frieda's husband) and, in his fiction, by the scenes with Baxter Dawes, the husband of the woman Paul Morel is involved with in *Sons and Lovers*. In both of these cases Lawrence is intuitively moving more toward a tribal approach to sex. For instance, Wilfred Pelletier explains the difference between sex on his Indian reserve in Canada and in the white world in this manner:

> My own introduction to sex was provided by a relative. I still look on that as one of the greatest and happiest experiences of my life. From that time on, it seems to me that I screwed all the time, without letup. Not just my relatives, who were not always available, but anywhere I could find it, and it always seemed to be there. . . . I have the impression that in white society, at least for those of my generation, sex and relating to girls was really rough. It was sinful and immoral, stuff like that. . . . On the reservation people were honest about their feelings and their needs, and as all the resources of that community were available to those who needed them, sex was not excluded. Sex

was a recognized need, so nobody went without it. It
was as simple as that.[71]

The rigid rules and traumas associated with marriage in our
culture developed only recently in the long history of the human
species, with the rise of agricultural societies, where the transfer of
land and property became important. To trace the underlying
importance of sexual activity it is necessary to turn to our primate
ancestors, where sex was not merely a reproductive process but
served as a bonding agent for the group. Contrary to most other
animals, female primates do not all come into heat at the same time;
they do have a peak season of births, but the mating game and sexual
activity continue throughout the year, thus freeing sexual energy
for social uses. One or another female is in heat at any given time.
The continuing courtship and copulation in primate groups acts as
a sort of bonding mechanism throughout the tribe. In general this
bonding action of sex continued in human cultures.[72] As the
psychologist Erik Erikson explains, a satisfying sexual act is "a
supreme experience of the mutual regulation of two beings that in
some way breaks the point off the hostilities and potential rages
caused by the oppositeness of male and female. . . . Satisfactory sex
relations thus make sex less obsessive, over-compensation less
necessary, sadistic control superfluous."[73]

A tribal society, which is based on kinship, is "universally
conservative and stable. Oddly enough, the most flexible bond seems
to be marriage itself. . . . not until the rise of agrarian cultures was
marriage subjected to the chains of public opinion, civil law, and
institutionalized religion. . . . For hunting-gathering people . . . the
kin structure is stable because the individual is born or initiated into
a group as durable as the plant or animal species taken by it as a
totemic emblem. Given the reality of flux in all human society, this
link to the natural throws people into closer intellectual and
emotional recognition of the one constant in their lives, the terrain
with its enduring natural community."[74]

Toward the end of his life, Lawrence wrote some of his ideas
about marriage in a letter to Brett, after reading a book on marriage

which she had sent him. "[W]hat a feeble lot of compromises! It's no good talking about it: marriage, like homes, will last while our social system lasts, because it's the thing that holds our system together. But our system will collapse, and then marriage will be different— probably more tribal, men and women being a good deal apart, as in the old *pueblo* system, no little homes. It all works back to individual property, even marriage is an arrangement for the holding of property together, a bore!"[75]

Primitive cultures provide helpful information on another aspect of sexuality in connection with Lawrence and his work. This is the speculation, through the years, concerning Lawrence and homosexuality. Particular scenes in a number of novels have been mentioned in this connection: in *The White Peacock*, where Cyril Beardsall (based on Lawrence) and George Saxton (modeled on Jessie's brother), bathe together in a pond; in *Women in Love*, the famous wrestling scene between Gerald Crich and Rupert Birkin (Lawrence); and in *Aaron's Rod*, Rawdon Lilly chafing Aaron Sisson back to health. In addition, there is Lawrence's suggestion of a "blood brotherhood" ceremony with Murry while they were living in Cornwall.

The idea horrified Murry; but it was not altogether out of context in Cornwall with its megalithic stone monuments. Catherine Carswell, one of Lawrence's oldest friends, wrote in her book *The Savage Pilgrimage* that "he cherished the deep longing to see revived a communion between man and man which should not lack its physical symbols. He even held that our modern denial of this communion in all but idea, was largely the cause of our modern perversions. To recover true potency, and before there could be health and happiness between man and woman, he believed that there must be a renewal of the sacredness between man and man.[76] More than fifty years later we finally have a book, *Sacred Manhood, Sacred Earth*, which dares to explore this essential concept. Joseph Jastrab explains: "This communion with all life—inner and outer—is precisely what a sacred manhood is all about. But so few of us today actually experience the mystery of this communion as a daily reality. The recovery of sacred manhood begins with noticing that we've turned our backs on selected parts of ourselves, others, and the Earth." He explains that "the need for beauty, or spiritual longing or wildness . . . are not just human desires and behaviors; these are acts of nature."[77]

After Lawrence's death Murry, in trying to explain what had happened between Lawrence and him there in Cornwall, reported that each of them had a totally different purpose. All Murry wanted was "the warmth and security of personal affection." Lawrence not only wanted that but he also wanted "an impersonal bond between us: that we should be servants of the same purpose, disciples of the same idea." Murry states that two elements went into Lawrence's idea that he did not understand at the time. "One was an instinctive, infra-personal sense of solidarity with men—the true, deep gregarious experience, which Lawrence had known as a child and longed to renew," and the other was a curiously intense preoccupation with "the animal of himself."[78] Murry considered himself a part of the intellectual community, which at that time tried to totally ignore every part of the human being, except the head, while Lawrence was interested in the whole being working as a unit.

Lawrence had experienced the joys of working together with close friends—the haying with Jessie's father and brothers and working together on the cabin and cutting trees for fuel with the Danes—in both cases, almost a tribal experience. Furthermore, he remembered his father and his father's mates. In "Nottingham and the Mining Countryside," written toward the end of his life, Lawrence wrote: "Under the butty system, the miners worked underground as a sort of intimate community, they knew each other practically naked, and with curious close intimacy, and the darkness and the underground remoteness of the pit *stall* and the continual presence of danger, made the physical, instinctive, and intuitional contact between men very highly developed, a contact almost as close as touch." He says his father "loved the pit . . . loved the contact, the intimacy." Above ground the colliers went to the pub to "continue the intimacy" and they roamed the countryside with a dog and "loved the countryside, just the undiscriminating feel of it." His father would sit on his heels and "watch—anything or nothing." In the essay, Lawrence criticizes the idea of each having "their own little homes," separate from everything else, thus causing a "great scrabble of ugly pettiness over the face of the land." He says that "we have frustrated that instinct of community which would make us unite in pride and dignity in the bigger gesture."[79]

In Taos there were two relationships which provided some speculation. One friend was Clarence Thompson, a protégé of Mabel Luhan. He is mentioned together with Lawrence in several anecdotes both by Mabel and by Dorothy Brett. Brett tells of a time when Clarence drove up to have tea and "during tea Clarence has the impertinence to make googoo eyes at you [Lawrence]. You make no sign of having noticed."[80] Mabel says that Clarence "began to turn all his attention upon Lorenzo" and that they "planned to ride off into the desert on horseback and never be seen again!" Frieda said, "Just let them try it."[81]

Neither the full story of Lawrence and Clarence or, for that matter, Lawrence and Jaime de Angulo will be known until Mabel Luhan's archives are opened. Some aspects of Jaime's life provide further insight into Lawrence's particular genius, so I will go into more detail here concerning de Angulo, who was born in Paris in 1887 of Spanish aristocracy and was raised speaking French. At eighteen, he broke with his father, sailed to the U.S. and worked as a cowboy on ranches in Colorado, Wyoming and later, California. Talked into getting some education by a Frenchman he met in California, he enrolled in the now defunct Cooper Medical College in San Francisco, and later got his M.D. from Johns Hopkins in 1912. About this time he married Cary Fink, who later left him and went to Zurich to study with Jung. Eventually, as Cary F. Baynes, she became one of the major translators of Jung's works. During World War I, Jaime was a doctor and a psychiatrist for the early air corps.

At one time Jaime owned a ranch near Alturas, California, and became friends with his Achumawi ranch hands, thus beginning his linguistic studies. In 1915 he drove a herd of cattle 500 miles south to the Big Sur country to homestead and it was here that he met Kroeber and Radin, both outstanding anthropologists of the time. Recognizing his linguistic talents, Kroeber got him to teach two courses at Berkeley, one in psychiatry and one on the mind of the primitive man. Jaime learned seventeen new Indian languages in the next fifteen years and published nearly thirty academic papers in the fields of anthropology and linguistics. He eventually married Nancy, his second wife, who was a scholar and an expert on the Miwok Indians. They traveled to Europe where his first wife introduced him to Jung, with whom he worked for a short time and "for whom he developed a warm liking and respect."[82] Henry Miller, who knew de Angulo on the Big Sur, wrote that "his spirit was as wild and unpredictable as this wild and lonely coast where he finally anchored. Cultured though he was, versed in so many things—medicine, folklore, magic, anthropology, language—what he really craved was a virginal world. . . ."[83]

Mabel brought de Angulo to Taos, having met him the previous winter when she and Tony Luhan, her husband, were living on Mt. Tamalpais near San Francisco. Mabel wrote so glowingly to Lawrence about de Angulo that Lawrence disliked him before he met him. Brett writes that Mabel was sure there would be a great rapport between Lawrence and de Angulo "so we are intrigued and impatient to see him." He showed up wearing "several shirts, a pair of Chinese pants, no hat, a wild fluff of curly hair blowing about . . . a thin, sensitive face."[84] Brett continues: "Jaime flits in and out of our lives. He is vivacious: his keen, energetic mind darts and probes like the beak of a humming bird. My awful English reserve irritates him, but he adds a note of gaiety to our lives." Brett adds that Lawrence "would chaff him endlessly about everything."[85]

The various accounts of the relationship between Jaime and Lawrence cannot possibly be reconciled so I will just give two of them as examples. D. L. Olmsted, in the brief summary of de Angulo's life in the introduction to *The Achumawi Dictionary*, states that "Lawrence was already jealous at long distance of de Angulo, because of Mabel's letter of praise. . . . in Taos, de Angulo did his best to appease Lawrence . . . but Lawrence, who basked in the idolatry of women, feared other men, particularly if they interrupted his monologues. Lawrence ridiculed de Angulo's attempts to write fiction, and eventually drove him off."[86] The poet Robert Duncan, who lived in the de Angulo household as the family typist in 1949 and 1950, says that he first heard of Jaime in the late thirties in Berkeley and that he was "the very young man that D. H. Lawrence had fallen in love with in Taos." De Angulo's "memory of D. H. Lawrence during that period was that Lawrence was an utterly repulsive man. Jaime hated him, but was never very clear why . . . ."[87]

The deeper relevance of this controversial relationship between Lawrence and de Angulo is that, in his later years, Jaime was considered a shaman. True to the shamanic type, de Angulo not only crossed the lines between the living and the dead but the sex line as well. He was a transvestite as part of his shamanic vocation. De Angulo's definition of sex has little to do with being specifically male or female, having more to do with generation. Children of any one couple belong to the whole tribe—not just that particular couple. And the Indians are concerned with being the "children of the world they are living in," which is why they venerate the tree or rock. In the Indian world, "the earth, and all its properties . . . become a large commune, larger than man."[88]

De Angulo had a great many personal tragedies and became something of a legend in his own lifetime. He called himself a "wanderer" in later life. According to Pit River Indians, in a time of great personal stress, when one finds his usual surroundings impossible to bear, he starts wandering—traveling on and on—living mostly in wild, lonely places. De Angulo explains, "Wandering is something that may unfortunately befall any man or woman, and it can take many, many forms. . . . When you have become quite wild, then perhaps some of the wild things will come to take a look at you, and one of them perhaps takes a fancy to you. . . . When this happens the wandering is over, and the Indian becomes a shaman."[89]

Not only does the concept of "wanderer" also describe Lawrence's life after the war, when he became so discouraged with England, but the concept of shaman fits him, too, in some very important ways.

Joan Halifax, a medical anthropologist specializing in psychiatry and religion, went through the demanding Huichol training for a shaman in the 1970s. She decided to do this, she told me, when she had some severe breakdowns in her personal life and recognized the shamanic manifestations. In her book, *Shamanic Voices*, she describes the central aspects of shamanic personality. The shaman "can be described not only as a specialist in the human soul but also as a generalist whose sacred and social functions can cover an extraordinarily wide range of activities." Parts of her descriptions of a shaman's functions apply to Lawrence. "Shamans are healers, seers, and visionaries who have mastered death. They are in communication with the world of gods and spirits. . . . they are poets and singers . . . [who] create works of art. . . . they are familiar with cosmic as well as physical geography; the ways of plants, animals, and the elements are known to them. They are psychologists, entertainers, and food finders. Above all, however, shamans are technicians of the sacred and masters of ecstasy."[90]

Most often, the crucial experience which causes a person to manifest shamanic tendencies is a severe illness where the person almost dies. For Lawrence this occurred the first time when he was sixteen and almost died of pneumonia. When he was twenty-two and teaching at Croydon his health broke and, again, he almost died. As a result of such illness, "The human spirit is oriented toward the cosmos, the ground of being is the universe." The shaman has "integrated many planes of life experience: the body and the spirit, the ordinary and the nonordinary." In writing of shamanic balance, Halifax says: "Just as twilight is the temporal threshold, shamanic equilibrium is the process occurring at that threshold."[91] Lawrence used Venus, the Evening Star, as the symbol of this balance between opposites in his *Plumed Serpent*. In this shamanic equilibrium contraries are dissolved—life and death, light and dark, male and female. Halifax gives examples of shamanic initiation where the spirits guide and teach the male shaman "in the woman's way." This transformative process can also involve an actual change in sex role.[92] Perhaps most interesting of all for an understanding of Lawrence is where Halifax writes that the "shaman's voice, whether raised in song or chant is most important." Through his voice can come the voices of the gods or the voices of creatures and the elements, the "numinous sounds of far-off stars."[93]

Given this shamanic background the so-called "problem" of homosexuality loses its importance. Whether a person is or is not homosexual is unimportant on this deeper level because it is a recognized stage in shamanic vision but not necessarily a part of every shamanic process.

The problem which Lawrence had to face, though, was that his special traits of heightened vision and clarity which in a primitive society would be considered so important that he would be a "sacred" personage, in a modern industrialized society only led him to be labeled neurotic or insane. Because Lawrence saw so clearly, he felt that he only needed to show others through his writing and they, too, would see and change. This is precisely what a shaman does as a "technician of the sacred" in a tribal culture. But this is not how it works in modern society, which has lost its center. The critic and novelist Richard Aldington, who knew Lawrence personally, remarks on his "delusion of immense personal power," referring to Lawrence's "extraordinary faith that by writing and publishing his books he would immediately have a decisive influence on human society."[94]

In a tribal culture, such as that of the Huichol Indians in Mexico, however, the shaman, Matsúwe, does maintain "balance in the human community as well as in the relationships between the community and the gods or divine forces that direct the life of the culture." Joan Halifax refers to Matsúwe as a "sacred politician."[95] Barbara Meyerhoff, another anthropologist who worked with the Huichol shamans, points out that the shaman lives in paradox. If we look at her definition of the shaman we find a remarkable correspondence with Lawrence's work. The shaman brings "the dark world of the 'unconscious' to the light of consciousness." He tries to find wholeness, a "dynamic equilibrium of living life's paradox, and the magical quest for meaning via stories and symbols—these are the shaman's heritage, as enriching and useful now as in the Old Stone Age."[96]

In her book on modern shamans, Ruth-Inge Heinz gives three categories for the role of a contemporary shaman: "1. They access different states of consciousness at will. 2. They perform services for their 'community' which otherwise are not available, and 3. They are the mediators between the sacred and the profane." Heinz has two studies of living Caucasian shamans: the ritualist, Elizabeth Cogburn, who lives in northern New Mexico, and the Polish theater director, Jerzy Grotowski. As Heinz mentions, although modern shamans do help people through consciousness changes and in healing, until the last few years their services went unrecognized and often they were considered mentally unbalanced.[97] Heinz's three categories fit Lawrence's work; but of course this shamanic aspect of his work could not be recognized until now.

Returning to Lawrence's search for a valid, deep relationship between men, in a letter written in the summer of 1919, he states; "I believe in 'manly love' the real implicit reliance of one man on another; as sacred a unison as marriage: only it must be deeper, more ultimate than emotion and personality."[98]

Only now, with Joseph Jastrab's work, do we have further insight into what Lawrence was trying to say so long ago. Jastrab explains: "A mature relationship with Eros is fundamental to the recovery of sacred manhood. By Eros I mean the felt experience, or em-body-ment, of that connection or union. The sacred is not a thing, and therefore, it cannot be found in any particular place. Being no-thing and no-where, it is gained or lost through the aperture of our openness toward life. To experience the enlivening warmth of Eros, a man must come to love the wildness of his physical and emotional body. . . . A sacred erotic sensibility has to do with establishing a love relationship with the entire universe through the body."[99]

Later, when the Lawrences traveled to the American Southwest and saw ritual Indian dancing, Lawrence saw a culture in which man related to man in a totally different way. For instance, in his essay "The Hopi Snake Dance," he writes of the young priest holding the corn cob in a particular way and "the old priest prancing strangely at the young priest's back in a sort of incantation, and brushing the heavy young shoulders delicately with the prayer-feathers." And again, watching a dance in Taos he mentions the older men "hover carefully, protectingly over the young men."[100] He saw the same underlying action in the races of the Taos Indians.

A large part of the male activity among many primitive tribes was the sweat lodge ritual held before every important ceremony, or for health, or for merely getting together. For instance the Potwasi Indians of California, who lived in the foothills of the Sierra, went several times a day to the sweat bath, just to meet and talk with other men.

One more widely misunderstood aspect of Lawrence's approach to sexuality in his work is concisely stated in a letter he wrote to Scottish poet J. O. Meredith in November of 1915: "One has oneself a fixed conscious entity, a self which one has to smash. . . . It is no good being sexual. That is only a form of the same static consciousness. Sex is not living till it is unconscious: and it never becomes unconscious by attending to sex. One has to face the whole of one's conscious self, and smash that."[101]

Michel Foucault, in his book *The History of Sexuality*, remarks that sexuality was constructed. It is not naturally given. Sex is natural but what we have done to it is sexuality. This "sexuality" created these new personages: the nervous woman, the frigid wife, the mother with obsessions, the impotent husband, the hysterical girl, "the precocious and already exhausted child, the young homosexual who rejects marriage or neglects his wife." Out of all this grew the realization that the family, "the keystone of alliance," was the "germ of all the misfortunes of sex."[102]

Foucault's book shows how it came to be that sex was cut off from its roots in the whole of the mind and body of the individual and, therefore, helps in understanding Lawrence's emphasis on the difference between "sex in the head" and true "phallic sex." One of the things many critics have found puzzling in Lawrence is the fact that he raged against not only "dirty stories" to do with sex, but also idle sexual gossip; while at the same time, through his books, he was urging the return to phallic sex. They see a dichotomy in this situation, whereas in reality, these are complementary aspects of the same approach.

In our culture we have "hooked most of the passion of living into sexuality, and that's the real trouble. Any time there is a total response in any situation, the "whole being is there and because the being is sexual, sexuality is always there in any total response. . . . It can occur in any relationship—with an animal, a flower, the world itself."[103] There is no problem until we bind this sexual energy into the genital area and thus cut off the flow throughout the person. This explanation from Joel Kramer's book, *The Passionate Mind*, illuminates another aspect of Lawrence. It becomes obvious that Lawrence related totally with his complete being, including the sexual aspect, with almost everyone and everything he came into contact with. For instance, in the incident which I mentioned in an earlier chapter, Ford Madox Ford, Lawrence's first editor, tells of Lawrence's "almost super-sex-passionate-delight" in flowers. Ford admits that Lawrence was "too disturbing" for him. This ability of Lawrence to relate totally—sexual aspect and all—was the reason not only for the dislike of some people, but also for the jealousy. When Lawrence first talked to Mabel Luhan, after he arrived in Taos, she later wrote, "In that hour, then, we became more intimate, psychically, than I had ever been with anyone else before . . ."[104] But she complains that Frieda would not allow the flow of energy from Lawrence to go out to anyone else. In other words Mabel felt that, because Lawrence could give her his flow, no one else was entitled to share it and Frieda in turn felt that only she was entitled to it.

Although Lawrence searched through several continents he never found a living culture which managed to preserve the sacredness and unity of sex within the whole of nature. The Etruscans were long dead and the American Indians had been infiltrated by Christianity for several centuries by the time he saw them. To find a culture which did preserve this unity until modern times, we must turn to Taoist China, with its basic understanding that the energy of the universe operates through the male and female. Joseph Needham, a biochemist at Cambridge University in England who devoted at least thirty years of his life to studying the science and civilization of China, writes: "The purpose of Taoist sexual techniques was to increase the amount of life-giving *ching* as much as possible by sexual stimulus. . . . Continence was considered not only impossible, but improper, as contrary to the great rhythm of Nature." There were special liturgies for the people of the entire village, called the "True

Art of Equalizing the Chhi's." The ceremony occurred on nights of the new moon and full moon, after fasting. It consisted of a ritual dance, the "coiling of the dragon and playing of the tiger; which ended either in a public hierogamy or in successive unions of the members of the assembly in the chambers along the sides of the temple courtyard." Needham says: that "naturally Buddhist asceticism and Confucian prudery were both scandalized" and they began a counter movement so that no more general Ho-Chhi festivals were held after the seventh century. But they "continued until the last century for lay people in general." In a footnote Needham says: "I always remember the reply given to me by one of the deepest students of Taoism at Chhengtu when I asked him how many people followed these precepts: 'Probably more than half the ladies and gentlemen of Szechuan.'"[105] This conversation occurred in the 1940s during the midst of the war, when Needham was in China to gather the manuscripts from Taoist monasteries so they would be safe from destruction in the revolutionary battles. Thus we see that a ceremony developed by the cultured, sophisticated, literate, aesthetic Taoists survived right down to modern times.

Needham provides an interesting summary in which he links Taoism with general primitive usage: "The recognition of the importance of woman in the scheme of things, the acceptance of equality of women with men, the conviction that the attainment of health and longevity needed the cooperation of the sexes, the considerable admiration for certain feminine psychological characteristics, the incorporation of the physical phenomena of sex in numinous group catharsis, free alike from asceticism and class distinctions, reveal to us once more aspects of Taoism which had no counterpart in Confucianism or ordinary Buddhism. There must surely be some connection between these things and the matriarchal elements in primitive tribal collectivism. . . ."[106] The juxtaposition of holiness, sex and nature inherent in Taoism produced the exquisite Chinese love poems wherein nature was an inclusive part of the sexual act.

Lawrence's "phallic vision" was completely misunderstood in the midst of the "flaming, hedonistic twenties" and the aftermath of the war. It becomes clear why he was totally misunderstood on all sides. As early in his life as 1908 he was working toward his "phallic vision," as shown in a letter to Blanche Jennings in which he said that most people marry "with their souls vibrating to the note of sexual love. . . . But love is much finer, I think, when not only the sex group of chords is attuned, but the great harmonies, and the little harmonies, of what we will call religious feeling (read it widely) and ordinary sympathetic feeling."[107] Many years later, after finding fulfillment with Frieda as well as experiencing many different cultures in the world, Lawrence was able to state more clearly what he felt to be true in this passage, written in 1929, the year before he died:

> Oh, what a catastrophe, what a maiming of love when it was made a personal, merely personal feeling, taken away from the rising and the setting of the sun, and cut off from the magic connection of the solstice and equinox! This is what is the matter with us. We are bleeding at the roots, because we are cut off from the earth and sun and stars, and love is a grinning mockery, because, poor blossom, we plucked it from its stem on the tree of Life, and expected it to keep on blooming in our civilized vase on the table.[108]

4

Mind and Nature

Nothing is born by taking thought.[1]
—D. H. Lawrence, in a letter to Bertrand Russell, 1916

For the same reasons that Lawrence fought against "sex-in-the-head," he battled against the supremacy of "rational" thinking. While the former brought down the wrath of the puritanical general public, the latter brought down the hostility of the leading intellectuals of the day, the Bloomsbury group. Some twenty years after his death, during a taped discussion of several people talking about Lawrence, Frieda remarked that some of his terrible rages had been directed at ideas supported by the Bloomsbury group, and she goes on to say, "I felt they could have wrung our necks, both of them." When the moderator asks why, Huxley answers, "It was entirely a critical society based on books, and thus a direct conflict with Lawrence." The Bloomsbury group, of course, included Middleton Murry, Vanessa and Clive Bell, Lytton Strachey, Maynard Keynes, and Virginia Woolf.[2]

Equally at odds with Lawrence were the Cambridge group and Bertrand Russell. Lady Ottoline Morrell brought Russell to meet Lawrence in February of 1915, during the time he was working on *The Rainbow*. Lawrence and Russell met together several times after that. The crucial event occurred when Lawrence visited Russell in his rooms at Cambridge University. At that time Russell introduced him to Maynard Keynes. Afterwards, Lawrence wrote that it made him "very black and down" to be there and that he couldn't bear "its smell of rottenness, marsh-stagnancy."[3] In June Lawrence had written that he and Russell were going to give joint lectures in the fall, but in August he wrote Cynthia Asquith, again telling her that Russell had sent him a synopsis of the lectures and "I can only think them pernicious." He goes on to say that Russell and the rest all want the same thing, "a continuing in this state of disintegration wherein each separate little ego is an independent little principality by itself." He says he has "a real bitterness" in his soul and that Russell and Lady Ottoline are traitors. They make him talk, and enjoy what he says, but it is just as though he were a sensation to be enjoyed. "They say I cannot think," he adds. [4] The lectures were called off and, in some later letters to Russell, Lawrence writes that Russell is the "enemy of all mankind." He continues, "It is *not* the hatred of falsehood which inspires you. It is the hatred of people, of flesh and blood."[5]

In one of his last letters (December 8, 1915) to Russell, Lawrence says he has been reading Frazer's *The Golden Bough* and *Totemism and Exogamy*. "Now I am convinced of what I believed when I was about twenty—that there is another seat of conciousness than the brain and the nervous system: there is a blood-consciousness which exists in us independently of the ordinary mental consciousness. . . . And the tragedy of this our life, and of your life, is that the mental and nervous consciousness exerts a tyranny over the blood consciousness and that your will has gone completely over to the mental consciousness, and is engaged in the destruction of your blood-being or blood-consciousness, the final liberating of the one, which is only death in result. Plato was the same."[6]

Once again, there were no words for what Lawrence was trying to say back then in 1915 and 1916. Some of the words he used through the years in different essays were "non-rational," "soul," "love," "mindlessness," "blood-consciousness," "the organic," "the dynamic," "the vital," and "darkness."

Russell in turn wrote that he felt Lawrence was a "positive force for evil" and that Lawrence came to have the same feeling about him. Russell said that he disliked Lawrence's "mystical philosophy of 'blood.' . . . it seemed frankly rubbish, and I rejected it vehemently."[7]

In the intervening decades since this controversy between Russell and Lawrence, Russell has been considered the authority and Lawrence's ideas generally dismissed. Only recently has the situation changed. In a paper given at the "Earthday X Colloquium" at the University of Denver in April of 1980, philosopher Ernest Partridge explained that logical atomism which drew both Bertrand Russell and the young Wittgenstein, was a "reiteration, refinement and elaboration of Hume's claim that our knowledge consists of discrete bits of data 'glued together' by external rules of association. But the atomists went further: the structure of our knowledge reflects the basic metaphysical structure of the world—i.e., a collection of 'atomic facts' joined only by *external* relations among them. Herein was a thoroughgoing rejection of the basic ecological maxim: 'everything is connected to everything else.' First, as most contemporary philosophers will acknowledge, logical atomism is virtually without adherents today. . . . Furthermore . . . the *holistic* systems approach and perspective is alive, well and flourishing in game and systems theory, cybernetics, and of course, in the compelling facts of the science of ecology."[8]

When Lawrence said that Russell's "will had gone over to the mental consciousness" and was destroying the other consciousness, with death as the result, his words were generally considered as the ravings of an unstable man. With the rise in ecological consciousness in the last two decades, the considered opinion of experts who have spent their lives studying the interactions of man and nature echo Lawrence's insight—for example, Gregory Bateson's statement in 1967 that rational consciousness alone, "is necessarily pathogenic and destructive of life."[9]

Russell, as noted above, had introduced Lawrence to Keynes, whose influence on our economy is still felt today, as well as to the philosopher G. E. Moore. All three men were members of a secret club called "The Society." The predominant influence was Moore, whose emphasis was on emotional reticence, unworldliness and intellect. Another aspect of this group was that it was either celibate or frankly homosexual.[10] After this meeting, Lawrence wrote to David Garnett: "when I saw Keynes that morning in Cambridge it was one of the crises of my life. It sent me mad with misery and hostility and rage. . . ."[11] David Garnett was not only the son of Edward Garnett, one of Lawrence's earlier editors, but he had also accompanied Frieda and Lawrence in their walk over the Swiss mountains some years before. Garnett had introduced Lawrence to Lady Ottoline Morrell and through her he met the others from Cambridge. In the above letter Lawrence was "ultimately telling me to break with him or with my friends," according to Garnett, so he broke with Lawrence. Much later Garnett read a memoir about Lawrence to a small group of friends who met regularly through the years. And shortly after that, in September 1938, just a year before World War II began, Keynes, one of this group, did a memoir on "My Early Beliefs" in which he referred to Lawrence. In the introduction to the published *Memoir*, David Garnett says, "I never met a writer who appeared to have such genius," and he admired several of his novels. "But I was a rationalist and a scientist, and I was repelled by his intuitive and dogmatic philosophy."[12]

Keynes writes that at the time he met Lawrence, "Cambridge rationalism and cynicism, then at their height, were, of course, repulsive to him [Lawrence]." Keynes admits that the fundamental intuitions of Moore's work under which they lived "are much too few and narrow to fit actual experience . . . [but] they furnish a justification of experience wholly independent of outside events." He continues that this has become "an added comfort, even though one cannot live today secure in the undisturbed individualism which was the extraordinary achievement of the early Edwardian days. . . ." He goes on to admit: "As cause and consequence of our general state of mind we completely misunderstood human nature, including our own. The rationality which we attributed to it led to a superficiality, not only of judgment, but also of feeling. . . . The attribution of rationality to human nature, instead of enriching it, now seems to me to have impoverished it." And he ends with a most interesting paragraph in which he remarks, "What a combination of qualities we offered to arouse his passionate distaste; this thin rationalism skipping on the crust of the lava, ignoring both the reality and the value of the vulgar passions . . . that is why I say that there may have been just a grain of truth when Lawrence said in 1914 that we were 'done for.'"[13]

Lawrence was correct, but the damage of ignoring his ideas went far deeper than anyone at that time could have predicted. Serge Latouche explains that "following the Great Depression with the vogue for Keynesian ideas and the interest in macro-economics the major industrial countries . . . entered upon the period of the Gross National Product as the criterion for judging a culture's success."[14] According to Jean Robert, "It was Keynes, who in 1936 first suggested that a country's total expenditures on final products—goods and services ready for consumption—could be the measure of its 'national product',"[15] and hence of that country's true value. However, the full horrors of the Keynesian economic system did not become apparent until after World War II "when Truman declared, in his inauguration speech, the Southern Hemisphere as 'underdeveloped areas." Wolfgang Sachs continues: "The label stuck and subsequently provided the cognitive base for both arrogant interventionism from the North and pathetic self-pity in the South."[16]

The World Bank, the Peace Corps, and other development schemes were supposedly for the good of the Third World countries; however, Ivan Illich gives a list of the environmental disasters resulting from "development" and continues: "But even more difficult to survive with these environmental changes is the horror of living with the habits of needing which four decades of development have established. The needs . . . that development kindles not only justified the despoliation and poisoning of the earth, but they also acted on a deeper level. They transmogrified human nature. They reshaped the mind and senses of *homo sapiens* into those of *homo miserabilis* . . . Needs have only very recently become a universal experience and just now have people come to speak of their needs for shelter, education, love and personal intimacy."[17]

Jean Robert provides the best summation of the problems when he writes: "Today, awakening from four decades of development dreams, we are forced to confront the credibility of the association of production with happiness or welfare. For we can now see the worldwide dislocation, suffering and alienation resulting from these dreams—or delusions. We are the witnesses of a war, a war against subsistence embedded in specific cultures, a war against nature itself."[18] Trying to repay loans from the World Bank forced the cutting of rain forests and other worldwide destruction of the natural environment—just to pay the interest on the loans with no hope of ever repaying the loans. Indeed, Lawrence was right when he said long ago that we are "done for."

I have gone into these matters at some length because they furnish a background for what Lawrence was up against. The Bloomsbury and Cambridge groups were composed of the leading intelligentsia of England, the ones with the most influence. Lawrence saw clearly that the ideas of these intellectual leaders were creating an "almost overwhelming incubus of falsity and ugliness on top of us, so that we are almost crushed to death," as he wrote to Russell.[19] But Lawrence was no match in educational credentials or reputation to this group, a fact which made him rage even more. Lawrence had played the intellectual game for awhile with great success. Huxley pointed out that in his youth Lawrence was "a tremendous passer of examinations." He *was* good at being an intellectual but he had realized its deadly limitations.[20]

There is an interesting insight into the ending of *The Rainbow* in Lawrence's letter written to Cynthia Asquith on August 16, 1915, which was just about the time he was finishing that book: "We are a nation which must be built up according to a living idea, a great architecture of living people, which shall express the greatest truth of which we are capable. . . . We must begin to choose all afresh, for the pure, great truth." And in another letter to her after the book was out, when the authorities had suppressed the sales and people he counted on to support it had disliked it, he wrote: "Your letter makes me sad. Believe me, my feet are more sure upon the earth than you will allow—given that the earth is a living body, not a dead fact."[21] It was not until some seventy years later that Lovelock's Gaia hypothesis made it intellectually acceptable to call the earth a living body. Here, mirrored in Lawrence's personal life, we can see the last lines of *The Rainbow*: "And the rainbow stood on the earth. . . . She saw in the rainbow the earth's new architecture, the old, brittle corruption . . . swept away, the world built up in a living fabric of Truth, fitting to the over-arching heaven."

During the controversy with Russell, Lawrence began writing his "philosophy." He mentions in a letter to Russell in March of 1915, "I was too sad to write my 'philosophy' (forgive the word) any more." Later he writes that he will write "all [his] philosophy again," pointing out that last time it came from the Christian camp but this time it will be from the early Greek philosophers.[22] Russell lent Lawrence a copy of John Burnet's *Early Greek Philosophy*, thus introducing him to the pre-Socratic philosophers.[23] When the lectures with Russell fell through, Lawrence decided to write "his philosophy" for the short lived little paper, *The Signature*. This was the origin of his essay "The Crown," which ran in the first three issues—all that were ever published.

In "The Crown," Lawrence uses the British symbol of the lion and the unicorn above the crown. Within this basic symbol he developed numbers of polarities which must be balanced, such as light and dark, unconscious and conscious. He says that the rainbow, "the iridescence which is darkness at once and light at once," is the symbol of this relatedness. "The true crown is upon the consummation itself, not upon the triumph of one over another, neither in love nor in power." He says that war is an almost inevitable outcome of the triumph of ego and will, "within the shell of our civilization," until eventually everything goes flat. Then comes the necessity of some extra stimulus: "Oh, give us the brush with death." He goes on to say that perhaps when men have had their fill of destruction and our civilization is broken then we "are at last born into the open sky, we shall have a whole new universe to grow up into and to find relations with." Near the end he points out that our universe is "not much more than a mannerism with us now." But if we break out we shall find that man and woman are more than they thought and the sun is greater and then we can begin the "one glorious activity of man: the getting himself into a new relationship with a new heaven and a new earth. Oh, if we knew, the earth is everything and the sun is everything that we have missed knowing. But if we persist in our attitude of parasites on the body of earth and sun, the earth and the sun will be mere victims on which we feed our louse-like complacency for a long time yet."[24]

In January, 1916, Frieda and Lawrence moved to Cornwall; there Lawrence began work on his *Studies in Classic American Literature.* In the first essay, "The Spirit of Place," he writes that "the deepest self is way down, and the conscious self is an obstinate monkey," and if one wants to be free and real one cannot follow the imposition of one's own will but instead follow "IT": "IT being the deepest whole self of man, the self in its wholeness, not idealistic halfness."[25] In the essay, "Herman Melville's *Moby Dick,*" he chants: "Doom! Doom! Doom of our whiteday." He goes on to say that Melville knew that our white civilization is doomed. Moby Dick "is the deepest blood-being . . . hunted by the maniacal fanaticism of our white mental consciousness. . . . Our blood-consciousness sapped by a parasitic mental or ideal consciousness."[26] In "Hawthorne and the *Scarlet Letter,*" he writes that when a person is split as in our culture, "the blood *hates* being KNOWN by the mind. It feels itself destroyed when it is KNOWN." And the mind "simply hates the dark potency of blood-acts: hates the genuine dark sensual orgasms, which do, for the time being, actually obliterate the mind and the spiritual consciousness, plunge them in a suffocating flood of darkness."[27]

Here in these works of Lawrence, written in the midst of the first World War, we find him groping toward an understanding of the human mind which has not been clarified until recently. This breakthrough began with Myer's and Sperry's experiments on cats, where it was found that when the corpus callosum was cut, each hemisphere of the brain could function independently as if it were a complete brain.[28] Some years later Dr. Bogen and P. Vogel developed a technique for cutting the corpus callosum of those people afflicted with uncontrollable epilepsy, thus preventing massive seizures. Working with such people provided knowledge of how the two hemispheres process information. Ornstein labels these processes "day consciousness" and "night consciousness," terms which Lawrence had used decades earlier. In the left hemisphere, consciousness is located in a place and events come one at a time and in order. Language, logic, and scientific analysis depend on this type of thinking. In the right hemisphere many different events can occur all at once. This kind of thinking is synthesis-oriented, non-verbal and intuitional. Artistic, musical, and spatial activities are handled in the right hemisphere.[29] Our culture puts great stress on rational hemisphere activities, so much so that Dr. Bogen claims that in denying the information coming to us from the right hemisphere, "we are all half-brained." The analytic left hemisphere can take an incoming event apart and analyze it, but cannot put it back together; this is the function of the other hemisphere. Bogen believes that it is possible to develop both hemispheres in a more balanced relationship, thus providing access to separate but complete information systems. Self and world could be seen as part of the same whole.[30]

Bogen has shown that certain other cultures, such as the Hopi, have a more balanced use of the two hemispheres.[31] Presumably other primitives also have this ability. Using the rational hemisphere, items of incoming information must be handled one at a time; while in the intuitional hemisphere much more information must be handled at once because it is absorbed in gestalts or patterned wholes. Too great a dependence on the linear, left-brain type of knowledge limits the human being because nature is *not* linear. Primitives such as the Kalahari bushmen are able to locate a buried ostrich egg full of emergency water in a featureless desert by depending on total body knowledge—a sensing of which way the wind blows at particular seasons, minute changes of color in the vegetation at different seasons, etc.[32]

Paul MacLean's "Triune Brain" theory is useful in explaining the interaction between the neo-cortex or new brain, the limbic or animal brain, and the old or reptile brain. MacLean explains that the human brain "amounts to three interconnected biological computers," each with "its own special intelligence, its own subjectivity, its own sense of time and space, its own memory, motor, and other functions." These three brains are different in structure and millions of years apart in evolutionary time. In effect, we experience the world through three different mentalities, "two of which lack the power of speech." The oldest brain, the reptilian, has a role in aggressive behavior, territoriality, ritual and the establishment of social hierarchies. Although the word "reptilian" seems abhorrent to westerners, in India, yogic techniques raise the kundalini energy, "serpent power," from the base of the spinal cord into the brain, producing powerful energy and sometimes enlightenment. Thus it connects the "abdominal brain" of the Oriental cultures with the triune brain in the skull. Likewise in T'ai Chi, the abdominal breathing of Taoism in China, rouses the "dragon power" lodged in the abdomen and sends it up by means of the "Greater Heavenly Circulation" to the crown of the head. The limbic brain is involved with the basic things needed to keep the individual organism functioning, and with emotions.[33]

Lawrence's "mind consciousness" can be equated to the rational, analytical left hemisphere of the neo-cortex, while his "blood consciousness" can be equated at times with the intuitional right hemisphere and at other times with the overall "knowing" of the three brains working harmoniously together. The "whole mental consciousness and the whole sum of the mental content of mankind is never, and can never be more than a mere tithe of all the vast surging primal consciousness, the affective consciousness of mankind," Lawrence wrote. Not that we have become too conscious, but rather, "we have limited our consciousness, tethered it to a few great ideas, like a goat to a post. . . . We insist . . . on what we know from one mere centre of ourselves, the mental centre."[34] In his "Introduction to These Paintings," he wrote, "Any creative act occupies the whole consciousness of a man. . . . The truly great discoveries of science and real works of art are made by the whole consciousness of man working together in unison and oneness: instinct, intuition, mind, intellect all fused into one complete consciousness; and grasping what we may call a complete truth."[35]

In a 1976 issue of *Man and World: An International Philosophical Review*, Hwa Y. Jung and P. Jung, referring to newer developments in phenomenology, write: "In its deepest sense, phenomenology is the possibility of embodied thinking—thinking in flesh and bones with the heart's desire rather than disembodied mind alone."[36] Thus we find, more than fifty years later, an echo of Lawrence's concepts in a modern philosophical journal.

By March 1920, Lawrence had finished *Fantasia of the Unconscious*, his next major attempt at outlining his philosophy. He notes that this "pollyanalytics" grows out of what he learns from the novels and poems which are "pure passionate experience."[37] Once again, Lawrence was faced with the difficulty of trying to articulate concepts for which there were not yet any acceptable words. He continues to inveigh against the over-rationalizing of human lives and pleads for a balancing of the analytical with the other ways of knowing, which come through love, art and religion. He begins with the development of the fetus from the center, which still in the adult human is beneath the navel, in the solar plexus. He then goes into a complicated system of development based on a fourfold polarity of objective consciousness, polarized in the cardiac plexus and the thoracic ganglion in the breast and lower, dynamic-subjective consciousness in the solar plexus area. Since his nomenclature is confusing because he adapted it from any system he could find which would help get his ideas across, it is not necessary to go further into it. What he is working toward is given quite clearly in his second chapter: "By idealism we understand the motivizing of the great affective sources by means of ideas mentally derived. . . . This motivizing of the passional sphere from the ideal is the final peril of human consciousness. It is the death of all spontaneous, creative life, and the substituting of the mechanical principle." Later on he says that if one mode is stressed more than the other, "corruption sets in," and he continues, "the two modes must act complementary to one another, the sympathetic and the separatist. . . . The goal of life is the coming to perfection of each single individual."[38]

From his reading of the early Greek philosophers, Lawrence had correctly attributed the beginnings of the emphasis on "ideas" as dating from the time of Plato. Farrington, in 1949, asked the basic question Lawrence was working toward: "What then, precisely, was the nature of the sin which had rendered Aristotelianism and so much else of Greek philosophy [after the Pre-Socratics] fruitless for good? It was the sin of intellectual Pride manifested in the presumptuous endeavour to conjure the knowledge of the nature of things out of man's own head, instead of seeking it patiently in the Book of Nature."[39] In the letter to Russell mentioned above, Lawrence wrote that he was no longer coming from a Christian position, but it is almost impossible for one man to break out of the thought patterns of several millennia so that he can clearly express the new position. What he was trying to get at, even though his terms are obscure, can perhaps be better understood by referring to certain Taoist concepts. Needham in his great work on Taoism in China clearly shows the difference between the European and the Taoist. It was not that the Taoists did not think there was order in nature, "but rather that it was not an order ordained by a rational personal being, and hence there was no conviction that rational personal beings would be able to spell out in their lesser earthly languages the divine code of laws which he had decreed aforetime. The Taoists, indeed, would have scorned such an idea as being too naive for the subtlety and complexity of the universe as they intuited it." They realized that the universal order was intelligible because they themselves had been produced by it, not because humans, by virtue of their rational minds, could impose an order on it. Human beings were part of the greater pattern, the *li*, of nature—not separate from it or above it. This concept is the base of the Chinese aphorism: "Heaven, Earth, and Man have the same *li*."[40]

One of the greatest thinkers of our time in the related fields of anthropology, biology, and psychiatry, Gregory Bateson, has spent his entire life on the problem of "the pattern that connects" humans and the rest of life. Finally, in 1979, at the age of seventy-five, his "major life's work" was published, *Mind and Nature: A Necessary Unity*. Early in the book he clearly outlines his stand: "This book is built on the opinion that we are parts of a living world." He goes on to say that there is no longer "a sense of unity of biosphere and humanity" as was once given to some degree by such religions as Christianity and Hinduism and totemism—"the sense of parallelism between man's organization and that of the animals and plants." He states that the purpose of his book is to "propose a sacred unity of the biosphere that will contain fewer epistemological errors than the versions of that sacred unity which the various religions of history have offered."[41]

Basically, how do things inside the head relate to those outside in the world of things and creatures, parts and wholes? Bateson states categorically that "there is no conventional method of describing such a tangle. We do not know where to begin." He continues:

> Fifty years ago, we would have assumed that the best procedures for such a task would have been either logical or quantitative, or both. But we shall see . . . that logic is precisely unable to deal with recursive circuits without generating paradox and that quantities are precisely not the stuff of complex communicating systems.
>
> In other words, logic and quantity turn out to be inappropriate devices for describing organisms and their interactions and internal organization. . . . [A]s of 1979, there is no conventional way of explaining or even describing the phenomena of biological organization and human interaction.[42]

Bateson's basic premise is that the mental world—the mind—is not limited to our skin. The information coming to us includes all the external pathways along which information travels, such as other minds, light, sound, temperatures, and all aspects of earth and sky. The basic unit of mind is not the rational individual but the relationships between all these aspects.

It is possible, now, to see why Lawrence had such a difficult time trying to explain his "pollyanalytics" fifty years ago. It took Gregory Bateson a full lifetime of more than seventy years to define the problem and attempt the beginnings of an answer. Furthermore, since Bateson often refers to the work of his father, who was a biologist and a pioneer geneticist, two lifetimes were involved in this project.

Given all these factors, it is remarkable that Lawrence managed to convey some understanding of this unity of mind and nature by means of the written word. The strange, haunting power of certain of his passages is due to the fact that they include the *total* human being—not just the rational mind or the emotions or the physical body—but the entire person in interaction with the whole of nature in the immediate vicinity.

The immediate state of nature around his characters—the texture of the air, the smell of the vegetation, etc., which most critics generally overlook or dismiss as mere scenery, are neither; these aspects are integral parts of Lawrence's holistic approach. Only now is it even possible to begin to understand what he was doing. As Bateson says, "We are beginning to play with ideas of ecology, and although we immediately trivialize these ideas into commerce or politics, there is at least an impulse still in the human breast to unify and thereby sanctify the natural world, of which we are."[43] This is why Frieda was correct when she endorsed A. S. Frere-Reeve's words: "Lawrence is like a man so far ahead on the road, that he seems small."[44]

There is one other aspect of Lawrence in which Gregory Bateson's work proves helpful. In an essay "The Logical Categories of Learning and Communication," Bateson categorized learning into three levels, remarking that the top level, Learning III, is "likely to be difficult and rare." It does sometimes happen in psychotherapy, and "in other sequences in which there is profound reorganization of character." He goes on to say: "Even the attempt at level III can be dangerous and some fall by the wayside." Some are labeled psychotic by authorities, but for the more creative who achieve this level, "the resolution of contraries reveals a work in which personal identity merges into all the processes of relationship in some vast ecology or aesthetics of cosmic interaction. That any of these can survive seems almost miraculous but some are perhaps saved from being swept away on oceanic feeling by their ability to focus in on the minutiae of life."[45] Now I am not claiming that Lawrence was a full fledged mystic or anything of that sort, but from the above it is obvious that at times he certainly operated at the level of Learning III and this, of course, accounts for some of the problems he had dealing with certain types of people, especially those locked into their limited egos.

When *Psychoanalysis and the Unconscious* was generally dismissed or ridiculed, Lawrence went ahead and wrote *Fantasia of the Unconscious*. In a letter to Brewster, he wrote that he was calling it "fantasia," "to prevent anybody tying themselves into knots trying to 'understand' it." Because a large part of it deals with educating children, I refer to an earlier Lawrence essay, "Education of the People." In August of 1918, Lawrence spent some time with the Carswells in the Forest of Dean. They had their young son John Patrick along. Catherine Carswell, writing a little later when John Patrick was a toddler and they were again visiting with Lawrence, said: "For the first time I had the chance to see how good Lawrence was with children. He made no special business of them, but knew how to include them warmly and naturally in his life. He was devoid of tricks with them, either old-fashioned or modern, and I was struck by the children's response." Anytime Lawrence was with children this same quality came out. During the earlier time when the Carswells and Lawrence were together and John Patrick was a baby, the three of them had many discussions on raising children; Donald Carswell suggested that Lawrence write some articles on education for *The Times Educational Supplement*.[46] Lawrence writes: "How to begin to educate a child. First rule, leave him alone. Second rule, leave him alone. Third rule, leave him alone. That is the whole beginning."[47] At the time he wrote this, in 1918, such a statement was incomprehensible. The vast educational bureaucracy was just getting into gear and it was deemed the salvation of the world. Now, since all the efforts of reform in the 1970s, some experts such as John Holt have decided that no school at all is the only answer for young children.

Needless to say Lawrence's "Education of the People" was never published in his lifetime, but writing it did lead eventually to writing *Fantasia of the Unconscious*.[48] In Chapter 7 of the latter work he states categorically: "No child should be sent to any sort of public institution before the age of ten years." He devotes some pages to discussing this matter. Lawrence remembered clearly the "anguish with which I wept the first day I was captured."[49] Later, as a teacher himself, he was forced to take part in the destruction of much of the child's spirit and natural learning ability, replacing it by the purposive stupidity induced by fear and conformity. His father's zest for life, untamed by school, was another factor influencing Lawrence's thinking on education.[50] During Lawrence's time, when schooling was essentially designed to produce workers for the ever-growing industrial system, it was felt that the children must be trained to meet the demands of the machine. "A wise and skilled Christian should bring his matters into such order that every ordinary student should know his place, and all should be . . . as the parts of a clock or other engine, which must be all conjunct and each right placed. [And] the school room is supposed to be a training ground for the 'habit of industry,' in which the children at the earliest possible age are 'habituated, not to say naturalized, to labour and fatigue.'"[51]

In the last few years a number of books indicate that Lawrence was correct in his analysis. Joseph Chilton Pearce, in his book *Magical Child*, is adamant when he says that "nothing is important except physical interaction with the world" during the early years. The child's physical actions *are* his thought processes. Play is how he learns. "Not only hard physical play but playing in imagination, fantasy and imitation. In this latter type of play lie the roots for true culture and religion later on." A few years later in the child's life, the middle childhood years, the child goes through a "period of intensive and ecstatic play in which varying the possibilities of one's survival tools is explored."[52] This is the joyous, peril-filled play with the earth itself—balancing activities such as walking tree limbs, jumping off roofs, or as Lawrence wrote, the "clue to early education: movement, physical motion, attuning of the kinetic energy of the motor centres to the vast sway of the earth's centre. Without this we are nothing."[53]

Reflecting Lawrence's much earlier thoughts, Pearce further states: "Forcing the early child to deal prematurely with adult abstract thought can cripple the child's ability to think abstractly later on. . . . The stage-specific period for bonding to the earth begins to fade at around eleven and disappears about fourteen or fifteen."[54]

As was noted in an earlier chapter, Edith Cobb, in her book *The*

Ecology of Imagination in Childhood, traced the roots of genius to a child's relationship with the natural world. The child's body becomes a way of knowing: "body and universe are engaged in some harmoniously integrated ongoing process . . . evoking a passionate response. . . . The exaltation that the child feels is a passionate response to an awareness of his own psychophysical growth potential as a continuity of nature's behavior."[55] Knowing and being are continuous with the larger processes of nature itself.

Paul Shepard points out that the activities which most attract children are precisely the ones through which they learn best: "In these crucial experiences of childhood play and exploration, in the impulse to name and classify and anatomize, in the yearning for skill tests, heroes, and the 'other,' in ceremonial revelation or workable myth . . . are the moments when the perception of nature is fixed and the heart of the hunter-gatherer comes to the surface."[56]

Lawrence said that the only two things which he really liked to teach to the boys in his classes were botany and drawing: botany having to do with "the impulse to name and classify and anatomize" and drawing having to do with developing the right hemisphere.

Lawrence wrote *Fantasia of the Unconscious* while sitting under a tree at the edge of the Black Forest in Bavaria and he devoted several pages to these great "full-bodied trees, with strange tree-blood in them, soundlessly drumming." He points out that it is no good just looking at a tree to know it; one must "sit among the roots and nestle against its strong trunk."[57] He says that's how he writes this, his "tree-book, really." The powerful presences of the trees undoubtedly encouraged him to write even more boldly against the limitations of mere ideas. The supreme lesson that must be learned is "how to live dynamically from the great Source, and not statically, like machines driven by ideas and principles from the head. . . . Education means leading out the individual nature in each man and woman to its true fullness: You can't do that by stimulating the mind. . . . Every extraneous idea, which has no intrinsic root in the dynamic consciousness, is as dangerous as a nail driven into a young tree."[58]

Fantasia of the Unconscious is a very uneven book; in some passages Lawrence presents matters of great importance for education which were not restated for decades; in other passages he relapses into sarcasm as though he knows no one will understand what he is trying to do. He has a long passage on dreams which is mostly nonsense; furthermore, he viciously attacks those who pay any attention whatsoever to dreams. Since dreams are one of the few ways the unconscious can communicate with the whole person, this section makes little sense until one realizes that at this time in his life, living with Frieda in Bavaria not too far from Munich, Lawrence was surrounded by talk about Freud. This was his way of lashing back. He uses mixed metaphors and sarcastically says: "And I wish I could mix a few more. . . ." He throws in some astrological jargon as well.

In *Fantasia of the Unconscious* Lawrence emphasized the great nerve center which "lies in the middle front of the abdomen, beneath the navel," called the solar plexus. He once told Rhys Davies, "When you have come to a decision, whatever your mental calculations tell you, go by what you feel here." Davies explains, "With his quick intent gesture he placed his hands over and around his belly—'go by that, what you feel deep in you, not by what your head tells you.'"[59] Lady Asquith wrote that it seemed to her as if Lawrence's "body thought." She explains that he thought "with his solar plexus rather than with his brain" and that he seemed to have a "strange perceptive sense of his own, which made it possible for him to probe into elements in a hidden world lying beyond the range of others."[60] Perhaps nothing has caused more critics to heap ridicule on Lawrence than his emphasis on the solar plexus. But in the last decade, with the growth of such disciplines as T'ai Chi, Aikido, and healing methods such as Rolfing and Feldenkrais, we know that Lawrence was right about the importance of this "other brain" as the Orientals call it: the *hara* in Japanese, *Tan tien* in Chinese. This particular area, when developed through any of the above disciplines, becomes a center of awareness so precise that it can register emotions of those nearby as well as danger from behind. It balances the energies of the entire mind and body. A recent study on subjects who had been through the entire rolfing procedure indicated that these people not only processed incoming data by more use of the right hemisphere activity; but also that there was considerable reflexive automatic spinal control of movement from the lower spinal area, in that the reflexes for some tasks went only between the spine and the lower extremities and not through the central brain process at all.[61] This accounts for the incredible ability of black belt Aikido experts to anticipate attacks from every side at once.

In a later essay, summing up his ideas on body knowledge versus mental-consciousness, Lawrence wrote: "There are many ways of knowing, there are many sorts of knowledge. But the two ways of knowing, for man, are knowing in terms of apartness, which is mental, rational, scientific and knowing in terms of togetherness, which is religious and poetic."[62]

Just after Lawrence finished writing *Fantasia of the Unconscious* he got his first letter from Mabel Luhan in Taos urging him to come there. He answered immediately (5 November 1921):

> I had your letter this afternoon. . . . I believe what you say—one must somehow bring together the two ends of humanity, our own thin end and the last dark strand from the previous, pre-white era. I verily believe that. Is Taos the place?
>
> I have already written the second book to *Psychoanalysis and the Unconscious*, and posted the MS. to Seltzer—called, provisionally, *Fantasia of the Unconscious*. I am satisfied with it for what it is. But it is the third book, which I have still to write, and which I can't write yet, not till I have crossed another border, and it is this that will really matter. . . . I think we will come to Taos.[63]

5

Taos Interlude

But the moment I saw the brilliant, proud morning shine high
up over the deserts . . . something stood still in my soul, and I
started to attend . . . a new part of the soul woke up suddenly,
and the old world gave way to a new.[1]

This passage from Lawrence's essay, "New Mexico," has been frequently quoted but often dismissed as the hyperbole of a neurotic man. This type of criticism began shortly after Lawrence made his statement and has continued intermittently through the years since. Most recently John Nichols, famous for his *Milagro Beanfield War* wrote that Taos's "most notorious visitor was D. H. Lawrence: though he spent but a handful of months in northern New Mexico, his presence dominates its aesthetic and scandal-oriented legacies."[2] Actually, Lawrence spent far more than a few months in Taos; but, more important, due to his lifelong awareness of the influence of place on human beings, he understood much more within a few weeks than most people are capable of understanding in years. The bioregional poet Gary Snyder has pointed out: "Local ecosystems speak to you if you know how to listen but you've got to listen well in one place, first."[3] This, Lawrence had learned to do as a child, through his deep attachment to his home valley.

To Lawrence, sensitized by a lifetime of immediate concrete

awareness, the landscape forms at Taos crystallized all his previous glimpses into the power of the land itself. Daily, he witnessed the ritual of the changing land and sky. He "used to stand on the porch of the house and watch the glowing sun sink deep behind the far mountains."[4] Brett writes of the evenings when Lawrence, Frieda and she, tired from the hard work of repairing the buildings, would walk slowly up to have dinner with Tony Luhan and the Indians around the big fire. "It is one of those magical evenings: a clear sky, a very young moon rising pale and dim out of the setting sun, a large star hanging below the moon. No sound, not a twig moves."[5] As Lawrence wrote in one of his short stories: "Ah, that was beauty!— perhaps the most beautiful thing in the world. It was pure beauty, absolute beauty! . . . at any hour of the day: whether the perfect clarity of the morning, or the mountain beyond the simmering desert at noon, or the purple lumping of the northern mounds under a red sun at night. . . . The landscape lived, and lived as the world of the gods, unsullied and unconcerned. . . . The great circling landscape . . . . "[6] Lest Lawrence's reference to the gods be idly dismissed, I want to point out the fact that both Taos and Tibet lie on the same degree of latitude (36°). At this latitude the quality of light experienced in the mountains is such that Tibetan scriptures describe "ultimate Reality" (God) as similar to the pure light of "the clear autumnal sky at midday."[7]

Later, in the short story "St. Mawr," Lawrence writes: "It's the beginning of something else, and the end of something that's done with. I *know*, and there's no altering it, that I've got to live differently . . . . I've got to live for something that matters, way, way down in me."[8] Lawrence was feeling his way deeper into his ideas on the relationship between human beings and the earth, trying out ideas which he later put into *The Plumed Serpent*.

It is difficult, at this late date, to fully appreciate the tremendous impact which the land in the West had on intelligent, sensitive Europeans in the early decades of this century. In a speech given at the University of California at Berkeley in 1911, the Spanish-born philosopher George Santayana said almost the same thing as Lawrence—but on a more abstract level—when he pointed out to the people of California that their easy access to the still undestroyed forests and mountains should lead them to a totally different philosophical approach: "In their non-human beauty and peace [these mountains] stir the sub-human depths and the superhuman possibilities of your own spirit. It is no transcendental logic that they teach; and they give no sign of any deliberate morality seated in the world. It is rather the vanity and superficiality of all logic, the needlessness of argument, the finitude of morals, the strength of time, the fertility of matter, the variety, the unspeakable variety, of possible life."

Santayana went on to mention that he had met a Californian (actually John Muir) who remarked that if philosophers had lived among the California mountains "their systems would have been different from what they are." Santayana said that he agreed with this and he further pointed out that such systems would be quite different from those systems "which the European Genteel Tradition has handed down since Socrates; for these systems are egotistical; directly or indirectly they are anthropocentric, and inspired by the conceited notion that man, or human reason, or the human distinction between good and evil, is the center and pivot of the universe. That is what the mountains and the woods should make you at last ashamed to assert. . . . It is the yoke of this Genteel Tradition itself, your tyrant from the cradle to the grave, that these primeval solitudes lift from your shoulders. They suspend your forced sense of your importance not merely as individuals, but even as men. They allow you, in one happy moment, at once to play and worship, to take yourselves simply, humbly, for what you are, and to salute, the wild, indifferent, non-censorious infinity of nature."[9]

This speech of Santayana's was immediately filed away and thus lost in the archives. William Everson discovered it while doing research for his 1976 book, *Archetype West*, and he felt that it was of such importance to the delineation of this archetype that he quoted it at length. In the appendix of his book, where he sums up the western archetype, Everson proclaims Robinson Jeffers "an apotheosis point" of this western archetype and further states that Jeffers "emerges as essentially reformist, dealing not with particular issues, but with the issue: man's corruption through alienation from Nature."[10] Because Everson is dealing with American writers here he does not mention Lawrence, although this issue was central to Lawrence's work as well.

Mabel Luhan had sensed the underlying similarity of certain aspects of the work of Lawrence and Jeffers and hoped to bring them together. She wrote to Jeffers: "You know, Jeffers, after I met you, I felt that you and Lawrence ought to know each other, that you would have liked and understood each other." She had asked him to send two books of poems to Lawrence but just at that time Lawrence died. She regrets that they never met; but writes: "I am going to try and tell you about Lawrence."[11] Ten years later, in the Foreword to a collection of Lawrence's poems titled *Fire and Other Poems,* Jeffers paid tribute to what Lawrence had tried to do when he wrote that although Lawrence was not a "'first-rate' poet . . . he was a man of genius." Jeffers points out that no writer since the author of *Pilgrim's Progress* has been so desperately convinced that the world was lost and society contemptible and that he would save them if they would hear him. Jeffers closes the Foreword with: "We have lost the way and we know it at last. We must just live as well as we can and listen to the Sybils mutter—the inspired persons: Lawrence is one of them."[12]

Actually it was not until the late 1970s that the culture toward which Lawrence was moving in the 1920s, evolved far enough so that Gary Snyder could articulate particular aspects of it when he wrote: "As a poet I hold the most archaic values on earth. They go back to the late Paleolithic: the fertility of the soil, the magic of animals, the power-vision in solitude . . . the love and ecstasy of the dance, the common work of the tribe. I try to hold both history and wilderness in mind, then my poems may approach the true measure of all things and stand against the unbalance and ignorance of our times."[13] "Snyder," Thomas Parkinson writes, "has effectively done something that for an individual is extremely difficult: he has created a new culture."[14] Although in some ways an inaccurate statement, because fishermen and forest workers from California and the Northwest as well as mountain climbers and other maverick types also had a hand in shaping this culture, still Snyder certainly has been its outstanding spokesman. Perhaps because so many of those involved are outdoor workers and not merely intellectuals and poets, the breadth of this movement has gone unnoticed, not only by opinion makers but by the general public. Gary Snyder, himself, was a fire lookout in Washington in the 1950s; (Linn) Freeman House, who coined the term "future primitive" was a fisherman in Washington at the time he wrote it. Parkinson, however, does defend Snyder against the charge most frequently leveled at him—that his concepts are irrelevant to the needs of an urban industrial civilization and are therefore "out of harmony with humanity as it is." Parkinson says: "There is no point in decrying Snyder's work as primitivism; it is merely good sense, for the ability to hold history and wilderness in the mind at once may be the only way to make valid measures of human conduct. A large and more humble vision of man and cosmos is our only hope."[15]

While the others mentioned in connection with this evolving culture are Americans, Lawrence, of course, was English; however, it was an American landscape, Taos, which was the culminating factor which led him to similar conclusions.

What is it about the landscape of Taos which is so powerful? It not only deeply influenced Lawrence but sent others into overwhelming enthusiasms such as John Marin's "My God! My God! That such a place exists. It engulfs you. . . . It's the best possible place to come alive. . . ."[16] Marin, a landscape painter discovered by Stieglitz, stayed with Mabel Luhan in Taos for a short time.

In essence, the Taos area combines in one unified, harmonious landscape the most compelling landscape forms in nature, forms which antedate *any* human culture but have affected the human psyche since Paleolithic times. In *Earth Wisdom*[17] I have discussed these forms at length; here I will only go into the matter enough to explain the Taos landscape. Legendary Taos Mountain itself is the most powerful Mother Goddess form—the rounded, double topped mountain with the inviting saddle. Almost directly in front of Taos Mountain and a little to one side is a cone-shaped Mother Goddess form. The surrounding lower-lying mountains form a semi-circle reaching almost around the entire valley, thus providing the encircling, protecting arms of the mother mountain. Right in the middle of this semi-circle, snug up against Taos Mountain, lies the Taos pueblo. Looking outward from the pueblo over the flat valley, the eye is drawn to numbers of small cone-shaped mountains and, in the far distance, to the great Rio Grande gorge, which has cut its way down into the lower country above Santa Fe. In ancient times this gorge would have been called the "cleft of the Goddess." The point where the opening between the walls of a gorge lead directly up to a combination of power forms was usually the site of a temple. To explain these landscape forms I refer directly to Vincent Scully's *The Earth, The Temple, and the Gods: Greek Sacred Architecture.* He begins by stating that the Cretan palaces and the sites on which they stand represent a late and full ritualization of the traditions of Stone and Bronze Age cultures. He states that from roughly 2000 B.C. onward in Crete there was a clearly defined pattern of landscape use at every palace site.

> [F]irst, an enclosed valley of varying size in which the palace is set; I should like to call this the "Natural Megaron"; second, a gently mounded or conical hill, on axis with the palace to north or south; and lastly a higher, double-peaked or cleft mountain some distance beyond the hill but on the same axis .... The double peaks or notched cleft seems essential to it. These features create a profile which is basically that of a pair of horns, but it may sometimes suggest the female cleft, or even, at some sites, a pair of breasts .... It forms in all cases a climactic shape which has the quality of causing the observer's eye to come to rest in its cup. .... [T]he cone would appear to have been seen as the earth's motherly form, the horns as the symbol of its active power. . . . [T]he horned mountain itself defined the consecrated site.[18]

Scully goes on to explain that the palace complex was unified in a "communally satisfying" way to include the human beings, the earth and the gods. The ritual "wove its dances of the labyrinth and the horns within the larger hollow of the protecting valley which was the goddess, and in view of the mounded hill which was her gentleness and the horned mountain which was her splendor and her throne." Possibly Scully's description of the sites of the temple and town of Gournia best explains Taos. At this site "one has the inescapable impression that human beings are conceived of as children who lie upon the mother's body, enclosed by her arms and in the deep shadow of her breasts. . . . To sleep within such a goddess shape, as the votaries apparently did at Malta and as the whole population obviously did at Gournia, would itself have been a ritual act."[19]

The later Greeks used the same landscape forms for their temples. The site of the Eleusinian Mysteries and that of the temple of Apollo at Delphi, which was originally an earth goddess site, were similar landscape forms. At both these sites the "gate of horn," the ritual association of human birth from the goddess's body, at both these sites is a cleft between deep rock walls, similar to that spot in the Rio Grande gorge where one looks between the walls up toward Taos.

In fact, the Taos site exceeds these Grecian locations in its natural sacred form in that the combination is even more fortuitous. Looking up the Rio Grande gorge one sees the broad lap of the goddess, the valley below the Pueblo, and the nourishing form, the cone just under the final horned form of Taos Mountain. To someone as sensitive as Lawrence, even though he did not have the words for it, such a sight would be awe-inspiring. From his Kiowa ranch, one can only see the sacred Taos Mountain from the side, but the double top is still obvious; in addition, from his ranch one looks out over the valley toward Tres Orejas ("three ears" in Spanish), which the Indians called Coyote Mountain after an animal which figures in almost all Indian mythologies. Several other cone-shaped mountains rim the horizon in this direction. Lawrence called it "the most dramatic landscape I have ever experienced."[20]

Taos Mountain (12,282 feet), sometimes in Lawrence's time called Pueblo Mountain, is in the Sangre de Cristo Mountains of northern

New Mexico. Just behind it is Wheeler Peak, the highest in New Mexico (13,151 feet). It is not visible from the valley. Between the two mountains lies Bear Lake in a high alpine bowl. The outlet stream from Bear Lake empties into the sacred Blue Lake stream that circles in front of Taos mountain and eventually flows between the two main adobe buildings of the Pueblo.

The alluvial fans of the tributaries to the Rio Grande, coming down from the mountains, form the Taos plateau, the broad flat valley. The Rio Grande at one time was below its present level; it was impounded by a lava flow and the level raised. A cycle of deposition began in which the alluvial plains which extend far up the tributaries were formed. Then it began cutting down again, thus forming steep walled arroyos. The present Rio Grande gorge is 1000 feet deep at the southern end of the Taos plateau.[21]

Many passages in Lawrence's works show that he had a feel for archetypal landscape forms. For instance, in *Women in Love*, Gerald Crich climbs up to a high valley, where he lies down and dies in the snow. The description of this valley states that the mountains rise up before them and that between their icy slopes lies a great white valley, a cul-de-sac of snow, which Lawrence called "the centre, the knot, the navel of the world, where the earth belonged to the skies . . . ," thus describing a classic "Mother Goddess" landscape form.[22] In *Sea and Sardinia* he writes of Trapani, the western part of Sicily: "And the hill near us was Mount Eryx—But why in the name of heaven should my heart stand still as I watch that hill which rises above the sea?" He says it was the site of the Venus of the aborigines, older than Greek Aphrodite. "This, one of the world centres, older than old! and the woman goddess, watching Africa!"[23] He also wrote of the power of Mount Etna. "They called her the Pillar of Heaven, the Greeks . . . Etna herself, Etna of the snow and secret changing winds . . . Etna, pedestal of Heaven."[24] Etna, being a volcano, was a "Mother Goddess" nurturing shape.

The inspiration which Lawrence received from Taos came primarily from the land itself, and only secondarily from the Indians. He did not make the mistake which other writers have done of claiming that the Taos culture was totally different from all others.

The Taos Indians speak Taos. It is a Tiwa language closely related to the Tiwa speech of three other New Mexico Pueblos: Picuris, Isleta and Sandia (close to Albuquerque). These Tiwa languages, in turn, are closely related to Tewa, which is spoken by six other groups of Pueblo Indians.[25] Taos Pueblo is thus rooted in the same culture as other Pueblos. The present Taos Indians came into the area around A.D. 1400; the two main buildings were built in 1450 A.D. There had been an earlier Basket Maker period around 900 to 1200 A.D., but for some time during the intervening period, the area had been abandoned. Taos Pueblo was probably settled by a northward shift of Tiwa-speaking groups during the period of A.D. 1325–1600.[26] Living under the sacred Taos mountain may have helped the Taos Pueblo to keep their culture viable. And this was what greatly interested Lawrence—the human and the non-human in relationship. Poet and critic Paula Gunn Allen, who was born in New Mexico near the Laguna and Acoma reservations, concisely explains these particular aspects of Native American literature:

> The tribes seek, through song, ceremony, legend, sacred stories (myths), and tales to embody, articulate, and share reality, to bring the isolated private self into harmony and balance with this reality, to verbalize the sense of the majesty and reverent mystery of all things, and to actualize, in language, those truths of being and experience that give to humanity its greatest significance and dignity. . . . The two forms basic to Native American literature are the Ceremony and the Myth. The Ceremony is the ritual enactment of a specialized perception of cosmic relationships, while the Myth is a prose record of that relationship.[27]

Some writers have disparaged Lawrence and claimed he did not really study the Indians so he knew little about them. Of course he did not study them; he was against forming any mental *ideas* of any sort. However, he had more living contact with them than many other white writers because Mabel Luhan's Taos husband, Tony

Luhan, brought several Taos Indians to work with Lawrence while he was remodeling the cabins. Together they rebuilt the larger house, making all the adobe bricks, and reshingled the roofs of all three cabins. Lawrence described this work in a letter to Catherine Carswell and continued, "There is something savage unbreakable in the spirit of place out here. The Indians, drumming and yelling at our campfire in the evening. But they'll be wiped out too, I expect—schools and education will finish them. But not before the world falls."[28] For many Europeans, as they set about conquering the so-called lower races, the drum was always that "infernal tom-tom" of the natives. They could hear no difference in drumming for war or drumming for celebration of new life in the spring. It was all the same to them. But Lawrence's experience under the pine tree by his house in the evening with Tony Luhan and the other Indians showed him the value of the drum. In *The Plumed Serpent* he wrote that bells call attention to the Christian Church standing there, focusing all power onto itself, while the drum connects humans with their "circumambient universe" and with nature's changing cycles.[29]

In his book *Mornings in Mexico*, Lawrence described the relationship created by ritual dancing to the drum: "The drums keep up the pulsating heart-beat . . . and for hours, hours it goes on: the round dance . . . in the dark, near the fire . . . the pine trees standing still, the everlasting darkness, and the strong lifting and dropping, surging . . . the pulsing incalculable fall of the blood, which forever seeks to fall to the centre of the earth . . . back to the great central source where is . . . unspeakable renewal."[30]

Once again, in his praise of the drum, Lawrence was way ahead of his time. It was not until the 1980s that people began discovering the power of the drum to help them, both psychologically and physically. The poet Robert Bly began using drumming in his men's workshops then and the anthropologist Michael Harner had workshops teaching drumming. In 1990 the real breakthrough occurred when Mickey Hart, the Grateful Dead's drummer, wrote *Drumming at the Edge of Magic*. He shows that drumming, natural to all humans when the Roman Empire became Christian, was damned as the work of the devil.[31]

John Collier, who was U. S. Commissioner of Indian Affairs from 1933 to 1945, lived next door to the Lawrences when they lived on the "other side of Mabel's alfalfa field." He wrote that the Indians "liked Lawrence, and so he must have understood them." But, since Lawrence was a crusader to restore real life to people such as the English middle-class, "he found nothing to crusade for" among the Indians since they were already living that life, so they didn't really need him.[32] The Indians called Lawrence "Red Fox" and Frieda, "Angry Winter."[33]

Originally, Lawrence liked Tony Luhan, Mabel's husband, but when Tony laughed at him while he was trying to learn to ride, Lawrence withdrew because his English working-class pride was hurt.[34]

Lawrence was not the usual sentimental Indian follower; he did not believe in a slavish imitation of the "red man," but rather in a living relationship to nature such as the Indians exhibited. In an article, "America, Listen to Your Own" published in the *New Republic* in 1920 before he went to Taos, Lawrence wrote that if Americans would accept the aboriginal spirit of the continent they would bring a "surpassing of the old European life-form . . . a departure from the old European morality ethic." The spirit of America's own dark, aboriginal continent, which the Pilgrims and the Spaniards thought was the Devil, "Americans must recognize again, recognize and embrace. The devil and anathema of our forefathers hides the Godhead which we seek."[35] In another article for *The New York Times* in 1922, he wrote that while the Indians cannot offer modern man a model for living, they can awaken into consciousness parts of the self which have been repressed in modern life. "The Indians keep burning an eternal fire, the sacred fire of the old dark religion. . . . [L]et us . . . take up an old dark thread from their vision, and see again as they see, without forgetting we are ourselves. . . . We have to feel our way by the dark thread of the old vision. Before it lapses, let us take it up."[36] When Lawrence wrote these praises of the Indian, the accepted stereotype of them was as drunken, worthless and becoming extinct anyway. Beginning with the 1960s people began to realize what we had lost in our industrial culture and began to look back to the Indians. Melissa Nelson, executive director of the Cultural Conservancy, a land conservation organization that works with traditional native communities, tells about the recent interest in "indigenous psychology." She says, "This term refers to both the thinking and healing practices of indigenous peoples and to those who adapt some of their rituals. . . . Most indigenous cultures have the deep conviction that their songs, prayers, dances, and ceremonies keep the earth in balance. Is it possible that we are facing such global crises today because western industrial society has forgotten the creative bond people have with each other and with the earth?"[37]

As Ralph Metzner explains: "Many people are aware that the technological-industrial civilization built upon the Euro-American world view is destroying the life-sustaining environment that has been our home since humans first evolved. While conservationists are trying to replicate the sustainable land-management practices of indigenous societies, ecophilosophers have pointed to the ecological wisdom inherent in the nature-reverencing spirituality of Native American and other traditional societies."[38] His *Well of Remembrance* helps us find our way back to the earth-reverencing religions of our ancestors in Europe.

A radical breakthrough in education comes from C. A. Bowers, Professor of Education at Portland State, who has spent fifteen years trying to understand why none of the environmental education which we have undergone has succeeded in making the necessary changes in mind-set to prevent further destruction. In his book *Critical Essays on Education, Modernity, and the Recovery of the Ecological Imperative*, he analyzes the problem and discusses what we can learn from such traditional cultures as the Hopi, Koyukan, Kwakiutl, Balinese and Australian Aborigine.[39] As mentioned above, Lawrence had already realized this in 1922. Finally, in the 1990s, we are listening.

In both the *The White Peacock* and *Sons and Lovers*, Lawrence relates in numerous passages how the life he lived was tied to his homeplace as a youth. Later on in his life there are several clearly documented times when he experienced on a small scale the joy and fulfillment of a kind of tribal life in close participation with nature. In September of 1912, the year he and Frieda began living together in Europe, they went on a walking tour with David Garnett (the son of Lawrence's editor, Edward Garnett) and Harold Hobson. They walked over the Alps to Italy from the Tyrol. Among their other adventures, David Garnett almost got swept over a waterfall and they had thunderstorms and slept in a hay hut during the rain. These episodes provide the source of the two short stories: "A Chapel Among the Mountains" and "A Hay Hut Among the Mountains."[40] The three collected specimens to add to Garnett's herbarium. After crossing the Pfitzer Joch they came down out of the snow into Italy during the grape and tobacco harvest. They parted there and David writes that though he saw Lawrence often in the next few years, "I never saw him so well or so happy, so consistently gay and light-hearted."[41]

Just before the war began he went on a walking tour with three other men: Koteliansky (Kot), who later became his close friend; Horne, who was an associate of Kot's at the Russian Law Bureau; and Lewis, an engineer who had walked through the Great St. Bernard Pass in the Alps with Lawrence the preceding June.[42] Writing to Lady Cynthia Asquith in January of 1915, he recalls that he had been "rather happy, with water-lilies twisted round my hat—big, heavy, white and gold water-lilies that we found in a pool high up." He tells her that they had crouched for shelter under a wall while the rain "flew by in streams" and the wind roared and "we shouted songs." Kot sang the Hebrew psalm *Ranani Sadekim Badanoi*, which means "Rejoice, O Ye Righteous." He tells her, "It seems like another life—we *were* happy—four men. Then we came down to Barrow-in Furness, and saw that war was declared."[43] Here in a microcosm is what Lawrence sought all his life—men in common pursuit within nature, lifted up together in natural spontaneous joy so great that the rain and the wind only added to it. Rananim, derived from the word of Kot's hymn, *Ranani*, became the name for Lawrence's hoped-for colony of like-minded people, which never materialized. He wrote of it often and made various tentative plans concerning it through the years.

When the Lawrences lived alongside the two Danish painters

Merrild and Gótzsche, that first winter in Taos up at the Del Monte Ranch, they worked and rode horses together and ate together. Merrild writes that as they rode together they never tired of singing "in sheer joy of being alive. To be alive through our senses! . . . And to be alive to the sight of beauty all around, and the spirit of the place, and the mystery and wonder of it all. To be alive, and to be alive TOGETHER!"[44]

Later Mabel wanted to give the little ranch, which her son used for hunting, to Lawrence. She gave it to Frieda, however, because "I knew he would rather I gave it to her." It was seventeen miles from Taos up on the slope of a mountain known as "The Lobo" or wolf, above the trading post of San Cristobal.[45] Mabel called it the Flying Heart Ranch. Lawrence changed the name, first to Lobo and later to Kiowa Ranch.[46] The Kiowa Indians, along with the Comanches used to make raids into Pueblo territory in the eighteenth and nineteenth centuries. During the fur trading era in Taos there was trade in beaver pelts with the Kiowas, who lived farther north along the Arkansas River.

When they left in the fall of 1925, Lawrence wrote: "It grieves me to leave my horse, and my cow Susan, and . . . the white cock, Moses—and the place."[47] They left because winter was coming on and Lawrence did not think he was strong enough after his illness in Mexico to face another winter there. Aldington visited them in a cottage where they were staying in England in 1926 and recalls: "He was evidently pining for his New Mexico ranch, for he talked of it constantly and with a nostalgic regret which made me quite unhappy on his behalf."[48] Later, in Port Cros, "one of the loveliest settings in Europe," Lawrence was staying with friends when he got a letter from Brett enclosing turkey feathers from the ranch. One of the friends present, Brigit Patmore, writes that Lawrence told them, "You think this place is beautiful. . . . It's nothing to those mountains. The light and clarity will kill you, but it's worth it. Other things seem small after you've lived on that plateau."[49]

Richard Aldington explains why Lawrence did not stay in Taos, since he loved it so much. "The answer is very simple. A visa to the United States is good for six months only, unless the person crossing the frontier of freedom comes as an immigrant 'on the quota' which . . . requires a medical examination. In the spring of 1925 Lawrence was refused admission on the Mexican-United States frontier for reasons of health, and was allowed in for six months only on the intervention of the U.S. Embassy in Mexico City. He never attempted to enter the country again."[50] In December 1928, Lawrence wrote to Mabel Luhan that Brett suggested he try to "creep into the U.S. unnoticed." But he did not want to do that.[51] Because a visa would allow him to stay in the U.S. for only six months, he thought that with his precarious health it was too far to travel for so short a visit. As late as January 30, 1930, just over a month before his death, he wrote: "If I can get well, I want to go to America, to the ranch, because I believe I should get better there. I wish it were possible to sail at the end of March. . . ."[52] Oddly enough he did sail by the end of March—in his "Ship of Death"[53] as he died on March 3.

In a letter to Mabel Luhan on 25 December 1928, he tells her that he has just written "quite a beautiful" article on New Mexico. "Writing it gave me a real longing to be back and I should like to come in spring even if only to stay the six months allowed by the passport."[54] In "New Mexico," Lawrence poured out all the longing he had for the land of Taos:

> But for a greatness of beauty I have never experienced anything like New Mexico. All those mornings when I went with a hoe along the ditch to the Canyon, at the ranch, and stood, in the fierce, proud silence of the Rockies, on their foothills, to look far over the desert sweeping grey-blue in between . . . the vast amphitheatre of lofty, indomitable desert, sweeping round to the ponderous Sangre de Cristo, mountains on the east, and coming up flush at the pine-dotted foot-hills of the Rockies! What splendour! . . . Never is the light more pure and overweening than there . . . arching with a royalty almost cruel over the hollow, uptilted world . . . but so beautiful, God! so beautiful! Those that have spent morning

after morning alone there pitched among the pines above the great proud world of desert will know, almost unbearably how beautiful it is, how clear and unquestioned is the might of the day. Just day itself is tremendous there . . . in New Mexico the heart is sacrificed to the sun and the human being is left stark, heartless, but undauntedly religious.[55]

Lawrence expressed his deepest feeling for the land through the words of Lou, in the short story "St. Mawr":

"For me," she said, as she looked away at the mountains in shadow and the pale-warm desert beneath . . . "For me, this place is sacred. It is blessed."[56]

6

The Blossoming of Relationship

Ecological thinking ... requires a kind of vision across boundaries.
The epidermis of the skin is ecologically like a pond surface or a
forest soil, not a shell so much as a delicate interpenetration. It
reveals the self ennobled and extended rather than threatened as
part of the landscape and the ecosystem, because the beauty and
complexity of nature are continuous with ourselves.[1]
—Paul Shepard

The revelation of the religious power of the land itself, which
came to Lawrence in Taos, gave a new dimension to his original
insight achieved at the end of *The Rainbow*, almost a decade before.
In that passage, Ursula sees in the rainbow the "new growth . . .
rising to the light and the wind . . . the world built up in a living
fabric of Truth, fitting to the over-arching heaven." As mentioned
earlier, Lawrence had at that point in his life the strong feeling that a
new relationship between man, woman and nature was the answer.
In the intervening years, from the time he finished *The Rainbow* until
he saw the "proud morning" of New Mexico, he had suffered
through the "nightmare" of the war years in England, the ongoing
confrontations with Frieda and the hedonistic and ideological
movements which were the aftermath of the war itself. The novel
Kangaroo, which Lawrence wrote in Australia just before coming to

Taos, provides an insight into his thinking at this time.

After some preliminary confrontations with Kangaroo (the fascist-type leader, also, ironically, filled with "Christian-love"), the main character, Somers (Lawrence) gets fourteen letters and a batch of European newspapers after the mail-boat comes in. He reads them, "with a sort of loathing" at the news of the German debt, Bolshevism, Communism, etc. "Never had Richard Lovat Somers felt so filled with spite against everybody . . . as now." He decides to quit "kicking himself" and goes off down to the shore. He knows the waves will make him forget; their "unconcern gradually soothed him of himself and his world." After a time the "disintegrative, elemental language" of the sea brings back simplicity and "inward peace" to Somers; he returns to his true self, "a quiet stillness in his soul, an inward trust." He realizes that, although most people seem to want to rush about in search of endless excitement of one sort or another, others "must stay by their own inmost being, in peace. . . . And there in the stillness listen, listen, and try to know, and try to obey."[2]

At tea-time it begins to rain once more and he is sitting on the verandah talking with Harriet (Frieda). She is referring again to the ongoing battle in his soul about joining with the Australian political movement headed by Kangaroo, and linked with this is the concept of the woman as the "Magna Mater," from Frieda's Munich days. Harriet asks: "Who is there that you feel you are with, besides me . . . ?" "'No one,' he replied. And at the same moment he looked up and saw the rainbow fume beyond the sea . . . the good symbol: of this peace. A pledge of unbroken faith, between the universe and the innermost. And the very moment he said 'No one' he saw the rainbow for an answer."[3]

Living in Taos taught Lawrence more about the relationship "between the universe and the innermost." He had learned through intimate living with nature—chopping his own wood, irrigating his fields, watching the ever-changing panorama of the rising and setting of the sun and the magnificent clouds and storms coming up over the sacred mountain. In short, he had been feeling his way toward an ecological understanding for which there were no words in the 1920s. The word, "ecology," did not surface as a common term until

"Earthday" in 1970, and even now, after all these years, we are only beginning to realize the possible implications of ecological understanding. Edith Cobb points toward just how rudimentary this understanding is when she writes:

> Even among naturalists and biologists the realization that in ecology as a biological science we have, for the first time in the history of thought, an instrument for the study of reciprocity and mutuality among categories of thought, as well as among divisions and levels in nature, seems strangely lacking.
>
> Ecology as a science permits us to evaluate reciprocal relations of living organisms with their total environment and with one another as living interdependent systems. This reciprocity ... extends into a counterpoint between universe and geographical place. Plants, animals, and humans must now be thought of as living in ecosystems, in a web of related, interacting, dynamic energy systems.[4]

More than fifty years ago, Lawrence wrote: "Everything in the world is relative to everything else. And every living thing is related to every other living thing." Ten years earlier still, Lawrence had written of the inevitable outcome of ignoring this seemingly obvious fact: "Anything that triumphs, perishes. The consummation comes from perfect relatedness." Gregory Bateson echoed this phrase in 1970 when he wrote: "[The] organism which destroys its environment destroys itself."[5]

Long after Lawrence's death, in 1944, Frieda wrote to Edward Gilbert, "To me his relationship, his bond with everything in creation was so amazing, no preconceived ideas, just a meeting between him and a creature, a tree, a cloud, anything."[6] This remarkable ability is shown in a passage where Lawrence has been talking about his relationship to his little brown hen on his ranch: he says that he calls it "relationship" but that the Greeks called it "equilibrium." He goes on to say that when they talked about being in equilibrium with a creature, for example, a horse, "the horse had to become nine-tenths human to accommodate them." That's not equilibrium, he says; instead, "we call it anthropomorphism." And, punning, he writes: "Too much anthropos makes the world a dull hole."[7] Del Ivan Janik explains in his article "D. H. Lawrence and Environmental Consciousness," that "D. H. Lawrence was both the first and the most prominent writer . . . to call anthropocentric and humanistic assumptions sharply into question."

Janik continues: "Lawrence and the other modern writers who in a sense are his followers in the development of a new environmental consciousness celebrate the whole of life, and recognize human potential for creative rather than destructive participation in it. Lawrence's post-humanism looks at the human species as part of a larger living whole, valuing that whole in its complexity and integrity. Posthumanism values all living things and the inorganic environment on which they depend, recognizing that all life and the conditions that sustain life are interrelated. It asserts that man can be, if he abandons his anthropocentric assumptions, a contributor to, rather than the destroyer of, the pattern of nature."[8] Janik quotes Lawrence's question: "What can a man do with his life but live it? And what does life consist in, save a vivid relatedness between the man and the living universe that surrounds him?" Lawrence remarks that we know for sure that "that which is good, and moral, is that which brings into us a stronger, deeper flow of life-energy: evil is that which impairs the life-flow."[9]

In this same essay, "Pan in America," written in Taos, Lawrence writes of the death of the great god Pan at the beginning of the Christian era and continues by stating that the idea and the engine came between human beings and all the other beings of the universe. Man was Pan along with everything else until that happened. The great pine tree in front of his ranch house is still Pan, especially at night, with the light shining out of the window onto it and "the great trunk dimly shows, in the near darkness, like an Egyptian column, supporting some powerful mystery in the over-branching darkness." The tree "gathers up earth power . . . and a roaming sky-glitter from above," and radiates this out, vibrating "its presence into my soul." He admits that he is changed, "vitally," by the tree and chants: "Give me of your power, then, oh tree! And I will give you of mine."

Watching the Indians race at the Taos Pueblo on St. Geronimo's day gave Lawrence further insight into this "power." The young men run with streaks of earth on them and a bit of eagle fluff, and the old men gently touch them with eagle feathers "to give them power." There is no competition involved; instead it is a "great cumulative effort" of the men of the tribe to come into contact with the "great cosmic source of vitality" which gives strength and power.[10]

Lawrence writes that power is not pushing someone around, hiring servants or getting your own way; rather, "Power is *pouvoir*: to be able to." We can't get real power by striving or forcing. It comes from the "unseen," the "unknown." For real power "we must put aside our own will, and our own conceit, and *accept* power, from the beyond."[11] This requires courage, discipline and "inward isolation." Among Indian tribes this "real power" has various names: *wakanda* for the Dakota tribes; *obi* for the Iroquois; and *manitu* for the Algonquins. The Huichol Indians of Mexico believe that a power circulates through men, ritual animals, and plants. The Melanesian concept of *mana* is similar. Jung explored this primitive energy-concept for more than twenty years and late in life wrote: "The existence of this remarkable correlation between consciousness and the phenomenal world, between subjective perception and objectively real processes, i.e., their energic effects, requires no further proof. . . . If these reflections are justified, they must have weighty consequences with regard to the nature of the psyche, since as an objective fact it would then be intimately connected, not only with physiological and biological phenomena, but with physical events, too."[12]

This is as far as Jung could go in his lifetime; however, the Jungian psychologist James Hillman made the real breakthrough in 1992. He begins with what he calls "soul-making" and reports that he "got the term from Keats and D. H. Lawrence." He explains that: "Soul-making and care of soul do not have to be identified with introversion and the spiritual denial of the world of matter, objects, things." Then he makes the radical statement: "Maybe the idea of self has to be redefined." He explains that the definitions we have now come from Protestant and Oriental traditions: "Self is the interiorization of the invisible God beyond. The inner divine . . . [but] it's still a transcendent notion, with theological implications, if not roots. I would rather define self as the interiorization of community, I would be with myself when I'm with others. . . . And others would not include just other people, because community as I see it, is something more ecological . . . a psychic field. And if I'm not in a psychic field with others—with people, buildings, animals, trees—I am not." Hillman does a brilliant take-off here from that infamous statement of Descartes: *I think, therefore I am.*

Hillman states categorically: "That's why I say therapy—even the best deep therapy—contributes to the world's destruction. . . . We have to have new thinking—or much older thinking—go back before Romanticism, and especially . . . out of Western history to tribal animistic psychologies that are always mainly concerned with the soul of things (environmental concerns, 'deep ecology,' as it's now called) and propitiary acts that keep the world on its course."[13]

Probably the most concise statement Lawrence ever wrote about this concept of relationship in his fiction occurs in the essay, "Morality and the Novel" (1925): "The business of art is to reveal the relation between man and his circumambient universe, at the living moment." Referring to Van Gogh and his painting of the sunflowers, Lawrence writes, "he reveals . . . the vivid relation between himself, as a man, and the sunflower, as sunflower" in that particular moment. It is neither the man himself nor the sunflower, as it can never be known what the sunflower in itself is. The painting itself is a "third thing" produced from the relationship between Van Gogh and that particular sunflower. "You cannot weigh nor measure nor even describe the vision on the canvas. It exists, to tell the truth, only in the much-debated fourth dimension. In dimensional space it has no existence."[14] A modern physicist, Fritjof Capra of the Berkeley Radiation Laboratories, stated in 1977 that in the fourth dimension where space and time are fused, "you never end up with things, only with interconnectedness, a web of relationship."[15]

In "Morality and the Novel" Lawrence went on to say:

> If we think about it, we find that our life consists in this achieving of a pure relationship between ourselves and the living universe about us. This is how I 'save my soul' by accomplishing a pure relationship between me and another person, me and other people, me and a nation, me and a race of men, me and the animals, me and the trees or flowers, me and the earth, me and the skies and sun and stars, me and the moon: an infinity of pure relations, big and little, like the stars of the sky: that makes our eternity, for each one of us, me and the timber I am sawing, the lines of force I follow; me and the dough I knead for bread, me and the very motion with which I write, me and the bit of gold I have got. This, if we knew it, is our life and our eternity: the subtle, perfected relation between me and my whole circumambient universe.
>
> And morality is that delicate, forever trembling and changing *balance* between me and my circumambient universe, which precedes and accompanies a true relatedness.[16]

Philosophy and religion try to get things down once and for all but only in the novel is it possible to show the "subtle inter-relatedness" of all. "Everything is true in its own time, place, circumstance," but untrue out of that particular relationship. Concerning the man/woman relationship, he says that "it is the *relation itself*" which is the "central clue to life"; neither the man nor the woman nor the children, coming from the union. The real morality is for the man to be true to his own manhood and the woman true to her own womanhood, then the relation itself will be true.

Using the metaphor of the crucifixion, Lawrence explains that to be moral one must not try to pin anything down—either the other person or the relationship, "which is forever the ghost of both of us." He continues: "But when you try to nail down the relationship itself, and write over it *Love* instead of *This is the King of the Jews*, then you can go on putting in nails for ever. Even Jesus called it the Holy Ghost."[17] In another essay he explains this "Holy Ghost" better: it is fifty percent me and fifty percent you "and the third thing, the spark, which springs from out of the balance, is timeless, Jesus, who saw it a bit vaguely, called it the Holy Ghost."[18]

This "fourth dimension" or the "Holy Ghost" is the topic of Lawrence's finest passage of all on relationship, occurring in "Reflections on the Death of a Porcupine." An "unfortunate Mexican's dog with its muzzle full of porcupine quills" arrives on the ranch one day. Lawrence tells Brett to get a rope. Putting a stick between its teeth and winding the rope around the muzzle, he proceeds to pull out the quills from the bloody muzzle. The dog writhes and whimpers and yelps in pain.[19] At the time of the next full moon, Frieda sees a porcupine lumbering along in the high grass. Lawrence goes back to get the little .22, which he has just recently learned to shoot while target practicing with Brett. "Now never before had I shot at any living thing: I never wanted to," but he knows the damage they do to trees. Indians, white men and Mexicans all agree they should be shot. The first shot missed, the second got him, but he stumbled on and so Lawrence finished the job with a cedar pole over the nose. Afterwards, musing on the killing, he admits he "always preferred to walk round my porcupine, rather than kill it." But he realizes that life lives on life. This is existence; it has to do with species and types, and there is a higher and a lower. But when it comes to single individuals, *beings*, it is different. Each individual is unique and cannot be compared to anything else— "that is the fourth dimension, of *being*."

"No creature is fully itself till it is, like the dandelion, opened in the bloom of pure relationship to the sun, the entire living cosmos." But Lawrence insists that "being is not ideal"; it depends on material. He proceeds to use the dandelion for an example. In the seed of the dandelion is the Holy Ghost. When it falls to earth this "Holy Ghost" calls to the sun rays and the earth's fertility and they come in. "So the sun in the seed, and the earthy one in the seed take hands, and laugh, and begin to dance." And out of this dance come the new little leaves growing up and the beginnings of roots growing down. Out of this embrace and dance, eventually comes the bud: from it the voice of the Holy Ghost crying, "I am lifted up! Lo! I am lifted up! I am here!" And the blossom comes forth from the bud and the Holy Ghost, the dandelion flower, says, "I am incarnate. . . . It is good!" But Lawrence goes on to say that there will be other incarnations just as wonderful; but the human being is hardly half grown yet, showing barely a stem for the blossom. If the human doesn't begin budding, the Holy Ghost will abandon him and all vitality will be gone. "The sun and the earth-dark will cease rushing together in him. Already it is ceasing. To many the sun is becoming stale, and the earth sterile." But only because humans have ceased moving toward blossoming: "Blossoming means the establishing of a pure, new relationship with all the cosmos. This is the state of heaven. And it is the state of a flower . . . and a man when he knows himself royal and crowned with the sun, with his feet gripping the core of the earth."[20] This "state of perfected relationship" is the fourth dimension. A full decade before, in his essay, "The Crown," Lawrence had written that immortality "is not a question of time, of everlasting life. It is a question of consummate being. . . . The perfect relation is perfect. But it is therefore timeless." We cannot hold onto this moment; it flows on into another moment. Trying to stop the flow is the sin. The flowering of the dandelion is the Holy Ghost, the "actual presence of accomplishing oneness, accomplished out of twoness. The true God is *created* every time a pure relationship . . . takes place."[21]

Lawrence was calling for a change in the basic underlying assumptions of our entire culture. European thought has always tended to find reality in *substance;* Taoist China remains the outstanding example of a culture based on relations. There were two basic origins of Taoism, according to Joseph Needham. The oldest one goes back to the ancient shamans of primitive groups on the southern and northern boundaries of the Chinese Empire. These peoples were followers of earth religions and got their power directly from nature. The more recent strand of Taoism was an outgrowth of the thinking of philosophers of the Warring States period (480 B.C. to 221 B.C.). Because of the disturbed condition of human affairs, a few intellectuals decided that, rather than stay at the courts of their feudal lords, they would withdraw into the wilderness and there seek to learn the Order of Nature. They felt that human society could never be brought into order before there was more knowledge and understanding of Nature, because human society was only a smaller part of the whole of nature.[22]

Chuang Chou points out that an animal or human body is not run by the conscious mind:

> It might seem as if there were a real Governor, but we find no trace of his being. One might believe that he could act, but we do not see his form. He would have [to have] sensitivity without form. But now the hundred parts of the human body, with its nine orifices and six viscera, all are complete in their places. Which should one prefer? Do you like them all? Or do you like some more than others? Are they all servants? Are these servants unable to control each other, but need another as a ruler? Or do they become rulers and servants in turn? Is there any true ruler other than themselves?[23]

Thus the Taoist sage knew that Nature was much too complex for human reason to fully comprehend, but he felt that by not imposing his preconceptions on Nature—and instead by exhibiting a receptive, yielding attitude—he would be able to observe and eventually understand. Taoists not only observed nature directly but, because of the rugged impassable nature of parts of China, there were always pockets of true "primitives" still living in a cooperative, undifferentiated village life right down to the late nineteenth century. The first historical Chinese dynasty was the Shang Kingdom (1520

B.C. to 1030 B.C.). Taoist intellectuals always had access to "primitive" culture—another way of doing things. Instead of the highly centralized bureaucracy of the Empire, they could see how much simpler and more fulfilling life was when lived in a primitive village type of agriculture where nature and man worked together in harmony. In contrast, about the time of the Taoist classic, the *Tao Te Ching* (around 300 B.C.), Aristotle was already old. All of Greece was tamed and civilized since it is only a very small peninsula jutting out from the larger peninsula of Europe, which, in turn, is merely a small appendage on the Eurasian continent. If we look at America, the first Jesuit missionaries had arrived in the heartland of America, the Mississippi valley, in the middle of the seventeenth century, and Ishi, the last aborigine untainted by contact with the white man, died in 1916 in California.[24] Primitive culture, in the form of fully functioning tribal units, was essentially wiped out in roughly 300 years.

The ongoing contact with primitivism in China led to the Taoist concept of "wu wei" which has been translated as "do nothing" but actually, according to Needham, means "do nothing contrary to nature."[25] The emphasis on yielding and understanding which developed out of these Taoist concepts led to an organismic viewpoint in which each individual, by following his own "tao," contributed to the good of the whole.

In contrast to the innate organism of Chinese thought, the Western heritage from both Greek philosophy and Christianity led to a dualism, which operated on many levels. Within the human being there was a mind-body or soul-body dichotomy; in physics, a mechanistic, reductionist attitude; while in biology, the logical place for organismic thinking, there raged the vitalism vs. mechanistic battle.

The biologist von Bertalanffy states that when he began his scientific work some forty years ago, biology was still in the midst of the mechanism/vitalism controversy. Some critics have stated that Lawrence was a vitalist. But he was far from that because, as von Bertalanffy explains, vitalism claimed that the parts of any organism were organized "by the action of soul-like factors, little hobgoblins, as it were, hovering in the cell or the organism."[26] This is precisely what Lawrence was struggling against by attempting to explain life in a more holistic fashion.

Actually, the way out of this impasse proved to be neither the mechanistic idea of a machine plus an invisible operator nor a reduction to lower integrative levels (reductionism). Bertalanffy advocated the "organismic viewpoint," which granted that organisms are organized things, so he set about trying to learn how they were organized, which led him to the so-called theory of open systems and steady states and then to a further generalization which he called "general systems theory." Although he first presented this idea in 1937,[27] there were no further developments until after WWII. The crucial event which occurred during the war was the advent of anti-aircraft guns with the necessity of aiming at a rapidly moving target, which meant the future position of the target must be anticipated on the basis of its location at a succession of positions. This eventually led to the rapid automatic computing machines and, further, to cybernetics and general systems theory.

In the past in the West, science had attempted to find the substance shared by all entities while, as Laszlo succinctly points out, "contemporary general systems theory seeks to find common features in terms of shared aspects of organization."[28] In other words, both Chinese and modern systems thinking, rather than dealing with substance, concentrate on how sets of events are structured and how they function in relationship to their environment. The systems approach allows for dealing with more than one set of relationships. It is possible to look at the relationships within a cell or an organism, or within a family; or, this can be extended to the level of the relationship of human beings and their particular ecosystem. "We are natural systems first, living things second, human beings third, members of a society and culture fourth, and particular individuals fifth," according to Laszlo.[29]

A natural system is not an amorphous pile of objects such as a sand pile. For instance, if one took the neutron, proton and electron of a hydrogen atom and combined them in an arbitrary manner, the chances are one would not get a hydrogen atom at all. The properties of the hydrogen atom are the result of the properties of its parts plus the exact relationship of the parts within the structure. It is not just random parts of a group which make the "system" but the mutual relationship of the members of the group—whether it is an atom, where communication of the parts is in terms of the interaction of fields of force potentials, or in a family, where communication is in gestures or words, or in nature, where the human being is a part within the whole of a particular ecosystem. In all these aspects, communication is by Laszlo's definition, "effective, mutually qualifying interaction between the members."[30]

"Our understanding of nature and our practice in regard to it has been radically altered by systems theory," according to the environmental poet Gary Snyder. "Specifically, systems theory as it comes through the science of Ecology, and in particular . . . Landscape Ecology. They provide some extraordinary detail to fill out the broader generalization that 'everything is connected.'"[31]

Perhaps the personal level is the simplest way to explain systems theory: for instance, the example of friendship or love between two people. There is Mike's friendship for Linda and Linda's friendship for Mike, but, even further, there is "the friendship" itself—the something more than either of them. This is the *love* which Lawrence was trying to define, where each remains an individual yet takes part in the greater whole. Each is enriched because each person is all that she is as an individual plus the "more than" of the relationship. In one of his earlier novels, *The Rainbow*, Lawrence was already feeling his way toward this concept when Lydia tells Anna, her daughter: "Between two people, the love itself is the important thing, and that is neither you nor him. It is a third thing you must create."[32] Lawrence explains more about the concept of relationship in the essay "We Need One Another," where he writes that "everything, even individuality itself, depends on relationship" and "We have our very individuality in relationship."[33]

Lawrence believed that each self in its distinctiveness has one purpose only: to come into the "fullness of its being" or "into the state of blossoming."[34]

Relying on his years of living and studying with primitive

groups, anthropologist Stanley Diamond writes: "The primitive realization of the person can be termed *individuation*, and it is the antithesis of ideological individualism." The latter is really *individualization*, a symptom of civilization, and it "denotes the increasingly mechanical separation of persons from each other, as a result of the shrinkage and replacement of primitive, organic ties by civilized, collective connections." Pathological loneliness is the psychological state caused by this civilized individualism. Diamond says that "primitive man is not a mere reflex of the group but instead the full development of the individual contributes to the group's unity." He gives an example of how this works by analyzing an African dance and notes that "the individual's sense of personal power and worth is immeasurably heightened by the communal nature of the event." The primitive society is a community, "springing from common origins, composed of reciprocating persons, and growing from within."[35] The power of primitive community is shown by James Lowan's account of an event in Australia. An aboriginal man sold a mountain to the mayor of a local town. The mayor offered the tribal owner a few sovereigns and a bottle of rum as payment for the mountain, which was to be used as a quarry.

> The first charge of gelignite set under the mountain unleashed a stream of black water which took many weeks to dry up. During the time the original tribal owner of the mountain fell sick and died. His dreaming had been so damaged by the explosion that the man himself was mortally wounded.
>
> It is virtually impossible for an Aborigine to deny his relationship with the earth, with his Dreaming, with his totem. The triad conditions his intellectual and emotional outlook. It also conditions his attitude towards his community. Though he does recognize the need to retire from the community on ceremonial occasions, the sense of solitude he engenders at this time is carefully orchestrated by way of myth and ritual. He therefore is never "alone" as such. So

complete and overreaching is the Dreaming that an Aborigine would find it difficult to break free and become "self-conscious" in the way we understand it, because his self cannot be detached from the web of relationships that he has with his mother, his father, his totemic kindred and the land which made him.[36]

Lawrence felt the same type of intense relationship with the circumambient nature around him. As mentioned above, he wrote: "everything, even individuality itself, depends on relationships. . . . Blossoming means the establishing of a pure, *new* relationship with all the cosmos."

It is remarkable that the Norwegian Arne Naess founder of Deep Ecology, also writes about the "equal right to live and blossom" of all beings—human and non-human. Explaining further, Naess says: "Maximum richness of life depends upon maximizing symbiosis rather than cut-throat competition or 'struggle for life'. . . . The easier one life form can blossom without destruction of any other, the more forms there can be in a finite environment."[37]

Among other themes in *Women in Love*, Lawrence tried to differentiate between these two types of individuality in the characters of Gerald Crich and Birkin. Gerald "had to fight with Matter, with the earth and the coal it enclosed. This was the sole idea, to turn upon the inanimate matter of the underground, and reduce it to his will. And for this fight with matter, one must have perfect instruments in perfect organization, a mechanism so subtle and harmonious in its workings that it represents the single mind of man, and by its relentless repetition of given movement will accomplish a purpose irresistibly, inhumanly. It was this inhuman principle in the mechanism he wanted to construct that inspired Gerald with an almost religious exaltation."

At the end of the book, Birkin concludes that "whatever the mystery which has brought forth man and the universe, it is a non-human mystery, it has its own great ends, man is not the criterion. Best leave it all to the vast, creative, non-human mystery. Best strive with oneself only, not with the universe."[38]

In his essay "Why the Novel Matters," Lawrence writes about science and how it takes one to pieces and then considers first one piece and then the other as really the person. He goes on, "Now I absolutely deny that I am a soul, or a body, or a mind . . . or a nervous system . . . or any of the rest of these bits of me. The whole is greater than the part. And therefore, I, who am man alive, am greater than my soul, or spirit, or body, or mind, or consciousness, or anything else that is merely a part of me."[39]

And in the *Apocalypse*, the last book he ever wrote, he simply and lyrically states: "We and the cosmos are one. The cosmos is a vast living body, of which we are still parts. The sun is a great heart whose tremors run throughout our smallest veins. The moon is a great gleaming nerve-centre from which we quiver forever."[40]

Today, biologists and physicists concur that the "*principle of hierarchic* order in living nature is a demonstrable fact. . . . Opposed to atomism and behaviorism, the systems view of man links him again with the world he believes in, for he is seen as emerging in that world and reflecting its general character."[41] Or, as the Chinese say, "Heaven, Earth and Man have the same *Li* (pattern)."[42] Martin Heidegger expressed the same concept even more forcefully when he wrote: "The appropriating mirror-play of the simple fourfold of earth and sky, divinities and mortals, we call the world."[43] Earth and sky, god and mortal, each mirrors in itself, in its own way, the presence of the others. This reciprocal relationship of each to the other is what makes up the human world in any particular ecosystem. Heidegger does not consider himself a philosopher, but instead a "thinker on Being." He says that this has not been attempted since the pre-Socratics. From the time of Plato, western thinking has been anthropocentric; by thus denying that we are part of nature, the human being becomes something other than human. In the context of nation-states, he becomes a cog in the war machine; in the context of machine technology he becomes another cog in the machine: material to be processed along with all the other beings in the world—trees, animals, soil—whatever can be processed and sold for money. To live as a full human being, we must learn what it means "to dwell" on the earth rather than exploit it for human ends.

"To dwell is to spare the earth, receive the sky, expect the gods, and have a capacity for death."[44]

Heidegger believes that truth is a function of the interrelationship of the fourfold: earth, sky, gods and man.[45] This concept of truth provides a further dimension to what Lawrence was trying to do in 1915 when he wrote the ending of *The Rainbow*: "And the rainbow stood on the earth . . . its arch the top of heaven. . . . She saw in the rainbow the earth's new architecture . . . the world built up in a living fabric of Truth, fitting to the over-arching heaven."

A modern American Indian, a member of the Kiowa tribe, M. Scott Momaday, expresses a concept very similar to Heidegger's in this passage:

> [T]he native American ethic with respect to the physical world is a matter of reciprocal appropriation: appropriations in which man invests himself in the landscape, and at the same time incorporates the landscape into his own most fundamental experience . . . . [T]his understanding of the relationship between man and the landscape, or man and the physical world, man and nature, proceeds from a racial or cultural experience. I think his attitude toward the landscape has been formulated over a long period of time, and the length of time itself suggests an evolutionary process perhaps instead of a purely rational and decisive experience. . . . His heritage has always been rather closely focused, centered upon the landscape as a particular reality. . . . The idea of "appropriateness" is central to the Indian experience of the natural world. . . . It is a basic understanding of right within the framework of relationships, and, within the framework of that relationship I was talking about a moment ago, between man and the physical world.[46]

Or, we can say, using terminology from hierarchy theory, each sub-system—earth and sky and gods and mortals—dominates its own subordinate, smaller parts within its own domain, restraining their degrees of freedom according to its own integral portion of the overall pattern; much as its own degrees of freedom have been restrained by the pattern of activities of the higher system—the fourfold itself or the world of which it is a part. In other words the mortals cannot impart order upon seemingly chaotic nature by laws—either human or so-called "natural laws"—derived from a God which is considered to be an ultimate law-giver; instead they, themselves, (the human beings) are part of an ordered system in which they are enclosed and within the patterned dynamics of which they interact.[47]

After this excursion through Taoism, modern psychological and anthropological research, systems theory and American Indian concepts, perhaps it is now possible to understand what Lawrence was up against when he tried to articulate these concepts in the 1920s. Only two years before his death, he wrote: "The last three thousand years of mankind have been an excursion into ideals, bodilessness, and tragedy and now the excursion is over. . . . It is a question, practically, of relationship. We *must* get back into relation, vivid and nourishing relation to the cosmos. . . . The way is through daily ritual, and the re-awakening. We *must* once more practice the ritual of dawn and noon and sunset, the ritual of the kindling fire and pouring water, the ritual of the first breath, and the last. . . . We must return to the way of 'knowing in terms of togetherness' . . . the togetherness of the body, the sex, the emotions, the passions, with the earth and sun and stars."[48]

In two passages of his works Lawrence gave a living example of his philosophy—where the human being is totally, completely a full individual self moving freely within the totally flowing allness of nature. These times are rare in any life. I can recognize the feeling from having achieved it with friends skiing together in powder snow. As we stand along the ridge, each of us makes the first turn. From then on no throught and no effort; gravity (the fall line) lays out each person's way down. The powder snow lifts the tip of the ski and gravity pulls it down. Once at the bottom, looking back up, we see the perfect curves nature gives us in the turns and there's no crossing of one another's tracks because there is only one fall line (one best line) gravity gives for each person's position along the ridge. In skiing powder, each human being is moving freely, but so sensitively responding to earth's gravity, conforming to the shape of the land and yielding to the snow, that the entire hillside seems to be one moving organism, moving together unthinkingly with no possible conflict. Lawrence concisely and clearly explained this feeling when he wrote: "Paradoxical as it may sound, the individual is only truly himself when he is unconscious of his own individuality, when he is unaware of his own isolation, when he is not split into subjective and objective, when there is no *me or you*, no *me or it* in his consciousness, but the *me and you*, the *me and it* is a living *continuum*, as if all were connected by a living membrane."[49]

He first wrote about this "living continuum" in his essay, "Dana's *Two Years Before the Mast*":

> Beautifully the sailing-ship nodalizes the forces of sea and wind, converting them to her purpose. There is no violation, as in a steam-ship, only a winged centrality. It is this perfect adjusting of ourselves to the elements, the perfect equipoise between them and us, which gives us a great part of our life-joy. The more we intervene machinery between us and the naked forces the more we numb and atrophy our own senses. Every time we turn on a tap to have water, every time we turn a handle to have fire or light, we deny ourselves and annul our being. The great elements, the earth, air, fire, water are there like some great mistress whom we woo and struggle with, whom we heave and wrestle with. And all our appliances do but deny us these fine embraces, take the miracle of life away from us. . . . When we balance the sticks and kindle a fire, we partake of the mysteries. But when we turn on an electric tap, there

is as it were a wad between us and the dynamic universe.[50]

And then, much later in his life after he had almost died in Mexico, he dictated a beautiful fragment of a story to Frieda while sailing back to Europe in October of 1925. In 1928 he read this fragment to the Brewsters. Later, Earl Brewster wrote: "As he read, it seemed to reach an ever higher and more serene beauty. Suddenly he stopped, saying: 'The last part will be regenerate man, a real life in this Garden of Eden.' When they urged him to finish it he said, 'I've an intuition I shall not finish that novel. It was written so near the borderline of death. . . .'"[51]

Lawrence's fictional character Gethin Day in "The Flying Fish" is on the way back to England, sitting for hours at the very tip of the bowsprit of the ship as it sails through the Gulf of Mexico "and the world was all strange white sunshine, candid, and water, warm, bright water, perfectly pure beneath him, of an exquisite frail green."

The flying fish "swept into the air, from nowhere, and went brilliantly twinkling in their flight of silvery watery wings rapidly fluttering away" over the surface of the sea and gone again. He lay there all morning watching them "on translucent wings swept in their ecstatic clouds out of the water, in a terror that was brilliant as joy, in a joy brilliant with terror. . . ."

On the third morning there are porpoises staying just below the surface of the water, "a spectacle of the purest and most perfected joy in life that Gethin Day ever saw." Because they were moving at the same speed as the ship, they seemed to hang motionless and the tail flukes of the last fish "exactly touched the ship's bows, underwater, with the frailest, yet precise and permanent touch." While neither ship nor fish seemed to move, the fish were changing places all the time, "and ever the others speeding in motionless, effortless speed, and intertwining with strange silkiness as they sped, intertwining among one another. . . ." He watched, spellbound by their perfect balance:

. . . mingling among themselves in some strange single

laughter of multiple consciousness, giving off the joy of life, sheer joy of life, togetherness in pure complete motion, many lusty-bodied fish enjoying one laugh of life, sheer togetherness, perfect as passion. They gave off into the water their marvelous joy of life, such as the man had never met before. And it left him wonderstruck.

"But they know joy, they know pure joy!" he said to himself in amazement. "This is the purest achievement of joy I have seen in all life. . . . Men have not got in them that secret to be alive together and make one like a single laugh, yet each fish going his own gait. This is sheer joy and men have lost it, or never accomplished it. . . . It would be wonderful to know joy as these fish know it. The life of the deep waters is ahead of us, it contains sheer togetherness and sheer joy. We have never got there."

There as he leaned over the bowsprit he was mesmerized by one thing only, by joy, by joy of life, fish speeding-in water with playful joy. . . . What civilization will bring us to such a pitch of swift laughing togetherness, as these fish have reached?[52]

7

"What the Human Heart Secretly Yearns After"

Primarily I am a passionately religious man and my novels must be written from the depths of my religious experience. . . .[1]

Nothing in Lawrence's controversial life and work has been more misunderstood and misinterpreted than his "passionately religious" nature, for it did not fit within the limited confines of Christianity. Instead, based as it was on his "religious experience" of nature, it was part of the ongoing continuum of human religious experience. To understand Lawrence's creative work of the last eight years of his life it is necessary to take a brief look at religious experience as manifested throughout most of humanity's time on earth.

In her book *The Gate of Horn: A Study of the Religious Conceptions of the Stone Age and Their Influence Upon European Thought*, Gertrude Levy deals not only with Upper Paleolithic cave art but also the remnants of Stone Age culture still remaining in undisturbed pockets of the world. She states: "What is remarkable in [these beliefs] is the spiritual and truly religious conception of a connection originally based upon the need for food and sufficiently effective to hold the group in social and economic cohesion."[2] Concisely summing up her decades of research, she defines religion as the "maintenance of abiding relationship."[3]

Later, in the Megalithic Age, it became the custom to bury the dead in massive communal tombs. According to the archaeologist Jacquetta Hawkes, such tombs symbolized "a return to the Earth Mother for rebirth, the association of death with fecundity, which inspires all the myths of the goddess and the dying god. In this sense they represented the timeless unity of the tribe, of its members, dead, living and unborn all enclosed within their common matrix, the rock and the earth."[4] As knowledge grew of the causes of seasonal change in sky phenomena, there developed the concept of deities of the sun and wind. Thus the Stone Age religion of reciprocity, which began with ceremonies concerning the birth and death of the hunted animals, developed further into ritual attunement to the rhythms of seasonal change. Ceremonies developed in which human beings ritually gave their energy to the process of assisting the new year to be born, the harvest to be cut, and the sun to rise or to return from his winter house and bring back the light and warmth.

As late as the Classical Age in Rome there was no real need to define religion because it was so closely bound up with life. The word *religio* existed, derived from the word *religere*, which meant to bind back or bind again, referring to certain religious practices to insure safety in particular places or at particular seasons of the year. Still later, Cicero wrote, "All those things pertaining to the worship of the gods are called religious."[5] By that time culture had become centralized in the city of Rome, loosening the ties of the people to their local place; thus the broader meaning of religion—involving the total relationship of human being, place, gods and ritual—was narrowed down to the worship of specific gods. The final step was the "death of the gods" when the "Christians set out to destroy the gods of the classical world,"[6] in order to co-opt the energy existing between the people, their land and the gods of a particular place. Libanius, one of the last of the cultured, educated pagans, tried to stop the wholesale destruction of the temples by the Roman Christian authorities with an appeal to the Emperor in 386 A.D. In his moving speech, "In Defense of the Temples," he pointed out that Christian "men in black . . . rush through country places like flood waters—ravaging them by the very fact that it is the temples that they destroy.

For every country place where they destroy a temple is a place made blind: a place knocked down, assassinated. For the temples, my Emperor, are the souls of the countryside."[7]

Although the Christians did succeed in destroying the temples, the worship of the old gods lingered on in the country places. In 589 A.D. the Inquisition began with the Council of Toledo.[8] Throughout the following centuries the clergy repeatedly warned the faithful of the devils lurking in the wild places. It is no wonder that the wilderness was feared and avoided. The deeper nature rituals survived, however, and were listed as the offenses of witches in the fifteenth century. These offenses included "the making of offerings at trees, rocks and springs, the blessings of fields."[9] This deliberately inculcated fear of nature continued so that by the time of the settling of America it came to be "fear of the idea of America . . . fear, indeed of the rivers, mountains, and ceaseless skies of the continent itself," as the philosopher Santayana explained it in 1911.[10] But always in natural places the gods lingered on.

Lawrence felt these influences in the remnants of Sherwood Forest where he roamed as a child. Of course, he was also exposed to Christian concepts both in his mother's "proper" Congregational chapel and in his father's Methodist chapel, which was the one most mining families attended. He became deeply imbued with Biblical symbolism, which provided the only terms he had to express his religious feelings, but throughout his life, he tried to break out of the limitations enforced on these natural concepts by Christianity. This can be seen in all his works, from *The White Peacock* to the last book he wrote, *The Apocalypse*; but his most intense effort occurs in *The Plumed Serpent*. Although growing directly out of Lawrence's relationship to the land of Taos and his exposure to Indian culture, indirectly *The Plumed Serpent* was the result of his life's search for authentic sacred ritual in tune with the natural world.

Councilor William Edward Hopkin, who was one of Lawrence's oldest friends in Eastwood, said: "When he went away from his native town 1908 he knew where he stood, but could not give it a name. . . . What was plainly manifest was that in D. H. Lawrence we had a man with beliefs and ideas at variance with accepted dogmas and theories, irreconcilably at variance, and therefore with few to understand his teachings or even prepared to try." Hopkin went on to say, "When he talked about his dark Gods I was lost entirely. . . . They were very real to Lawrence."[11]

There is a pervading sense of reverence for nature in all three of his earlier novels: *The White Peacock, The Trespasser* and *Sons and Lovers*. For example, in this passage from *The White Peacock*, his first novel, Lettie and Cyril find hosts of little white flowers called snowdrops. Lettie (based on his sister) asks Cyril (Lawrence), "What do you think they say—what do they make you think, Cyril?" He answers, "I don't know. Emily says they belong to some old wild lost religion. They were the symbol of tears, perhaps, to some strange-hearted Druid folk before us." Lettie replies that they are "more than tears, they are so still. Something out of an old religion, that we have lost. . . . They belong to some knowledge we have lost, that I have lost and that I need. . . . Do you think, Cyril, we can lose things off the earth . . . things that matter—wisdom?"[12]

By the time Lawrence wrote his fourth novel, *The Rainbow*, after he met Frieda, he was moving toward a more specific statement of the basic religious problem created by the narrowing of natural religious concepts to fit Christianity. The crucial scene takes place in Chapter 7, "The Cathedral," where Anna and Will have gone to Lincoln Cathedral. He is swept away in "perfect, swooning consummation, and his soul remained, at the apex of the arch, clinched in the timeless ecstasy, consummated." Anna, although moved by the beauty of the cathedral will not "consent to the knitting of all the leaping stone in a great roof that closed her in, and beyond which was nothing." She remembers the open sky above, not just a blue vault hung with lamps "but a space where stars were wheeling in freedom." She draws Will's attention to the impish little faces carved in stone, which "winked and leered, giving suggestions of the many things that had been left out of the great concept of the church." What before had been an "absolute" to Will now became only a world shut off from the greater world "of the whole blue rotunda of the day." And when he thinks about it the Grecian temple was never perfectly a temple unless it was "ruined and mixed up with the winds and the sky and the herbs. . . . There was life outside the Church."[13] Paul Shepard, in *Man in the Landscape*, points out that "The great period of building cathedrals followed the peak of clearing forests in Europe. . . . A metaphor of forms and spaces within suggests nostalgia and profound emotion linking cathedral and the post-Pleistocene primeval forest."[14]

Writing in 1921 about the classical age in his *Movements in European History*, Lawrence says that gifts were offered and people danced to the gods, hidden in the springs and sacred groves, and concludes with "everything that was wonderful had its gods, the Greeks and Romans were not jealous of strange gods. Religion was a part of life with festivals and sacred rituals for every purpose; but the Christians kept apart, afraid to offend their own God."[15] Much later he wrote, "The Greeks, being sane, were pantheists and pluralists, and so am I."[16]

His rejection of Christianity culminates in the Australian novel, *Kangaroo*. Halfway through the book, after Somers (based on Lawrence) has already become somewhat involved with the movement headed by Kangaroo Jay, a friend brings him to meet Struthers, a labor leader in Australia, who tries to convince Somers to join them by appealing to the bond between working class men. Somers muses on this new "cohesive principle," this "new passion of a man's absolute trust in his mate, his love for his mate" and he comes to the conclusion that "love is the greatest thing between human beings" when it happens naturally, but when it is used as an ideal to "lock individuals together, it is just courting disaster." Love as the highest ideal is as bad as any other ideal. He decides that "Any more love is a hopeless thing, till we have found again . . . the great dark God who alone will sustain us in our loving one another." Somers tries to explain this to Struthers by telling him that it needs more than the limited belief of "men in each other"; it needs "some sort of religion." Struthers is open to this idea because, as he says, "[A]ll the churches are established on Christ. And Christ says 'Love one another.'" Struthers is quite willing to use Christ for his purposes. That presents no problem, but the "great dark God, the ithyphallic, of the first dark religions. . . . Struthers had no use for him." Somers's heart is heavy and he evades all Struthers' attempts to get him to commit himself by saying he'll see him tomorrow. Somers leaves, feeling as if he had just been in the same kind of medical examination as that which happened to him during the war. When he gets outside and sees the sun and the flowers "suddenly the whole thing switched right away from him." He called a hansom cab and told Jay that he wanted to drive round the Botanical Gardens and out to the spit. He tells Jay that he is not going to join Kangaroo. He felt like a "child escaped from school . . . from the necessity to *be* something and to *do* something." He enjoys the palm trees and the wild birds and the blue water of the harbor. "It's wonderful to feel this blue globe of emptiness of the Australian air. It shuts everything out."

Lawrence writes that "in the evening of this memorable day," Somers went to dine with Kangaroo. The clarity of his decision, made amid the palm trees and birds in the Gardens, is still with him, enabling him to confront Kangaroo on what turns out to be his final meeting with him. They clash over Kangaroo's "sympathy" and "love" for all men. "But you're such a Kangaroo, wanting to carry mankind in your belly-pouch." Somers continues: "You're a Jew, and you must be Jehovah or nothing. We're Christians, all little Christs walking with our crucifixes. . . . I'm tired, tired. I want to be a man, with the gods beyond me, greater than me. I want the great gods." Somers, feeling the intense hatred of Kangaroo coming at him, is engulfed in a growing horror, not fully explained in the book. It makes more sense, however, when one understands that in this scene, Lawrence is not only rejecting all the two thousand years of Christianity with its gospel of "love one another" and "meekness and mildness" but at some deeper level facing up to the fear, implanted in him as a child, of the idea of eternal damnation. At the end of this passage Lawrence writes that Somers very carefully and quickly moves to the door and unlocks it and moves on down the stairs hoping Kangaroo will not catch him.[17]

"The Nightmare" chapter follows, in which Somers relives the war years in England and the horror of mob rule, which is the wrong kind of power. By the end of the chapter he feels clear of all ties: "Without a people, without a land." He continues with a statement of what he believes in—"the inward soul, in the profound unconscious of man. Not an ideal God. The ideal God is a proposition of the mental consciousness, all-too-limitedly human." The God he believes in is "forever dark, forever unrealisable"; but "every living human soul is a well-head to this darkness."[18] In this statement Lawrence comes closest to defining what he means by his "dark gods."

Further light on Lawrence's "dark gods" comes from Ralph Metzner in *The Well of Remembrance.* "In the Goddess-worshipping farming communities of Old Europe and the Mediterranean, black is the color of the richly fertile earth, which brings forth new vegetative growth and nourishment. Residues of the black Earth-goddess appear in the imagery of the Black Madonna of which over five hundred examples can be found in Christian churches all over Europe, testifying to her persistence."[19] For the Neolithic people, black was identified with the good black soil, source of abundance, but for the Christians, when they took over, black was evil and connected with the devil.

Lawrence believed in the "inward soul, in the profound unconscious [sic] of man." Metzner explains that we can once again get in touch with the old gods and goddesses of our ancestors. "It is a task of remembering something we once knew and practiced. . . . Our animistic, shamanistic ancestors had . . . awareness of symbiotic relatedness with the natural world."[20] Through listening and reflecting on their ancient stories, we may be able to reawaken the nature goddesses and gods slumbering in the inner recesses of the collective unconscious. Further on in this chapter, I recount some of the pagan remnants still operating among the seemingly Christian peasants in Southern Europe.

What Lawrence discovered through the process of writing *Kangaroo* is that neither the ideal of love nor the ideal of a particular political movement was the answer to a fulfilling life. The one aspect of life which he always found fulfilling was his deep relationship to nature. Throughout *Kangaroo* there are passages of extraordinary beauty concerning the sea, which "talked all the time to him in its disintegrative, elemental language."[21] Thus when he arrived in

America and was captivated by the "brilliant, proud morning" of the desert of New Mexico he was singularly receptive to the Indian's religious relationship to his land. He wrote:

> A vast, old religion which once swayed the earth lingers in unbroken practice there in New Mexico ....For the whole life-effort of man was to get his life into direct contact with the elemental life of the cosmos, mountain-life, cloud-life, thunder-life, air-life, earth-life, sun-life. To come into immediate felt contact, and so derive energy, power, and a dark sort of joy. This effort into sheer naked contact, without an intermediary or mediator is the real meaning of religion.[22]

In a letter to Else, from the ranch, Lawrence wrote about the Indians and the "intense religious life they keep up.... This animistic religion is the only live one, ours is a corpse of a religion."[23]

He hoped to write a novel while in America but perhaps because of the pressure he felt from Mabel Luhan he was not able to start it in Taos. In her book Mabel frankly explains what she wanted from Lawrence: "I wanted Lawrence to understand things for me. To take *my* experience, *my* material, *my* Taos, and to formulate it all into a magnificent creation."[24]

When he got to Mexico he wrote to Catherine Carswell: "Mexico has a certain mystery of beauty for me, as if the gods were here. Now, in this October, the days are so pure and lovely, like an enchantment, as if some dark-faced gods were still young."[25] Catherine Carswell, in her book *Savage Pilgrimage*, explains that when Lawrence visited the old monastery at Monte Cassino in 1919 he was tempted by the atmosphere of the Middle Ages which still lingered there. But he made the decision that he "must live in the hard and often loathsome present, an individual man's life, with all its needs, contradictions and error proclaimed as it went along: and at the same time he must be an unswerving conduit from the very origins of life—so far back that they were lost—to the undiscovered future, in some way that transcended, while it never eliminated or absolved the individual. The conception, I believe, is new and it is potent. But a kind of sensitiveness akin to the sensitiveness of Lawrence, which is a thing far removed from emotionalism, has to be acquired before either the novelty or the potency becomes apparent."[26]

Although Lawrence was both fascinated and repelled by the Aztec ruins and sculptures which he saw in Mexico, they led him to begin work on the novel which later became *The Plumed Serpent*. Working on it on the shores of Lake Chapala in Mexico, he grafted what he knew of the New Mexican Indians onto all that he found good in the Mexican peasants. His central motif was a revival of the old Mexican gods. Before he finished the final draft he had tried out some of his ideas in two short stories: "St. Mawr" and "The Woman Who Rode Away."

In "St. Mawr" Lou finds, when she buys a ranch in New Mexico, that "There's something else for me . . . and it's here, on this ranch. It's here, in this landscape. It's something more real to me than men are, and it soothes me, and it holds me up. I *know*, and there is no altering it, that I've got to live differently."[27] In "The Woman Who Rode Away," a bored white woman in Mexico half consciously allows herself to be kidnapped by Indians while she is riding in the hills and later, she is sacrificed by them to restore the connection between them and the sun, which was broken by the white man. The sacrifice takes place in a cave, which is modeled on one not far from Lawrence's ranch above Taos.[28]

Lawrence and Mabel Luhan had ridden their horses up from Taos to the hill above the village of Arroyo Seco to see the cave. She explains: "It is a place the Indians feel very strongly about." She describes what they found: "a vast pelvic-shaped aperture faces the west and yawns upward to the sky; and over it descends the mountain water, falling thirty feet across the face of the entrance to form an icy pool below." They climbed up to an "altar-like ledge where there is a faint sun painted high up to the east of it. One by one we climbed to the high altar and looking before us, we saw the clear fall of water across the opening, green and transparent." Mabel felt a mixture of awe and fear in the place and says: "I can never go back there without a shudder."[29]

Personally, I can testify to the power of this cave. One year during the Winter Solstice, when I joined the all-night ritual drumming and dancing with Elizabeth Cogburn, the ritualist, at her place above Taos, all of us drove up the road and took the trail to the cave. We had rattles and a small drum with us. We were sitting along the ledge facing the west, looking out through a gigantic, glittering, blue-green icicle waiting for the sun to set. Toward sunset, the sun moved directly behind the icicle so that we were looking through blue-green ice as the sun set. To see through the ice the Solstice, the turn-around point of the sun in its journey back toward summer, was a rare experience. Such a powerful land form as this cave would certainly inspire Lawrence to use it in one of his works.

What Lawrence was trying to do in the stories he wrote in New Mexico was to resacralize the natural cycles so that human beings flowed within the whole as all other beings do. He realized, even while writing it, that what he was attempting was almost impossible using a linear method to tell about an experience which could only be felt by the brain/body as a whole. About halfway through *The Plumed Serpent*, he writes of Ramón, sitting with a "sense of heaviness and inadequacy" beside Kate. He had "gnashed himself almost to pieces" before he had found the way to the "Quick of all being and existence, which he called the Morning Star, since men must give all things a name." To find the way to the "bright Quick of all things: is very difficult and needs great strength and courage." But when some people "drag at his entrails" to hold him back, pleading love of him, and others try to hold him back with the "hands of hate . . . it becomes almost impossible."[30] When Lawrence wrote of "those pleading love" he was probably referring to Frieda and Mabel, while the "hands of hate" refer to all those he knew would vilify the book and not understand what he was trying to do.

The Plumed Serpent tells the story of Don Ramón, a graduate of Columbia University, and Don Cipriano, a graduate of Oxford, and their efforts to rediscover the wholeness of the "old ways" after confronting the limitations of rational thinking and "ideal" politics and religion in their own lives. The opening scene in which Kate, an Irish widow, attends a bullfight in Mexico City with two American friends, provides Lawrence with a vehicle for showing the lifelessness and mob psychology of humanity when it is reduced to its lowest common denominator. Equally horrified by the mob and the senseless cruelty to animals, Kate leaves early and is helped through the rain to a taxi by Don Cipriano. Later at tea with Mrs. Norris she formally meets both Don Cipriano and Don Ramón. Mrs. Norris is based on Zelia Nuttall, an archaeologist at whose home Lawrence could have seen a number of books on Mexican myths.[31]

"The Gods of Antiquity Return to America" is the headline in a newspaper which Kate sees shortly after tea at the Norris home. The article informs her of an astonishing event which has just occurred at a village on the Lake of Sayula, where people still find little idols of baked clay, which were long ago thrown into the water by natives who worshipped the spirit of the waters. The article goes on to relate that some women washing clothes in the lake saw a naked and bearded man, whose body shone like gold, rise up out of the lake and wade toward shore. Putting on a pair of cotton pants, from the laundry drying in the sun, he tells the protesting women that he has come out of the lake to tell them that "the gods are coming back to Mexico." The article concludes with the statement that "Don Ramón Carrasco, our eminent historian" was going to investigate the incident.[32]

Later, traveling along the lake by boat, Kate first sees the town of Sayula beyond a "mound of a hill standing alone, dotted with dry bushes, distinct and Japanese-looking."[33] She takes a house in Sayula and at night in the plaza she first sees the men of Quetzalcoatl with their drum. A man with a banner of the sun tells of the new coming of the gods in a legendary manner. He tells of the lake calling for men but "there were no men. . . . So one of the gods with hidden faces walked out of the water, and climbed the hill," pointing toward the round hill at the back of the village. From the hill, he looked up at the sun and behind it to the dark sun that made all things and he asked, "Is it time?" The narrator continues, "The man on the top of the hill, who was a god" said he was Quetzalcoatl and that long ago he had brought the people many good things but the people forgot him so he had cried to the dark sun, "Let me go home." The dark sun lifted him into the sky and then "beckoned with a finger" and brought the white man out of the east, who brought with him his dead god on a cross. But now it is time for Jesus and his mother, Mary, to go home behind the Sun. Now, the bright Morning Star is here and says, "It is I, the Morning Star, who . . . was Quetzalcoatl," returning to the earth. All the men surrounding the banner began to sing a hymn with flute and drum.[34]

Lawrence's choice of the "mound of a hill" behind the town for the appearance of "the man . . . who was a god" again shows Lawrence's feeling for the sacred places of the earth. In a photograph of the village[35] along Lake Chapala in Mexico, which Lawrence used as the setting for *The Plumed Serpent*, the mounded hill is a true nourishing Mother Goddess form, the exact shape of the hills on which the Cretans built their temples. Lawrence's brief reference to the hill as "distinct and Japanese-looking" refers to the fact that in Oriental prints one always sees a shrine on just such a hill.

Kate, in the story, is eventually drawn into the group surrounding Don Ramón and Don Cipriano, eventually marrying Don Cipriano, "in Quetzalcoatl"; thus becoming Malintzi,[36] the goddess and third member of the pantheon. Throughout the book she continually vacillates between her old life and the new world of Don Ramón. Kate muses that the aboriginal life in America was that of humanity "before the mental-spiritual world came into being." When the white men came to this country their "mental-spiritual life flourished like a weed in this virgin soil but will probably wither and die as quickly. Then there is the possibility of a new type of human life which combines 'the old blood-and-vertebrate consciousness' with the modern white 'mental-spiritual consciousness'. . . . The sinking of both beings, into a new being."[37]

Don Ramón's next step is to reverently remove the Christian gods from the church, load them on a boat and ritually burn them on an island in the lake. Later the drum is heard instead of the bells and the church is rededicated to Quetzalcoatl with rituals and dancing.

The book closes with Kate vacillating once more and wondering if she should go back to England for its security and limited life, or whether she should stay where there is real, full life but all is deep and unknown and sometimes frightening. At the very end of the book she pleads with her husband Cipriano, "You won't let me go!" and she stays.

The bare outline of the story can give no idea of the full effect of Lawrence's writing. By drawing together the work of a number of people, I hope to further elucidate what I feel Lawrence was trying to do in this book, which he claimed was "the most important of all [his] novels," but that he hated "sending it out into the world."[38]

The wonder is that Lawrence somehow managed by words alone to convey the way he felt when he was immersed in nature as the Indians sang to the soft thudding of the drum around the fire while the Evening Star hung in the west over his ranch.[39] Venus, the central symbol in *The Plumed Serpent*, had always been important to him. He had used it in many of his works throughout the years, though not always mentioning it by name. In *The Trespasser*, Helena and Siegmund are lying in the sand, looking out over the water, waiting for the moon to rise. "Each was looking at a low, large star which hung straight in front of them, dripping its brilliance in a thin streamlet of light along the sea almost to their feet. It was a star-path fine and clear, trembling in its brilliance, but certain upon the water." To Siegmund it seems like a lantern hanging at a gate to light someone home, and he wondered what would he find if he followed the "thread of the star track."[40] In an early short story, "Witch à la Mode," a young man comes back to the town of a former girl friend. As he enters the town "looking west, [he] saw the evening star advance, a bright thing approaching from a long way off, as if it had been bathing in the surf of the daylight, and now was walking shorewards to the night. He greeted the naked star with a bow of the head, his heart surging."[41] When Lawrence was in Sicily, he wrote, ". . . oh, regal evening star, hung westward flaring over the jagged rock precipices of tall Sicily."[42]

Through the intervening years Lawrence wrote of Venus often but he used it with greatest effect in *The Plumed Serpent*, where it becomes the symbol of balance and equilibrium. It is "central between the flash of day and the black of night. . . . The mystery of the evening-star brilliant in silence and distance between the downward-surging plunge of the sun and the vast, hollow seething of inpouring night. The magnificence of the watchful morning-star, that watches between the night and the day, the gleaming clue to the two opposites."[43] In this passage he shows the influence of the many times he watched the evening sky over the desert near Taos. Search as diligently as one can, there is no star in the sky—until suddenly, it is there, like magic, where nothing was before. It requires just enough darkness before it can be seen; and then it is gone a short time later because it has set. Thus it provides the symbol for that moment of perfect relationship. The Morning Star was an important symbol for the Indians in the western part of the United States. Black Elk, the Sioux medicine-man, called it "day-break star," and he always got up early to watch for its coming. When it appeared he said: "Behold the star of understanding."[44] The Pawnee Indians had a ceremony called "The Hako" in which they kept vigil all night waiting for the dawn. When the first glimmer of light came, they sang the "Birth of the Dawn" song, and when the Morning Star appeared they sang a second song to it:

> The star comes from a great distance, too far away for us to see the place where it starts. At first we can hardly see it; we lose sight of it, it is so far off; then we see it again, for it is coming steadily toward us all the time . . . nearer and nearer. The Morning Star comes still nearer and now we see him standing there in the heavens, a strong man shining brighter and brighter. The soft plume in his hair moves with the breath of the new day, and the ray of the sun touches it with color. As he stands there so bright, he is bringing us strength and new life.
>
> As we look upon him he grows less bright; he is receding, going back to his dwelling place whence he came. We watch him vanishing. . . . The day is

close behind, advancing along the path of the
Morning Star and the Dawn.[45]

Lawrence not only intuitively grasped the central importance of
the Morning Star in American Indian mythology, he also added still
another dimension in the following passage from *The Plumed Serpent*,
where it stands for the "more than" present when all the parts of a
particular entity are in true relationship. When Kate first visits
Ramón's hacienda on a day when the Men of Quetzalcoatl are
meeting, they chant with the drum and then Ramón tells them of
the Morning Star, Lord of the two ways:

> There is no giving, and no taking. When the
> fingers that give touch the fingers that receive, the
> Morning Star shines at once, from the contact, and
> the jasmine gleams between the hands. And thus
> there is neither giving nor taking, nor hand that
> proffers nor hand that receives, but the star between
> them is all, and the dark hand and the light hand are
> invisible on each side. . . . Think neither to give nor to
> receive, only let the jasmine flower.[46]

The underlying theme throughout *The Plumed Serpent* is
expressed in Kate's words: "No! It's not a helpless, panic reversal. It
is conscious, carefully chosen. We must go back to pick up old
threads. We must take up the old, broken impulse that will connect
us with the mystery of the cosmos again, now we are at the end of
our tether."[47] This same theme is stated in a somewhat different
manner in a poem which Lawrence wrote about this time, with the
title, "Reach Over."

It begins with the lines, "Reach over, reach over / across the chasm
in the dark." He says there is a chasm which still lies between him
and "men dumb in the dusk but men / and dearer to me than
everything else." He is referring here to primitive cultures. Two
important stanzas follow:

I have come back to you, for I never left you.
Half-way round the circle now
I feel I'm coming near.

I never left you.
I went the opposite way round the circle,
Because it was the surest way of meeting you at last. . . .[48]

In both Kate's thoughts and in the poem, "Reach Over," Lawrence was trying to define a concept similar to that of "future primitive." This does *not* mean attempting to go back and imitate a past culture; rather it means acknowledging the body and nervous system, which we have inherited from past ages, and beginning again to live the life which harmonizes this body and mind with the surrounding environment. Paul Shepard, retired professor of Human Ecology, succinctly explains: "We are Pleistocene beings living in an impoverished culture, one that no longer offers us the diversity that our genetic makeup expects in order to grow up in a healthy fashion."[49]

Gary Snyder presents this same concept from a long-range point of view when he points out that during the middle and late Pleistocene, big game hunting was the usual way of life. Nomadic hunters roamed throughout large areas. "With the decline of the ice age—and here's where we are, most of the big game hunters went out of business." It is important to remember that we *are* now in an inter-glacial period. Snyder continues: "Countless local ecosystem habitation styles emerged. People developed specific ways to *be* in each of those niches: plant knowledge . . . smaller animals, smaller tools. From steep jungle slopes of Southwest China to coral atolls to barren Arctic deserts—*a spirit of what it was to be there* evolved, that spoke of a direct sense of relation to the land—which really means, the totality of the local bio-region system, from cirrus clouds to leaf-mold. . . . So, inhabitory peoples sometimes say 'this piece of land is sacred'—or 'all the land is sacred.' This is an attitude that draws on awareness of the mystery of life and death; of taking life to live; of giving life back—not only to your own children, but to the life of the whole land." Snyder continues, somewhat sarcastically, to point out: "Some time in the last ten years the best brains of the Occident discovered to their amazement that we live in an Environment." We now know that "We must find our way to seeing the mineral cycles, the water cycles, air cycles, nutrient cycles, as sacramental."[50]

This is precisely what Lawrence was trying to do in *The Plumed Serpent* more than fifty years ago, and the effort it took almost killed him. After three years of struggling to get his ideas down on paper he fell critically ill. The following spring, writing from Kiowa Ranch, he said: "I managed to finish my Mexican novel, *Quetzalcoatl*, in Mexico: the very day I went down, as if shot in the intestines. . . . I daren't even look at the outside of the MS. It cost me so much. . . ."[51]

Another aspect of the natural cycles is presented in the chapter, "Malintzi," where Kate is mulling over Don Ramón's insistence that "Alone you are nothing . . . But together we are the wings of the Morning." She wonders if she must "admit that the individual [is] an illusion." Perhaps only in the mechanical world individuals are real and effective. "In the vivid world all are 'fragments' or 'halves'. The only whole is the Morning Star, which can only rise between two: or between many."[52]

With that statement Lawrence had touched on an important aspect of American Indian culture. Vine Deloria explains this concept in his book, *God Is Red*: "[A]ll things are related. This fundamental premise undergirds all Indian tribal religions and determines the relationship of all parts of creation one to another. . . . If all things are related the unity of creation demands that each life form contribute its intended contribution. Entities are themselves, because they have been made to be so. Any violation of another entity's right to existence in and of itself is a violation of the nature of the creation and a degradation of religious reality itself." Furthermore, Deloria equates healing with relationship when he writes: "Healing may indeed be a means of determining the extent to which a religion is strong or weak. In none of the three areas of land, ethnicity, or healing is any set of beliefs required in the traditional sense which Western religious thinkers have defined beliefs. The transition from traditional Western and Christian categories is not then a matter of learning new facts about life, the world, or mankind's history. It is primarily a matter of participation in terms of the real factors of existence—land, a specific community, and religious men with special powers existing within that community."[53]

In *The Plumed Serpent*, Ramón says emphatically to Cipriano, "Above all things I don't want to acquire a political smell. . . . The surest way to kill it [their revival of the ancient religion] . . . is to get it connected with any political party." It is beyond politics in that it appeals directly to the *spirit of place* itself. He says he wishes that the "Teutonic would think in terms of Thor and Wotan, and the tree Igdrasil." The Druidic world should return to the mystery of the mistletoe and revitalized gods of ancient Greece should return to the Mediterranean. He grounds this specifically by using the symbolism of blossoming flowers: "The hibiscus and the thistle and the gentian all flower on the Tree of Life, but in the world they are far apart: and must be." Different soils and climates produce different flowers. "But the Tree of Life is one tree, as we know when our souls open in the last blossoming. . . . The men and women of the earth are not manufactured goods, to be interchangeable."[54] Rather they flourish best when developing from their own roots in their own soil and with their own archetypes growing out of that soil. Finally, some sixty years later, those of us of European descent are beginning to remember our ancient gods and goddesses. Ralph Metzner explains how these ancient sacred beings "did not survive the onslaught of Christianity. The old gods and goddesses were desacralized and demonized. . . . The symbolic climax of this brutal forced conversion of an entire people occurred in the year 772 A.D., when the Frankish emperor Charlemagne massacred thirty thousand Saxons who had refused to convert and ordered the cutting down of the Irminsul, the sacred pillar representing the world-tree Ygdrasil, the holy axis of the Germanic-Nordic religion." The old sacred beings did not die of course. "We could say that they became dormant or withdrew from human affairs, as humans ceased to speak of them, denying their reality," Metzner explains. Continuing, he says: "In Jungian terms, we would say the archetypes that supported our ancestors' sense of living connectedness with all of nature became submerged in the dark, unconscious underworld of the collective psyche."[55] But now that the forests of the world are in such danger, the "old ones" are re-emerging as we write and sing and dream of them.

Deep inside, Lawrence felt the power of these old sacred beings within the trees he loved and tried to bring that power out in his work.

Vine Deloria wrote that what is needed is a "major revolution in theological concepts. . . . While Christianity can project the reality of the after life—time and eternity—it appears to be incapable of providing any reality to the life in which we are here and now presently engaged—space and the planet Earth." Christianity "views creation as a specific event while the Indian tribal religions could be said to consider creation as an ecosystem present in a definable place . . . the interrelationship of all things." The purpose of a tribal religion "is to determine the proper relationship that the people of the tribe must have with other living things" in their particular place. Deloria insists that "a fundamental element of religion is an intimate relationship with the land on which the religion is practiced." This should become a major premise "of future theological concern."[56]

Recently another Sioux, George Barta, said: "We believe that land and people are one. We believe that only people with an integral relationship to the land can survive. We consider the land as our church, thus the destruction of the land is equal to the destruction of the cathedrals of Europe and the temples of Asia."[57]

Because of Lawrence's unique sensitivity to place he somehow intuited these concepts long ago. In a letter to Rolf Gardiner on July 4, 1924, from Kiowa Ranch, Lawrence said: "Myself, I am sick of the farce of cosmic unity, of world unison. It may exist in the abstract—but not elsewhere . . . as soon as it comes to experience, to passion, to desire, to feeling, we are different. . . . The spirit of place always triumphs. . . . To me it is life to feel the white ideas and the 'oneness' crumbling into a thousand pieces, and all sorts of wonder coming through. It is painful—much more painful. . . . I know there has to be a return to the older vision of life. But not for the sake of union. And not done from the *will*. It needs some welling up of religious sources that have been shut down in us: a great yielding, rather than an act of will: a yielding to the darker, older unknown, and a reconciliation. Nothing bossy. Yet the natural mystery of power."[58]

These ideas, which he poured out to the sympathetic ear of Rolf Gardiner, surface in *The Plumed Serpent*, providing some background to the sudden yielding of Kate to Cipriano. While Ramón is the "living Quetzalcoatl," Cipriano is the "living Huitzilopochtli." The celebration on the night dedicated to the god Huitzilopochtli is taking place in Ramon's "church." Meanwhile, Kate is sitting alone in her room in the village. Suddenly she hears footsteps. It is Cipriano, his black eyes blazing but at the same time smiling "in a dazzling, childish way." He tells her to come, put on the green dress and come. "I cannot be the Living Huitzilopochtli without a bride."

Kate sees that he is all "flickering and flashing and strangely young, vulnerable." No will at all. Sensitively calling her only with "the living, flickering, fiery *Wish*." She, who was only used to fighting for her own against individualist men, is uncertain and disconcerted. It was not that he was seeking her for his own individual end; instead, it was a yielding in him to something greater and a wish or a need for her to be with him in this yielding.

They go to the church and perform a brief ritual—each pouring oil into a lamp, together lighting it—each with a candle, "with the flames dripping and leaping together." The "blue bud" of flame rises higher and Cipriano says: "It is our Morning Star—the slow light ... of [our] united lives floating." She is amazed. "There are more ways than one of becoming like a little child." Cipriano naively brings his flame to her flame in an innocence which is "virginal." She muses, "when one finds one's virginity, one realises one is among the gods. He is of the gods, and so am I." They are met together in the realms of the dark gods, where life is continually renewed. But this cannot be reached by will alone—only by yielding.[59]

Because what Lawrence is trying to do here and in his descriptions of other rituals in *The Plumed Serpent* may easily be misunderstood by people in a modern industrial culture, I will turn again to China for further elucidation. In an earlier chapter I mentioned the word *li*, sometimes translated as "pattern"; but in the larger sense, as used by Chu Hsi, it is the principle of cosmic organization. The earliest meaning of *li* came from the pattern in which fields were laid out for cultivation in order to follow the lay of the land. Hence the earth itself is the ordering principle of a particular place.[60] The word *li* later became used to describe the pattern in things such as the markings in jade or the fibers in muscles. When asked, "How do you distinguish between Tao and Li?" Chu Hsi answered, "Tao is a road, Li is like the veins of bamboo. . . . The content of the word Tao is wide; Li consists of numerous vein-like principles included in the term, Tao. . . . The term Tao calls attention to the vast and comprehensive; the term Li calls attention to the minute."[61] Human beings follow the same *li* as the rest of the universe, not by following any laws laid down by a celestial law-giver but by following the pattern of nature in themselves within a particular place, as laid down by the interaction of land and sky (weather). *Li* also means "holy ritual" or "sacred ceremony." In a proper ceremony, "each person does what he is supposed to do according to a pattern. My gestures are coordinated harmoniously with yours—though neither of us has to force, push, demand, compel or otherwise 'make' this happen." If all are together in the underlying meaning of the rite then the only thing needed is "an initial ritual gesture in the proper ceremonial context; from there onward everything 'happens.' What action did Shun (the Sage-ruler) take? 'He merely placed himself gravely and reverently with his face due south; that was all.'"[62]

This concept, so elusive and yet so all-pervading, is what is behind the truly ceremonial action which "takes place" or happens "of itself." *Li* works through "spontaneous coordination rooted in reverent dignity."[63] This makes possible the coordination of the practical, the intellectual and the spiritual in one act, harmonized by the feeling for the underlying pattern or *li*. It was possible for the old Chinese sages to make any action, such as serving tea or eating a meal, into a ceremony. Yen Yuan, a Neo-Confucian (1635–1704) wrote: "The ancients taught men to do housework, and while doing housework to practice reverence. They taught the proper ways of dealing with people, and in these to practice reverence. They taught rituals, music, archery, riding, reading, and mathematics, but in arranging the order of the rituals, in the laws of the notes, in steadying the bow . . . there was nothing without the practice of reverence."[64]

Lawrence followed precepts such as these in his daily life to a remarkable extent. Many people have remarked on the importance of the ritual observation of tea-time by Lawrence. As for housework, William Gerhardi, an English novelist who met Lawrence in 1925, wrote: "Mrs. Lawrence dislikes housework; her husband excels in it. Lawrence, a beam on his face, which was like a halo, brought in the dishes out of the kitchen, with the pride of a first-class chef in his unrivaled creations: no, as if cooking and serving your guests were a sacrament, a holy rite."[65]

In *The Plumed Serpent*, Lawrence introduced this aspect of ritual into many scenes: for instance, the weaving of fabric at Don Ramón's hacienda, and Cipriano instilling cleanliness and care in the daily routine of his men.

In his fantasy, an "Autobiographical Fragment," which I quoted in Chapter 1, Lawrence wrote of life in the soft, curving, yellow buildings: "There was an instinctive cleanliness and decency everywhere, in every movement, in every act. It was as if the deepest instinct had been cultivated in the people to be comely. The soft, quiet comeliness was like a dream, a dream of life at last come true."[66]

Throughout their life together, wherever he and Frieda lived, they held nature rituals. Katherine Mansfield refers to one in Cornwall. "Always, when I see foxgloves, I think of the Lawrences. Again I pass in front of their cottage and in the window—between the daffodil curtains with the green spots—there are the great, sumptuous blooms. 'And how beautiful they are against the whitewash!' cry the Lawrences. As is their custom, when they love anything, they make a sort of Festa. With foxgloves everywhere. And then they sit in the middle of them, like blissful prisoners, dining in an encampment of Indian braves."[67]

In the first place he and Frieda lived together, the Isartal in Bavaria, they spent most of their time outside. "We had lost all ordinary sense of time and place . . . the fireflies at night and the glow-worms, the first beech leaves spreading on the trees like a delicate veil overhead, and our feet buried in last year's brown beech leaves, these were our time and our events."[68]

Throughout Lawrence's life he celebrated the cycle of the seasons. Passages in *The White Peacock*, his first novel, dwell ritually on seasonal change. Many scenes of the Morel family in *Sons and Lovers*, during the time Paul Morel (Lawrence) was growing up, celebrate the ritual of the seasons in Christian terms. These seasonal motifs continue in most of his works. In *The Plumed Serpent* he returns the cycle of the day to nature when he has Don Ramón replace the bells in the church with the drum beat. Kate, sitting down by the lake shore, hears the drum beat and thinks: "But the world was somehow different; all different." There is no ringing of church bells throughout the day and no clock striking; instead there is the drum. In a few sentences Lawrence hints at the enormous changes implicit in moving from rigid clock time with metallic bells to drums timed to the natural rhythms of the day: dawn, first sun showing, sun highest in the sky and sunset, when the command is, "Lift your hand, say Farewell! . . . The sun is in the outer porch." Kate decides: "The drums seemed to leave the air soft and vulnerable, as if it were alive. Above all, no clang of metal. . . ." Don Ramón's verses say, "Metal for resistance / Drums for the beating heart."[69]

Don Ramón says: "We can do nothing with life, except live it." Life itself will bring the change, not dead ideals. "Therefore we turn to life; and from the clock to the sun and the stars, and from metal to membrane." The drum recalls that "life is vulnerable . . . only metal is invulnerable."[70]

When Kate first heard the drums on the day the church was dedicated to the new gods, she remembered hearing them in Ceylon: "The sound that waked dark, ancient echoes in the heart of every man, the thud of the primeval world . . . acting on the helpless blood direct."[71] In a later essay Lawrence wrote of the *primal, integral* I, which is for the most part a living *continuum* of all the rest of living things . . . as if all were connected by a living membrane."[72] Here in *The Plumed Serpent* he has the membrane of the drum connecting man with his "circumambient universe." The bells called attention to the Christian Church standing there focusing all power onto itself;

the drum connects humans with their circumambient universe and with nature's changing cycles. "Successful culture is a semi-permeable membrane between man and nature," Gorsline and House state in "Future Primitive."[73]

The drum is not a return to past ages; rather it is a remembrance of who we really are. During the most important part of our lives, the first nine months in the womb, we lived to syncopated beating. It has been found that the womb, filled with amniotic fluid, powerfully amplifies sound. The fetus's heart beats roughly twice as fast as the mother's; thus there is a powerful, syncopated double beat during the most crucial part of our lives. The drum has always been the center for sacred rituals in every culture in the world. The drum is the vehicle for ritual dancing as well. Lame Deer, the Sioux medicine man, said: "All our dances have their beginnings in our religion. They started out as spiritual gatherings. . . . Dancing and praying—it's the same thing."[74] In ritual dancing, Stanley Diamond points out, the "individual's sense of personal power and worth is immeasurably heightened by the communal nature of the event." The bodily movements and expressions vary in each person, the "individual style comes through"; yet each person also seems to be "expressing an energy beyond his own"—the group energy.[75]

In a letter to Rolf Gardiner, in October 1926, after Lawrence had returned to Europe, he is again talking about establishing a place where "we might slowly evolve a new rhythm of life . . . and learn to dance and sing together." He continues: "One cannot suddenly decapitate oneself. If barren idealism and intellectualism are a curse, it's not the head's fault." The Christian love ideal is not thrown out; rather "it means expanding it into a full relationship, where there can be also physical and passional meeting, as there used to be in the old dances and rituals. We have to know how to go out and meet one another, upon the third ground, the holy ground."[76]

Perhaps the most succinct way to explain what Lawrence was trying to do when he wrote Plumed Serpent and much of his work after that is to quote, once again, from his essay, "New Mexico." "For the whole life-effort of man [is] to get his life into direct contact with the elemental life of the cosmos, mountain-life, cloud-life,

thunder-life, air-life, earth-life, sun-life. To come into immediate *felt-*
contact, and so derive energy, power, and a dark sort of joy."[77] These
words provide a lyrical description of the movement which Arne
Naess defined more than fifty years later as Deep Ecology.

Returning by ship to England, after his almost fatal illness in
Mexico, Lawrence saw below him in the water, the very thing he
had tried so hard to show in his novel, *The Plumed Serpent.* Down
below the surface of the water, the dolphins were "speeding in
motionless, effortless speed, and intertwining with strange silkiness
... giving off the joy of life ... togetherness in pure complete motion."
Each one going its own way but all moving in "swift laughing
togetherness."[78]

Lawrence never fully recovered from this illness. He died only
five years later. All his life he knew he had a limited time to live.
Many years before, Catherine Carswell, dissatisfied with her work,
told Lawrence how unproductive her life was when compared to
his. "'Ah, but you will have so much longer than I to do things in!'
he answered quickly and lightly."[79] Now he knew that time was
running out. When *The Plumed Serpent* met with the general
condemnation he felt it would get, there was no longer enough time
left to point toward a totally new way. All he could do was try to
reinterpret the basic symbols which Christianity had co-opted from
the pagan religions, and thus attempt to restore some of their original
life-giving meaning. This is why he returned to using the Church as
a norm, in such passages as this: "The rhythm of life itself was
preserved by the Church, hour by hour, day by day, season by season,
year by year ... down among the people." He lists the Church festival
days such as Christmas, Easter and others. He continues: "This is
the wheeling of the year, the movement of the sun through solstice
and equinox, the coming of the seasons, the going of the seasons."[80]
In my book *Earth Wisdom,*[81] I have shown in detail how the Church
co-opted the natural earth festival days by putting Church feast days
on the same dates: Christmas (winter solstice), Easter (spring
equinox), St. John's Day (summer solstice), All Saints and All Souls
(cross quarter day between fall equinox and winter solstice). This
"wheeling of the year" was the underlying theme of Lawrence's next

novel, *Lady Chatterley's Lover*.

After he got back to England he drove through his own home country of the Midlands again and was horrified at how much more industrialized it was. This may well have been the immediate cause of his attempting another book.[82] He remained in England only a short time. Richard Aldington sums up his impressions of Lawrence's feelings from a 1926 visit to England: "The only thing to do Lawrence insisted, was to get out and stay out. . . . He was evidently pining for his New Mexico ranch, for he talked of it constantly and with a nostalgic regret which made me quite unhappy on his behalf. But meanwhile before everything crashes—and he was intuitively certain that it would crash sooner or later—we must have just a *little* more of Italy."[83]

The Lawrences eventually settled into Villa Mirenda in the hills above Florence. Lawrence was interested in this area because south and west of Florence were the tombs of the ancient Etruscan civilization. And, according to Mark Schorer, the Villa Mirenda offered him the isolation and good view which he required.[84]

Lawrence had been interested in the Etruscans since 1922 when Frieda's sister, Else, sent him Ludwig Klages's book, *Vom Kosmogonischem Eros*.[85] Klages was a member of the Cosmic Circle, which was based on Bachofen's *Mutterrecht* theory, which is discussed more fully in Chapter 3. The Etruscan culture was the source of much of Bachofen's theories concerning matriarchy and erotic religion. Bachofen refers to the "poignant beauty of the Etruscan tombs."[86] Martin Green points out that Klages, like Lawrence, was interested in primitive peoples, especially those before Greek rationalism became dominant. The art forms they most approved of were the folk song and folk dance, "but it was the even more 'primitive' arts like Indian tribal dances that they loved."[87]

Lawrence's first mention of Etruscans was in a poem titled "Cypresses," published in October 1923. In the first part of the poem he writes: "Tuscan cypresses / What is it? . . . Is there a great secret?" He mentions the "dusky, slim men" that Rome called "vicious." They are all dead and gone—the only things remaining are the "shadowy cypresses / And tombs." He continues by pointing out that "much of the delicate magic of life" has been buried by us. In the last verse he asks: "Evil, what is evil? / There is only one evil, to deny life." All the way through the poem are veiled references to phallicism.[88]

The last works of fiction which Lawrence wrote—the novel, *Lady Chatterley's Lover*, the short novel, *The Man Who Died*, and the two essays, *"Etruscan Places"* and the *"Apocalypse"*— are all interconnected by the underlying themes which developed out of Lawrence's visit to the Etruscan tombs with Brewster.

What is not generally recognized is that the peasants of the part of Italy called Tuscany still unconsciously followed the "Old Ways." Charles Godfrey Leland, an American expert on the gypsies, lived in Florence in 1885. He found that the Tuscan peasants "retained the primitive shamanism more than any of the people in Europe except the Sicilians and the gypsies. . . . The peasants of the Romagna Toscana had lived since prehistoric times with very little change, and they had preserved, under Etruscan, Latin and Christian rule, their primitive religion." The country people went to the priests and Christian saints for the big holidays but most of the time they used the old magic, concealing from the educated "everything that related to the old religion for the priests taught that all spirits not sanctioned by the Church were devils." By talking to the old women, Leland gathered "a mass of obscure old legendary names that poured down upon him like the Arno from the mountains of the Romagna Toscana. Divinities who had been supposedly extinct for fifteen hundred years lived on as real among old witches, and in the mountains all the names of the old Etruscan gods were still remembered by the peasants."[89]

On October 1926, Lawrence had finished the first draft of *Lady Chatterley*, a "comparatively harmless" one in which the gamekeeper is more a comic figure, similar to Annable in *The White Peacock*. The following spring he and Earl Brewster visited the Etruscan tombs in Volterra and Chiusi. They were together in Volterra near Easter when Lawrence saw a toy white rooster in a shop window which suggested the title, "The Escaped Cock," later changed to *The Man Who Died*.[90] Lawrence wrote to Brewster in late April that he had begun the story and in his next letter on the third of May he tells Brewster that it is about the Resurrection, "where Jesus gets up and feels very sick about everything and can't stand the old crowd any more—so cuts out—and as he heals up, he begins to find what an astonishing place the phenomenal world is, far more marvelous than any salvation or heaven."[91]

Before going to the tombs in 1927 Lawrence had visited the Brewsters in their house in Ravello, Italy, in early spring. Achsah Brewster describes the day they left for the tombs: "It was a radiant afternoon as we drove down the winding road, the sun full in our faces, the sea burning blue at our feet. The fig-trees had spurted out two green flames from the tip of each bare twig which delighted Lawrence."[92] Lawrence's delight was increased by the fact that he was with long-trusted friends and was about to start on a walking tour for the first time in years. After seeing the Etruscan tombs, where death was treated as a part of life and just as beautiful, Lawrence made the entire experience of that spring the focus of all his remaining work.

The main character in *The Man Who Died* comes out of a rock tomb and takes shelter with a peasant who owns a cock. The next morning as the man came out to lie in the sun to recover, the cock crows. The man "looked nakedly on life, and saw a vast resoluteness everywhere flinging itself up in stormy or subtle wave crests, foam-tips emerging out of the blue invisible, a black and orange cock, or the green flame-tongues out of the extremes of the fig-tree. They came forth, these things and creatures of spring, flowing with desire and with assertion. They came like crests of foam, out of the blue flood of the invisible desire, out of the vast invisible sea of strength." He thinks with nausea of his old life where he had "tried to lay the compulsion of love on all men."

Eventually, he meets a priestess of Isis, the goddess who looks for the fragments of the dead Osiris to reassemble them and restore him to life. The priestess has served the goddess for seven years but is unable to find "the last reality, the final clue to him, that alone could bring him really back to her." Lawrence writes that Isis is "the womb" which waits for the "touch of that other inward sun that streams its rays from the loins of the male Osiris." To the priestess, the "man who died becomes Osiris and the phallus is the clue, the living link between male and female and all of life."

The man and the priestess of Isis meet on the little pine-covered hill where the temple is. After she feeds him and rubs healing oil on his wounds, "he knew her and was one with her" and is healed. One day much later "under the trees, when the morning sun was hot, and the pines smelled sweet," she tells him that she has conceived of him. Because of the trouble that will come from the authorities if he stays, he leaves, but tells her that he will come again just as the sun comes back in the seasons.[93]

Lawrence finished the second half of this story sitting under the pine trees of Bavaria. He writes to Brewster about this time that he loves "the stillness of innumerable trees . . . silently growing, and pressing themselves on the air so softly and yet so indomitably."[94]

A further impetus toward Lawrence's "phallic vision" came from the fact that "when Lawrence returned from the tour of the Etruscan tombs on April 12, 1927, he found waiting for him a copy of Koteliansky's translation of Rozanov's *Solitaria*.[95]

In Lawrence's letter to Kot (April 13, 1927), he says that *Solitaria* "looks quite thrilling."[96] In his review of the book, Lawrence wrote for the first time of "the phallic vision." He states that "Rozanov has more or less recovered the genuine pagan vision, the phallic vision, and with those eyes he looks, in amazement and consternation, on the mess of Christianity." It is "as if the pagan Russian had wakened up in Rozanov . . . and was just staggering at what he saw."[97]

About this time (February 27, 1927), Lawrence wrote to Brewster concerning the paintings he was doing: "I stick to what I told you, and put a phallus, a lingam you call it, in each of my pictures somewhere. And I paint no pictures that won't shock people's castrated social spirituality." He goes on to say that he believes "the phallus is a great sacred image. . . . [I]t represents a deep, deep life which has been denied in us, and still is denied."[98]

Between the time that Lawrence finished the first version of *Lady Chatterley* and the time he finished the third and last version in January 1928, he had been influenced not only by the phallic reality of the Etruscan tomb paintings and the book by Rozanov but also by his own paintings. By the time the third version of the novel was completed he had tapped into the underlying meanings of the phallic symbol.

His essays on the Etruscan tombs, unpublished until after his death, were written after he had finished the second draft of *Lady Chatterley* but before he wrote the third draft. He begins the first essay with a few brief sentences about the Etruscans and how they were wiped out by the Romans. Then he goes on to say that one can read all sorts of books but never see a single word about the most noticeable image of all in their tombs, "that is, the phallic symbol," and he tells of seeing it everywhere, big and little.

He says in this essay that the ancients saw "the everlasting *wonder* of things." To them, the "living cosmos itself" was divine. The Etruscans were famous for their art of divination by means of watching the flight of birds or studying the entrails of freshly killed animals. He points out that anyone who deals with life must practice divination of one sort or another, because if you live by the cosmos, "you look in the cosmos for your clue." Those who believe in a personal god pray to him, instead. What really matters "is the amount of *true*, sincere, religious concentration you can bring to bear on your object. An act of pure attention, if you are capable of it, will bring its own answer."[99] Once the Etruscans were defeated it was the end of the old religion: "the profound attempt of man to harmonise himself with nature, and hold his own and come to flower in the great seething of life." With the Greeks and Romans came the desire to dominate nature by means of "mental cunning" and "mechanical force."[100]

Having realized how completely the phallic vision had been lost, Lawrence was determined that his treatment of this vision in *Lady Chatterley's Lover* be made available to the public. He purposely squandered some of his remaining strength seeing personally to its publication in Florence because he knew an unexpurgated version would not be published for years, if ever. (In the United States such a version was not published until 1959.) Some critics wonder at the excessive zeal of his efforts to get such a "sexual novel" published; others attribute it to a raging desire to succeed, which they attribute to his tuberculosis. Actually, to get some understanding of the importance of the phallic vision is a difficult matter, because so little has been published on its historical aspects. One of the best sources today is a recently republished edition of an old book which was first published in 1786, *Discourse on the Worship of Priapus*. In his introduction to this new edition, Ashley Montagu, the editor, admits that "a thoroughgoing systematic treatment of such beliefs and practices is still wanting at the present day," adding that since the book has long been out of print to have it once more available is a "great boon to scholars."[101]

Julian Press published together in a single volume two very old books. Ashley Montagu edited the entire volume. The first book is titled, *A Discourse on the Worship of Priapus and its Connection with the Mystic Theology of the Ancients*. It was written by Richard Payne Knight, a collector of antiquities who began studying the matter when a friend told him of a celebration on the feast of St. Cosmo and Damiano which was held each year (until 1780) in Isernia, on the confines of Abruzzo in the old Kingdom of Naples. Relics of the saints were carried in procession and *ex-voti*, little figures of the "male organ" molded in wax, were presented to the saint by women. Knight says that the female sexual organ was symbolic of the generative power of nature; while the male organ was symbolic of the generative power of God.[102] He explains that the lotus became symbolic of the productive power of water. The lotus has a unique seed case in which the top openings are too small for the ripe seed to escape. The seed germinates within the case, sending forth new plants through the holes. These plants grow until they are big enough to release and float away. Because it was "productive of itself," the lotus was adopted as a symbol by most peoples in the northern hemisphere, including the Tartars, the Japanese and certain sects in India.

In some of these cultures, the lotus is the symbol of the goddess Isis. She holds the stem of the plant, "surmounted by the seed-vessel in one hand, and the cross, representing the male organ of generation in the other: thus signifying the universal power, both active and passive, attributed to that goddess." He goes on to say that the cross, "the least explicit representation of the male organ of generation," was nevertheless a phallic symbol long before it was co-opted by Christianity.[103] The fig was consecrated to Priapus among the Romans on account of its productiveness.[104] Lawrence wrote of the saving actions of Isis in his short novel, *The Man Who Died*. He also wrote an erotic poem, titled "Fig," which deals with the deep sexual symbolism of this fruit.

The second work included in this volume is a continuation of Knight's work, titled, *The Worship of the Generative Powers During the Middle Ages of Western Europe*, published in 1866. The author, Thomas Wright, states that the general form of Priapus worship "prevailed throughout Southern and Western Europe largely during the middle ages" and in some parts was hardly extinct in his day. It was so "implanted in human nature, that . . . it continued to exist, accepted and often encouraged by the mediaeval clergy."[105] Furthermore, he says that "we have clear evidence that the phallus . . . was worshipped by the mediaeval Christians." The Roman settlement which once occupied the site of the modern city of Antwerp was one of the most remarkable sites of phallic worship, which continued there until about 1631.[106] "Antiquity had made Priapus a god, the middle ages raised him into a saint, and that under several names." In the south of France, one of those names was St. Foutin. Even at the beginning of the seventeenth century, waxen images of the organs of both sexes were offered at his chapels and hung there suspended from the ceiling.[107]

Wright tells of the festival of Palm Sunday in the town of Saintes in France. The festival was called the *fête des pinnes*—the word *pinne*, being a popular vulgar term for the male penis. In the procession held on this day, the children carried small cakes, baked in the form of a phallus, on the end of their palm branches. In other parts of the Mediterranean these cakes were in the form of the female vagina. When the Christians took over the Easter festival, formerly a fertility festival, they marked these cakes with the Christian symbol of the cross, hence the name *hot cross buns*. "Multitudes of people still believe that if they failed to eat a hot-cross-bun on Good Friday they would be unlucky the rest of the year."[108] The phallus was often built into the portals of Christian churches such as those of Toulouse and Bordeaux. Many leaden amulets in the form of a phallus have been found in the Seine River. "Such figures are found not only among Roman, Greek and Egyptian antiquities, but among every people who had any knowledge of art."[109] The editor of *The Worship of Generative Powers*, Montagu, concludes that: "The worship of the reproductive organs" ritually solemnized "the fertilizing, protecting, and saving power of nature."[110]

I have devoted considerable space to this material because it is fairly certain that some of these ideas had remained with the rural peasants of Italy down to Lawrence's time. In Charles Leland's 1892 book on Etruscan magic, he explains that he learned of these matters from talking to the working people of Florence.[111] Living in the Villa Mirenda near Florence, Lawrence might also have heard some of these legends from the peasants.

Further help in understanding the deeper philosophy behind the "phallic vision" comes from the Taoist idea that, since human beings were produced by nature, nature must be good in the larger sense and therefore nature is to be trusted. Furthermore, since the *li* or pattern of the individual human was part of the whole pattern of nature, for the human being to follow his own, deepest nature, including his sexual nature, was to take part in the whole of nature's generative power. It comes down to the fact that if the people of a particular culture learned to trust nature *without*, in the environment, they also learned to trust nature *within* themselves as well.

In *Lady Chatterley's Lover*, Lawrence tries to show this inter-relationship between man and woman and nature. All of the sexual scenes take place either in a secluded part of the forest or in the gamekeeper's hut deep inside the wood; the power of the novel lies in these long descriptive passages where man, woman and nature are united in a flowing whole. The story concerns Connie, married to Clifford Chatterley, who has returned from the wars a cripple. In this novel his affliction symbolizes the deadness of industrial England, as well as his own "deadness." Connie meets Mellors, the gamekeeper, a role which throughout Lawrence's life stood for the one who guards the forest, the one who is potent within himself.

Through Mellors's love Connie is awakened and they consummate their love in the forest in a number of tender love scenes. In the final chapter of the book Mellors goes off to find work elsewhere and Connie, now pregnant, waits to rejoin him when he is settled.[112]

Lawrence wrote the book in a grove of the umbrella pines near Villa Mirenda, sitting under a tree "with his knees drawn up and a thick exercise-book resting on them and nearly touching his beard."[113] That he still missed Taos is clear from a passage in *Lady Chatterly* in which Connie has gone to Venice on a holiday which is spoiled by a letter from her husband. "How foul these low people were! How nice it was here, in the sunshine . . . compared to that dismal mess of that English midlands! After all, a clear sky was almost the most important thing in life."[114] In 1928, when clear skies were not so rare as they are now, this statement was not as obvious as it is today.

After finishing the novel, Lawrence devoted much of his time to the effort of getting it published by Orioli in Florence. Thereafter he did no major work; however, he did produce some essays and his final *Apocalypse*. In one of these late essays, "Matriarchy," published in October of 1928, there is an important passage regarding his feelings as a "future primitive." He is writing of the Indian:

> The real life of the man is not spent in his own little home, daddy in the bosom of the family, wheeling the perambulator on Sundays. His life is passed mainly in the khiva, the great underground meeting-house where only the males assemble; where the sacred practices of the tribe are carried on; then also he is away hunting, or performing sacred rites on the mountains, or he works in the fields. But he spends only certain months of the year in his wife's house, sleeping there.

He continues by advocating a "drift" back to matriarchy so that the men can have a "new foregathering ground, where they can meet and satisfy their deep social needs . . . which are deep as religion in a man."[115]

Very shortly after Lawrence returned to England from New Mexico, he visited Frederick Carter in Shropshire, an artist who had been accumulating information on the astronomical significance of the symbols in the Apocalypse of the Bible. Lawrence had read Carter's manuscript of *The Dragon of the Alchemists* and had come to talk about getting it published. Carter says that he and Lawrence talked of dragons and symbols and much else, there beside the oak log fire. He remarks: "How he [Lawrence] stormed at St. John and maintained with the fullest extravagance of Laurentian rage the author's blasphemy against the great phallic urge to power."[116] Lawrence admired Carter's house in the churchyard with its windows above the gravestones and the surrounding slopes leading toward Wales. Carter says that Lawrence used some of that landscape in scenes in *Lady Chatterley.*[117]

Later, Carter visited Lawrence at his house, Beau Soleil, in the south of France. Lawrence told him that he was writing a lengthy introduction to Carter's book. This introduction ultimately became Lawrence's own book, *Apocalypse.*[118] On December 15, 1929 Lawrence wrote to Carter that he had roughly finished his introduction and was hoping to have Brewster's daughter type it for him.[119]

During the time Lawrence was working on *Apocalypse,* he *knew* time had run out for him, so he no longer temporized but instead outrightly condemned the Christian church for breaking the old living connection to the cosmos. He writes that although the landscape and the sky have become only a background to our personal life, "to the pagan . . . the cosmos was a very real thing. A man *lived* with the cosmos, and knew it greater than himself." We must "go back to the great living cosmos of the 'unenlightened pagans'. . . . The great range of responses that have fallen dead in us have to come to life again. It has taken two thousand years to kill them. Who knows how long it will take to bring them to life?"[120] He further claims that the "modern Christian State is a soul-destroying force, for it is made up of fragments which have no organic whole, only a collective whole. In a hierarchy each part is organic and vital, as my finger is an organic and vital part of me." A democracy, he says, is made up of millions of "disunited fragments." Here at the end of his life, Lawrence gives a definite formulation of hierarchy theory with the words: "We and the cosmos are one. The cosmos is a vast living body, of which we are still parts."[121]

Lawrence has been criticized for the inaccuracy of some of his ideas in *Apocalypse*. Admittedly, the book has little value as a commentary on the Revelations of St. John in the Bible; but that is not what Lawrence was trying to do. Although he became so ill that he had to stop working on the book, the last few pages he wrote succeeded in pulling together his entire life's effort of trying to show the unity of humanity and nature. On February 4, 1930, he sent a postcard to Carter saying that he was going into a sanatorium and would have to quit working on his essay on Revelations. Carter states that it is "strange, and more strange" that Lawrence, trying to discern the path through the heavens and writing to the last minute, left his house named Beautiful Sun (Beau Soleil) to go to the sanatorium Ad Astra (House of Stars) to die.[122]

Up to the very end, Lawrence was thinking of ways to bring his message to the world. In a letter to Mabel Luhan on January 6, 1930, he wrote: "We talk and make plans: plans of coming back to the ranch . . . and perhaps having a sort of old school, like the Greek philosophical talks in a garden—that is, under the pine-trees. . . . I might perhaps get going with a few young people, building up a new unit of life . . . making a new concept of life. . . . Perhaps now I should submit, and be a teacher."[123] The very morning before Lawrence left for the sanatorium, Achsah Brewster writes, he was "propped up in bed, galley sheets piled thick about him, correcting proof for his Nettles." He told Achsah that he would be "coming back soon to stay in our pine grove."[124]

The Rananim, the center or school that Lawrence always hoped to found, never happened in his life. Not until the 1970s was a center such as he had envisaged possible. It took another world war and further catastrophes beyond anything the people of the 1920s could imagine, before the world could glimpse the possibilities inherent in the concept of "future primitive." Now we have centers such as Michael Todd's New Alchemy Institute and William Irwin Thompson's Lindisfarne, which are both based on aspects of living as a "future primitive." Thompson concisely states: "The whole structure of civilization which emerged in Sumeria in the fourth millennium B.C. is transcended. Life becomes a highly 'civilized' way of returning to wildness, to 'savagery.' We become hunters and gatherers again, gatherers of wind and sun. We end up with a Taoist culture of simplicity, not of poverty."[125]

In the summer of 1980, exactly fifty years after Lawrence's death, Lindisfarne was moved from New York to Crestone, Colorado, a tiny town below the Crestone Peaks, the mountains at the northern end of the Sangre de Christo range. Lawrence's Taos lies just below the peaks at the southern end of this same range. Lawrence was pointing the way to such centers as he lay dying in 1930, when he wrote in *Apocalypse*: "We are unnaturally resisting our connection with the cosmos. . . . [W]e cannot bear connection." But the very frenzy of resistance shown in *Apocalypse* indicates "what the human heart secretly yearns after." He continues, "What man most passionately wants is his living wholeness," not just the salvation of his isolated soul. The entire last section of *Apocalypse* so concisely sums up Lawrence's work that I must quote it in full:

> For man, the vast marvel is to be alive. For man, as for flower and beast and bird, the supreme triumph is to be most vividly, most perfectly alive. Whatever the unborn and the dead may know, they cannot know the beauty, the marvel of being alive in the flesh. The dead may look after the afterwards. But the magnificent here and now of life in the flesh is ours, and ours alone, and ours only for a time. We ought to dance with rapture that we should be alive and in the flesh, and part of the living, incarnate cosmos. I am part of the sun as my eye is part of me. That I am part of the earth my feet know perfectly, and my blood is part of the sea. My soul knows that I am part of the human race, my soul is an organic part of the great human soul, as my spirit is part of my nation. In my own very self, I am part of my family. There is nothing

of me that is alone and absolute except my mind, and we shall find that the mind has no existence by itself, it is only the glitter of the sun on the surface of the waters.

So that my individualism is really an illusion. I am a part of the great whole, and I can never escape. But I can deny my connections, break them, and become a fragment. Then I am wretched.

What we want is to destroy our false, inorganic connections, especially those related to money, and re-establish the living organic connections, with the cosmos, the sun and earth, with mankind and nation and family. Start with the sun, and the rest will slowly, slowly happen.[126]

Epilogue

Six weeks after they met, Lawrence and Frieda left England for Bavaria where they lived in a peasant house in the Isartal, alongside the icy waters of the Isar River, which came tumbling down from the glacier high above. Here, Lawrence first encountered the alpine gentian. Frieda reported this occasion in her book: "I remember feeling as if he had a strange communion with it, as if the gentian yielded up its blueness, its very essence, to him."[1]

The alpine gentian has so impressed the mountain people that it appears in peasant embroidery, architectural decoration, songs and myths throughout the entire alpine region of Europe. It provides a startling contrast to most alpine plants, which produce masses of tiny flowers that hug the ground to escape the fierce winds. On a rocky patch of hillside suddenly one sees a large, deep, incredibly blue cup, which grows darker and darker as you peer into the bottom. This single blue flower seems to be an isolated miracle because at first glance there is no stem and there are no leaves. The leaves are merely a flat rosette, lying on the ground below the cup.

During his many visits to the alpine region Lawrence always searched for the alpine gentian. It was so tied to the mountain region of Europe that he was astonished when he discovered a gentian while riding up a dusty trail in Taos. In her book, Brett describes the occasion when Lawrence suddenly jumped off his horse and stopped to pick a flower. "You turn to me triumphantly. 'You have never found anything like this before!' And you hold up a small, intensely blue gentian."[2]

Many years later, the year before his death in 1930, Lawrence's precarious health suddenly became much worse. He and Frieda left the heat of Florence for Tegernsee in Bavaria to be near Max Mohr, the playwright and physician. It was autumn and Lawrence spent most of his time resting. "I remember some autumn nights," writes Frieda, "when the end seemed to have come." She lay awake, listening for his breath all night. "In the dim dawn an enormous bunch of gentians I had put on the floor by his bed seemed the only living thing in the room."[3]

During this time in Tegernsee, Lawrence wrote of his beloved gentians leading him on his return to Persephone and Pluto and the "dark gods."

BAVARIAN GENTIANS

Not every man has gentians in his house
in soft September, at slow, sad Michaelmas.

Bavarian gentians, big and dark, only dark
darkening the day-time, torch-like with the smoking blueness of
    Pluto's gloom,
ribbed and torch-like, with their blaze of darkness spread blue
down flattening into points, flattened under the sweep of white day
torch-flower of the blue-smoking darkness, Pluto's dark-blue daze,
black lamps from the halls of Dis, burning dark blue,
giving off darkness, blue darkness, as Demeter's pale lamps give off
    light,
lead me then, lead the way.

Reach me a gentian, give me a torch !
let me guide myself with the blue, forked torch of this flower
down the darker and darker stairs, where blue is darkened on
    blueness
even where Persephone goes, just now, from the frosted September
to the sightless realm where darkness is awake upon the dark
and Persephone herself is but a voice
or a darkness invisible enfolded in the deeper dark

of the arms Plutonic, and pierced with the passion of dense gloom,
among the splendour of torches of darkness, shedding darkness on
the lost bride and her groom.[4]

David Herbert Lawrence died on March 2, 1930, at Vence in the south
of France, and was buried in a little cemetery overlooking the sea.
Later his ashes were transferred to his Kiowa Ranch at Taos, where
they lie today midst the pine trees on Lobo Mountain.

Appendix

Trees and Lawrence

"Perhaps when I have a *Weh* at all, my *Heimweh* is for the tree in front of the house, the overshadowing tree whose green top one never looks at." —Lawrence, writing of his beloved tree in front of the ranch house near Taos in "A Little Moonshine with Lemon."

Lawrence was deeply attached to trees throughout his life. Whenever possible he preferred to write outdoors, sitting under a tree. Listed below are the works which he wrote under specific trees, as documented in biographies and letters.

1. Apple tree in England—"The Fox."
2. Lemon tree in Italy—*The Lost Girl.*
3. Fir trees at Ebersteinburg in Bavaria—*Fantasia of the Unconscious, Aaron's Rod,* and the Review of *Solitaria* by V. V. Rozanov.
4. Willow tree in Mexico—*The Plumed Serpent.*
5. Pine trees at Taos, New Mexico—"St. Mawr," "The Woman Who Rode Away" and "Pan in America."
6. Umbrella pines in Italy—"The Nightingale" and *Lady Chatterley's Lover.*
7. Pear tree in Switzerland—*The Man Who Died* and most of the twenty two articles later published under the title "Assorted Articles" in 1930.

Notes

Through the years there have been several different editions of each of Lawrence's major novels. Some of them have been published by a number of different publishers as well. To avoid confusion chapter numbers are given instead of page numbers for all the novels. The only exception is for the novel *The Plumed Serpent*, where the quotes need to be specifically located. See the Bibliography for the particular edition I used. For all other material, such as essays and stories, I give page numbers, where possible. If no page number is listed, there have been a number of editions of this material and I have consulted several of them. For definitive information see *The Cambridge Edition of the Works of D. H. Lawrence*, an on-going project of Cambridge University Press, London.

Preface

1. Raymond Dasmann, "Future Primitive." Note: Jeremiah Gorsline and Freeman House wrote the original "Future Primitive." The word, *primitive*, is analyzed by Stanley Diamond (*In Search of the Primitive*, pages 123–25). He states that the English word comes directly from the medieval-modern French word *primitif*. The first known appearance in print of the word in English occurs in a work on surgery, written about 1400, in which it is spelled *prymytiff* and has the meaning of "primary" or "original." In a statement by Henry VII at York about 1486 it occurs again in this phrase: "primative patrons." Diamond states: "Here *primitive* implies 'earliest,' 'original' and 'primary,' not only in time but in rank." The French word, *primitif* is derived from the medieval Latin *primitivus* (*primus* = first + *ivus*, a later adjectival ending), meaning earliest or oldest.

It seems that all the major European languages except Greek have adopted the word *primitive* from a medieval Latin source. Primitive does not have the negative associations of such words as *barbarian* or *uncivilized*. Primitive signifies "merely a prior state of affairs, a relative sense of origins." Following a brief overview of culture from its initial appearance in the Lower Paleolithic era, Diamond sums the matter up by saying: "*Primitive*, then, refers to widely distributed, well-organized institutions that had already existed just prior to the rise of ancient civilizations; it does not imply historically an inchoate time of cultural origins." He further states that no primitive group ever voluntarily gave up its way of

life; instead they were conquered. (See Bibliography also.)
2. Sybille Bedford, *Aldous Huxley*, p. 210.
3. Aldous Huxley, ed., *The Letters of D. H. Lawrence*, p. xxx.
4. D. H. Lawrence, "Study of Thomas Hardy."
5. Vivian de Sola Pinto and Warren Roberts, eds., *The Complete Poems of D. H. Lawrence*, p. 764.
6. Richard Adlington, *Life for Life's Sake*, p. 305.
7. D. H. Lawrence, "Indians and Entertainment."
8. Del Janik, "D. H. Lawrence and Environmental Consciousness."

Chapter 1

1. D. H. Lawrence, [Autobiographical Fragment].
2. D. H. Lawrence, "Nottingham and the Mining Countryside."
3. Harry T. Moore, ed., *The Collected Letters of D. H. Lawrence*, vol. 1, p. 11; E. T. (Jessie Chambers), *D. H. Lawrence: A Personal Record*, p. 23; May Chambers Holbrook, "The Chambers Papers," p. 583; Harry T. Moore, *The Priest of Love*, p. 173.
4. May Chambers Holbrook, "The Chambers Papers," p. 580.
5. D. H. Lawrence, [Autobiographical Fragment].
6. D. H. Lawrence, *Sons and Lovers*, ch. IV.
7. V. de Sola Pinto and W. Roberts, eds., *Complete Poems*, p. 853.
8. D. H. Lawrence, *Lady Chatterley's Lover*, ch. 8.
9. D. H. Lawrence, [Autobiographical Fragment].
10. C. G. Jung, *Memories, Dreams, Reflections*, p. 20.
11. Ibid., pp. 179, 189, and 195–97.
12. Ada Lawrence and G. Gelder, *Young Lorenzo*, pp. 24 and 26.
13. Ford Madox Ford, *Portraits from Life*, p. 75.
14. D. H. Lawrence, "Enslaved by Civilization."
15. Emily Lawrence King, BBC Third Programme's "Son and Lover."
16. Norman Shrapnel, "Eastwood Turns the Immortal Memory to Account," 7.
17. D. H. Lawrence, "Autobiographical Sketch."
18. Ada Lawrence and G. Gelder, *Young Lorenzo*, p. 9.
19. William Edward Hopkin, "D. H. Lawrence: A Personal Memoir."
20. May Chambers Holbrook, "The Chambers Papers," pp. 572–73.
21. Ibid., p. 578.
22. Earl and Achsah Brewster, *D. H. Lawrence: Reminiscences and Correspondence*, pp. 254–55.
23. Rhys Davies, "D. H. Lawrence in Bandol."

24. Earl and Achsah Brewster, *D. H. Lawrence: Reminiscences and Correspondence,* p. 310.
25. Ada Lawrence and G. Gelder, *Young Lorenzo,* pp. 26 and 43.
26. Emily Lawrence King, BBC Third Programme's "Son and Lover."
27. D. H. Lawrence, *Sons and Lovers,* ch. 4.
28. William Edward Hopkin, "D. H. Lawrence: A Personal Memoir."
29. D. H. Lawrence, "Enslaved by Civilization."
30. Mabel Thurlby Collishaw, in Edward Nehls, *D. H. Lawrence: A Composite Biography,* vol. 1, pp. 29–32.
31. May Chambers Holbrook, "The Chambers Papers," p. 562.
32. E. T. (Jessie Chambers), *D. H. Lawrence: A Personal Record,* p. 118.
33. D. H. Lawrence, *Sons and Lovers,* ch. 5.
34. Edith Cobb, *The Ecology of Imagination in Childhood,* p. 30.
35. Kenneth Rexroth, *An Autobiographical Novel,* p. 337.
36. C. S., Lewis, *Surprised by Joy,* p. 19.
37. Edith Cobb, "The Ecology of Imagination in Childhood."
38. Edith Cobb, *The Ecology of Imagination in Childhood,* p. 44.
39. Ibid., p. 46.
40. Paul Shepard, *The Tender Carnivore and the Sacred Game,* p. 268.
41. E. T. (Jessie Chambers), *D. H. Lawrence: A Personal Record,* p. 154.
42. D. H. Lawrence, *Sons and Lovers,* ch. 7.
43. Ibid.
44. Ibid., ch. 9.
45. Harry T. Moore, *The Priest of Love,* pp. 50 and 54.
46. Ada Lawrence and G. Gelder, *Young Lorenzo.* p. 44.
47. George H. Neville, "The Early Days of D. H. Lawrence."
48. E. T. (Jessie Chambers), *D. H. Lawrence: A Personal Record,* p. 31. Note: Although Jessie's father called him Bert, others called him by various names. In a letter in 1908 Lawrence wrote, "I am called Bertie, Bert, David, Herbert, Billy, William and Dick." Jessie Chambers, his closest friend in his youth, called him Lawrence because he told her, "I like it better." But she also called him David. May Chambers Holbrook, Jessie's sister, wrote: "It was by his initials (D. H. L.) he prefers to be called." The artist, Tony Cyriax, first gave Lawrence the nickname of Lorenzo. The peasants in Italy also called him Lorenzo and, soon after moving there, Frieda began calling him Lorenzo.
49. Ibid.
50. Aldous Huxley, in H. Mori, ed., *A Conversation on D. H. Lawrence,* pp. 18 and 19.
51. D. H. Lawrence, *The White Peacock,* Part 3, ch. 3.

Chapter 2

1. Gary Snyder, poetry reading, University of Washington, Seattle, Washington, 1976.
2. D. H. Lawrence, *The Trespasser*, ch. 5.
3. Ibid., ch. 8.
4. Helen Corke, *Lawrence and Apocalypse*, p. 4.
5. Helen Corke, an extract from a letter to the editor (20 February 1952). In Edward Nehls, *D. H. Lawrence: A Composite Biography*, vol. 1, p. 97.
6. Catherine Carswell, *Savage Pilgrimage*, p. 51.
7. D. H. Lawrence, *Studies in Classic American Literature*, pp. 8–9.
8. Frieda Lawrence, in H. Mori, ed., *A Conversation on D. H. Lawrence*, p. 24.
9. Frieda Lawrence, *Not I But the Wind*, p. 130.
10. W. Siebenhaar, "Reminiscences of D. H. Lawrence," in Edward Nehls, *D. H. Lawrence: A Composite Biography*, vol. 3, p. 107.
11. Walter Wilkinson, Solicited memoir written in 1954, in Edward Nehls, *D. H. Lawrence: A Composite Biography*, vol. 3, p. 63.
12. Frieda Lawrence, *Not I But the Wind*, p. 202.
13. Vernon Lee, in Aldous Huxley, ed., *The Letters of D. H. Lawrence*, p. xxx.
14. Ford Madox Ford, *Portraits from Life*, pp. 78–79.
15. Cecil Gray, *Musical Chairs*, p. 141.
16. Maurice Lesemann, "D. H. Lawrence in New Mexico."
17. Stanley Diamond, *In Search of the Primitive*, p. 170.
18. Frieda Lawrence, *Memoirs and Correspondence*, p. 131.
19. Norman Douglas, *Looking Back*, no paging.
20. Franz Schoenberner, "When D. H. Lawrence Was Shocked," in book by same title.
21. Herbert Asquith, *Moments of Memory*, pp. 189 and 192.
22. Cynthia Asquith, *Remember and Be Glad*, p. 133.
23. Mark Spilka, *The Love Ethic of D. H. Lawrence*, p. 41.
24. D. H. Lawrence, *The Rainbow*, ch. 15.
25. C. G. Jung, *Memories, Dreams, Reflections*, pp. 267–69.
26. Ibid., p. 250–52.
27. Frank Waters, *Pumpkin Seed Point*, p. 76.
28. C. G. Jung, *Memories, Dreams, Reflections*, pp. 250 and 252.
29. Stan Steiner, "The Sun Is Becoming Darker: The Ultimate Energy Crisis."
30. Michel Gauquelin, *The Cosmic Clocks*, pp. 141–44.
31. D. H. Lawrence, "Sun."
32. D. H. Lawrence, *Apocalypse*, p. 200.
33. Jessie Chambers, quoted in Richard Aldington, *Portrait of a Genius But...* p. 60.
34. D. H. Lawrence, *Sons and Lovers*, ch. VII.

35. D. H. Lawrence, *The Trespasser*, ch. 12.
36. D. H Lawrence, *The Rainbow*, ch. 4.
37. Ibid., ch. 15.
38. Vivian de Sola Pinto and Warren Roberts, eds., *The Complete Poems of D. H. Lawrence*, p. 139.
39. Alexander Marshack, "The Compleat Calendar."
40. D. Huff, *Cycles in Your Life*, as quoted in Michel Gauquelin, *The Cosmic Clocks*, p. 149.
41. Michel Gauquelin, *The Cosmic Clocks*, p. 150.
42. William Petersen, *Moon, Weather, Sun*, no paging.
43. D. Huff, *Cycles in Your Life*, as quoted in Michel Gauquelin, *The Cosmic Clocks*, p. 151.
44. Rhys Davies, "D. H. Lawrence in Bandol."
45. Ralph Metzner, *The Well of Remembrance: Rediscovering the Earth Wisdom Myths of Northern Europe*, pp. 2 and 3.
46. D. H. Lawrence, *Apocalypse*, p. 43.
47. Mabel Luhan, *Lorenzo in Taos*, p. 39.
48. Ada Lawrence and G. Gelder, *Young Lorenzo*, p. 8.
49. Jessie (E. T.) Chambers, *D. H. Lawrence: A Personal Record*, p. 28.
50. Aldous Huxley, ed., *The Letters of D. H. Lawrence*, p. 432.
51. Ibid., p. 439.
52. Frieda Lawrence, *Not I But the Wind*, p. 94.
53. D. H Lawrence, *Fantasia of the Unconscious*, ch. IV.
54. Paul Shepard, *The Tender Carnivore and the Sacred Game*, p. 102.
55. Henry Bailey Stevens, *The Recovery of Culture* and Vincent Scully, *The Earth, The Temple and the Gods*.
56. Witter Bynner, *Journey with Genius*, p. 113.
57. D. H. Lawrence, *The Plumed Serpent*, ch. VI.
58. Mark Schorer, "Two Houses, Two Ways."
59. D. H. Lawrence, "St. Mawr," in *St. Mawr* and *The Man Who Died*.
60. Dorothy Brett, *Lawrence and Brett*, p. 242.
61. Ibid., p. 82.
62. Joseph Foster, *D. H. Lawrence in Taos*, p. 158.
63. Dorothy Brett, *Lawrence and Brett*, pp. 107 and 123.
64. D. H. Lawrence, "A Little Moonshine with Lemon."
65. Earl Brewster, *D. H. Lawrence: Reminiscences and Correspondence*, p. 228.
66. Knud Merrild, *With D. H. Lawrence in New Mexico*, pp. 344 and 345.
67. Edward Nehls, *D. H. Lawrence: A Composite Biography*, vol. 2, p. 279.
68. D. H. Lawrence, "Mercury."
69. D. H. Lawrence, *Sea and Sardinia*.
70. Frieda Lawrence, *Not I But the Wind*, p. 185.
71. Chizhevskii, A. L., "Atmospheric Electricity and Life."

72. Dolores LaChapelle, *Earth Wisdom*, p. 57.

73. D. H. Lawrence, "Reflections on the Death of a Porcupine."

74. Richard Leviton, "How the Weather Affects your Health."

75. Lyall Watson, *Heaven's Breath: A Natural History of the Wind*, pp. 287–94, and Ron Cowen, "Receptor Encounters: Untangling the Threads of the Serotonin System."

76. Graham Hough, *The Dark Sun*, pp. 201–202.

77. Ibid., p. 205.

78. D. H. Lawrence, "…Love Was Once a Little Boy."

79. D. H. Lawrence, Review of *Gifts of Fortune* by H. M. Tomlinson.

80. Aldous Huxley, ed., *The Letters of D. H. Lawrence*, p. 643.

81. Rhys Davies, "D. H. Lawrence in Bandol."

82. Vivian de Sola Pinto and Warren Roberts, eds., *The Complete Poems of D. H. Lawrence*, p. 339.

83. Ibid., p. 351.

84. Edward O. Wilson, *The Diversity of Life*, p. 349.

85. D. H. Lawrence, "The Hopi Snake Dance."

86. David Garnett, *Golden Echo*, p. 247.

87. D. H. Lawrence, *The Lost Girl*, ch. XVI.

88. D. H. Lawrence, "Flowery Tuscany."

89. Brewster Ghiselin, "D. H. Lawrence in Bandol."

90. E. O. Wilson, *The Diversity of Life*.

91. Walter Christie, "Embracing Biophilia."

92. E. O. Wilson, *Biophilia*.

93. D. H. Lawrence, *The Rainbow*, ch. 16.

Chapter 3

1. Frieda Lawrence, *Not I But the Wind*, p. 83.

2. Aldous Huxley, ed., *The Letters of D. H. Lawrence*, pp. 191 and 192.

3. Frieda Lawrence, *Not I But the Wind*, p. 40.

4. Edward Nehls, *D. H. Lawrence: A Composite Biography*, Vol. 1, p. 302.

5. Joseph Chilton Pearce, *Magical Child*, p. 104.

6. Ada Lawrence and G. Gelder, *Young Lorenzo*, p. 26.

7. J. D. Chambers, intro. to E. T. (Jessie Chambers), *D. H. Lawrence: A Personal Record*, pp. xv–xvi.

8. Frieda Lawrence, *Not I But the Wind*, p. 56.

9. D. H. Lawrence, *Sons and Lovers*, ch. 11.

10. Vivian de Sola Pinto and Warren Roberts, eds., *The Complete Poems of D. H. Lawrence*, p. 915.

11. D. H. Lawrence, "Witch `a la Mode."

12. Vivian de Sola Pinto and Warren Roberts, eds., *The Complete Poems of D. H. Lawrence*, pp. 264 and 265.

13. D. H. Lawrence, *Sons and Lovers*, ch. 13.

14. D. H. Lawrence, *Love Among the Haystacks*.

15. Barbara Weekley Barr in Edward Nehls, *D. H. Lawrence: A Composite Biography*, vol. 1.

16. Frieda Lawrence, *Not I But the Wind*, p. 3.

17. Martin Green, *The Von Richthofen Sisters*, p. 10.

18. Ibid., p. 46.

19. Ibid., p. 43.

20. Ibid., p. 60.

21. Ibid., p. 47.

22. Ibid., p. 49.

23. Cynthia Asquith, *Remember and Be Glad*, p. 136.

24. Knud Merrild, *With D. H. Lawrence in New Mexico*, p. 355.

25. Barbara Weekley Barr in Edward Nehls, *D. H. Lawrence: A Composite Biography*, p. 58.

26. Harry T. Moore, *The Priest of Love*, p. 140.

27. Dorothy Brett, *Lawrence and Brett*, p. 256.

28. Frieda Lawrence, *Frieda Lawrence: The Memoirs and Correspondence*, p. 309.

29. Vivian de Sola Pinto and Warren Roberts, eds., *The Complete Poems of D. H. Lawrence*, p. 250.

30. William Gerhardi, "Literary Vignettes II," is quoting Ghiselin.

31. Josephine Miles, *Eras and Modes in English Poetry*, Appendix.

32. Stanley Diamond, *In Search of the Primitive*, pp. 123–24.

33. Stanley Diamond, *Primitive Vision of the World*, p. viii.

34. Dorothy Brett, *Lawrence and Brett*, Epilogue, p. 11.

35. Martin Green, *The Von Richthofen Sisters*, p. 4.

36. Rhys Davies, "D. H. Lawrence in Bandol."

37. A. L. Rowse, *The English Past*, pp. 217–37.

38. Dorothy Brett, *Lawrence and Brett*, p. 257.

39. Frieda Lawrence, *Frieda Lawrence*, p. 333.

40. Frieda Lawrence, in H. Mori, ed., *A Conversation on D. H. Lawrence*, p. 45.

41. Aldous Huxley, ed., *The Letters of D. H. Lawrence*, p. 95.

42. Harry T. Moore, ed., *The Collected Letters of D. H. Lawrence*, vol. 1, p. 326.

43. Stewart Brand, "Native American Church."

44. D. H. Lawrence, "St. Mawr."

45. Knud Merrild, *With D. H. Lawrence in New Mexico*, p. 187.

46. D. H. Lawrence, *Kangaroo*, ch. 2.

47. John Manchester, "Introduction" in Dorothy Brett, *Lawrence and Brett*,

p. xiii.

48. Paul Delany, *D. H. Lawrence's Nightmare*, pp. 327–30 and 294–96.
49. Frieda Lawrence, *Frieda Lawrence*, p. 320.
50. John Manchester, "Introduction" in Dorothy Brett, Lawrence and Brett, p. xiv.
51. Frieda Lawrence, *Frieda Lawrence*, p. 321.
52. Ibid., p. 320.
53. Frieda Lawrence, *Not I But the Wind*, p. 179.
54. Angelo Ravagli in Edward Nehls, *D. H. Lawrence: A Composite Biography*, vol. 3, p. 18.
55. Kenneth Rexroth, *An Autobiographical Novel*, p. 272.
56. Idella P. Stone in Witter Bynner, *Journey with Genius*.
57. Joseph Foster, *D. H. Lawrence in Taos*, p. 29.
58. Harry T. Moore, ed., *The Collected Letters of D. H. Lawrence*, vol. 1, p. 169.
59. Ibid., p. 565.
60. Dorothy Brett, *Lawrence and Brett*, p. 133.
61. D. H. Lawrence, "Apropos of *Lady Chatterley's Lover*."
62. R. B. Lee and I. Devore, "Introduction," in *Man the Hunter*.
63. Carleton Coon, *The Hunting Peoples*, pp. xvii and 393.
64. Robert Waller, "Out of the Garden of Eden."
65. Paul Shepard, *The Tender Carnivore and the Sacred Game*, ch. 3 and 4.
66. Roy A. Rappaport, "Energy and the Structure of Adaptation."
67. Marshall Sahlins, *Stone Age Economics*.
68. Gary Snyder, *The Old Ways*, p. 21.
69. David Whyte, *The Heart Aroused*, p. 262.
70. Harry T. Moore, *The Priest of Love*, pp. 112–13.
71. Wilfred Pelletier and Ted Poole, *No Foreign Land*, pp. 76–78.
72. Paul Shepard, *The Tender Carnivore and the Sacred Game*, pp. 56–57.
73. Erik Erikson, *Childhood and Society*, no paging.
74. Paul Shepard, *The Tender Carnivore and the Sacred Game*, p. 132.
75. Aldous Huxley, ed., *The Letters of D. H. Lawrence*, p. 685.
76. Catherine Carswell, *Savage Pilgrimage*, p. 95.
77. Joseph Jastrab, *Sacred Manhood, Sacred Earth*, p. 16.
78. Middleton Murry, *Son of Woman*, no paging.
79. D. H. Lawrence, "Nottingham and the Mining Countryside."
80. Dorothy Brett, *Lawrence and Brett*, p. 125.
81. Mabel Luhan, *Lorenzo in Taos*. p. 222.
82. "Introduction" in D. L. Olmsted, *Achumawi Dictionary*, p. 3.
83. "The Jaime de Angulo Library" from Turtle Island Foundation (no date).
84. Dorothy Brett, *Lawrence and Brett*, p. 202.
85. Ibid., p. 60.
86. D. L. Olmsted, *Achumawi Dictionary*, pp. 3–4.

87. Bob Callahan, "The World of Jaime de Angulo" in *A Jaime de Angulo Reader*.
88. Ibid.
89. Bob Callahan, "Introduction" to *A Jaime de Angulo Reader*, pp. xiii and xiv.
90. Joan Halifax, *Shamanic Voices*, pp. 3–4.
91. Ibid., pp. 18–19.
92. Ibid., p. 23.
93. Ibid., p. 34.
94. Richard Aldington, "Foreword" in Edward Nehls, *D. H. Lawrence: A Composite Biography*, vol. 3.
95. Joan Halifax, *Shamanic Voices*, p. 21.
96. Barbara G. Meyerhoff, "Balancing Between Worlds: The Shaman's Calling."
97. Ruth-Inge Heinze, *Shamans of the 20th Century*, p. 24.
98. Edward Nehls, *D. H. Lawrence: A Composite Biography*, vol. 1, p. 501.
99. Joseph Jastrab, *Sacred Manhood, Sacred Earth*, p. 63.
100. D. H. Lawrence, "The Hopi Snake Dance."
101. Harry T. Moore, ed., *The Collected Letters of D. H. Lawrence*, vol. 1, p. 374.
102. Michel Foucault, *The History of Sexuality*, vol. 1: An Introduction, p. 68.
103. Joel Kramer, *The Passionate Mind*, pp. 89, 90, 92 and 93.
104. Mabel Luhan, *Lorenzo in Taos*, pp. 60 and 72.
105. Joseph Needham, *Science and Civilization in China*, vol. 2, pp. 147, 149, 150, 151.
106. Ibid., p. 151.
107. Harry T. Moore, ed., *The Collected Letters of D. H. Lawrence*, vol. 1, p. 23.
108. D. H. Lawrence, "Apropos of *Lady Chatterley's Lover*."

Chapter 4

1. Harry T. Moore, ed., *The Collected Letters of D. H. Lawrence*, vol. 1, p. 442.
2. H. Mori, ed., *A Conversation on D. H. Lawrence*, p. 34.
3. Harry T. Moore, ed., *The Collected Letters of D. H. Lawrence*, vol. 1, p. 330.
4. Ibid., p. 350 and pp. 360–62.
5. Ibid., p. 367.
6. Ibid., p. 393.
7. Bertrand Russell, "Portraits from Memory—III: D. H. Lawrence."
8. Ernest Partridge, "Environmental Ethics: Obstacles and Opportunities."
9. Gregory Bateson, "Style, Grace, and Information in Primitive Art."
10. Paul Delany, *D. H. Lawrence's Nightmare*, pp. 77–79.

11. John Maynard Keynes, *Two Memoirs*, p. 77.
12. Ibid., p. 76.
13. Ibid., pp. 79, 94, 95, 101 and 103.
14. Serge Latouche, "Standard of Living."
15. Jean Robert, "Production."
16. Wolfgang Sachs, "Introduction," *The Development Dictionary*.
17. Ivan Illich, "Needs."
18. Jean Robert, "Production."
19. Harry T. Moore, ed., *The Collected Letters of D. H. Lawrence*, vol. 1, p. 362.
20. Aldous Huxley, in H. Mori, ed., *A Conversation on D. H. Lawrence*, p. 18.
21. Harry T. Moore, ed., *The Collected Letters of D. H. Lawrence*, vol. 1, p. 361 and p. 377.
22. Ibid., p. 330 and p. 351.
23. Paul Delany, *D. H. Lawrence's Nightmare*, p. 118.
24. D. H. Lawrence, "The Crown."
25. D. H. Lawrence, "The Spirit of Place."
26. D. H. Lawrence, "Herman Melville's *Moby Dick*."
27. D. H. Lawrence, "Hawthorne and *The Scarlet Letter*."
28. Michael S. Gazzaniga, "The Split Brain in Man."
29. Robert E. Ornstein, *The Psychology of Consciousness*, p.82.
30. Joseph E. Bogen, "Educating Both Halves of the Brain."
31. Joseph E. Bogen, "The Other Side of the Brain IV. The A/P Ratio."
32. Gary Snyder, *The Old Ways*, p. 60.
33. Marilyn Ferguson, ed., "MacLean's 'triune' theory describes brain hierarchy."
34. D. H. Lawrence, "Education of the People."
35. D. H. Lawrence, "Introduction to These Paintings."
36. Hwa Y. Jung and Petee Jung, "Towards a New Humanism."
37. D. H. Lawrence, *Psychoanalysis of the Unconscious*, p. 57.
38. Ibid., ch. 5.
39. G. Farrington, *Francis Bacon*, p. 146.
40. Joseph Needham, *Science and Civilization in China*, vol. II, p. 581.
41. Gregory Bateson, *Mind and Nature: A Necessary Unity*, pp. 17–19.
42. Ibid., p. 20.
43. Ibid., p. 18.
44. Frieda Lawrence, *Not I But the Wind*, p. 83.
45. Gregory Bateson, "The Logical Categories of Learning and Communication."
46. Earl and Achsah Brewster, *D. H. Lawrence: Reminiscences and Correspondence*, p. 35.
47. Catherine Carswell, *Savage Pilgrimage*, pp. 117–18.
48. D. H. Lawrence, "Education of the People."

49. D. H. Lawrence, *Fantasia of the Unconscious.*
50. D. H. Lawrence, "Enslaved by Civilization."
51. Ibid.
52. Joseph Chilton Pearce, *Magical Child*, p. 92 and 176.
53. D. H. Lawrence, "Education of the People."
54. Joseph Chilton Pearce, *Magical Child*, p. 27.
55. Edith Cobb, *The Ecology of Imagination in Childhood*, p. 32–33.
56. Paul Shepard, *The Tender Carnivore and the Sacred Game*, p. 259.
57. D. H. Lawrence, *Fantasia of the Unconscious*, ch. 7.
58. Ibid., ch. 6.
59. Rhys Davies, "D. H. Lawrence in Bandol."
60. Cynthia Asquith, *Remember and Be Glad*, pp. 144 and 189.
61. Valerie V. Hunt, "A Study of Structural Integration from Neuromuscular, Energy Field, and Emotional Approaches."
62. D. H. Lawrence, "Apropos of *Lady Chatterley's Lover.*"
63. Mabel Luhan, *Lorenzo in Taos*, pp. 5 and 6.

Chapter 5

1. D. H. Lawrence, "New Mexico."
2. John Nichols, *If Mountains Die*, p. 92.
3. Gary Snyder, poetry reading, University of Washington, Seattle, Washington, 1976.
4. John C. Neff, "A Visit to Kiowa Ranch."
5. Dorothy Brett, *Lawrence and Brett*, p. 71.
6. D. H. Lawrence, "St. Mawr."
7. Giuseppi Tucci, *The Theory and Practice of the Mandala*, p. 32.
8. D. H. Lawrence, "St. Mawr."
9. George Santayana quoted in William Everson, *Archetype West*, pp. 57–59.
10. Ibid., p. 166.
11. Mabel Luhan, *Lorenzo in Taos*, p. 3.
12. Robinson Jeffers, "Foreword," in D. H. Lawrence, *Fire and Other Poems.*
13. Gary Snyder, quoted in Thomas Parkinson, "The Poetry of Gary Snyder."
14. Thomas Parkinson, "The Poetry of Gary Snyder."
15. Ibid.
16. John Marin quoted in Joseph Foster, *D. H. Lawrence in Taos*, p. xv.
17. Dolores LaChapelle, *Earth Wisdom*, ch. 5.
18. Vincent Scully, *The Earth, The Temple, and the Gods*, pp. 10 and 11.
19. Ibid., pp. 18 and 19.
20. D. H. Lawrence, "New Mexico."
21. T. Gahusha and John Blick, "Stratigraphy of the Santa Fe Group, New

Mexico."
22. D. H. Lawrence, *Women in Love.*
23. D. H. Lawrence, *Sea and Sardinia.*
24. Ibid.
25. John J. Bodine, *Taos Pueblo.*
26. Elsie Parsons, *Taos Pueblo.*
27. Paula Gunn Allen, "The Sacred Hoop: A Contemporary Indian Perspective on American Indian Literature."
28. Catherine Carswell, *Savage Pilgrimage*, pp. 230 and 231.
29. D. H. Lawrence, *Plumed Serpent.*
30. D. H. Lawrence, *Mornings in Mexico.*
31. Mickey Hart, *Drumming at the Edge of Magic.*
32. John Collier, quoted in Edward Nehls, *D. H. Lawrence: A Composite Biography*, vol. 2, p. 199.
33. Dorothy Brett, *Lawrence and Brett*, p. 87.
34. Mabel Luhan, *Lorenzo in Taos*, p. 76.
35. D. H. Lawrence, "America, Listen to your Own."
36. D. H. Lawrence, "Certain Americans and an Englishman."
37. Melissa Nelson, "Reclaiming an Indigenous Mind."
38. Ralph Metzner, *The Well of Remembrance*, p. 1.
39. C. A. Bowers, *Critical Essays on Education, Modernity, and the Recovery of the Ecological Imperative.*
40. Lawrence, "A Hay Hut Among the Mountains."
41. David Garnett, *Golden Echo*, pp. 244–46.
42. George J. Zytaruk, "Introduction," in *The Quest for Rananim*, p. xviii.
43. Harry T. Moore, ed., *The Collected Letters of D. H. Lawrence*, vol. 1, p. 309.
44. Knud Merrild, *With D. H. Lawrence in New Mexico*, p. 25.
45. Mabel Luhan, *Lorenzo in Taos*, p. 192.
46. Ibid., p. 195.
47. Harry T. Moore, ed., *The Collected Letters of D. H. Lawrence*, vol. 1, p. 343.
48. Richard Aldington, *Life for Life's Sake*, p. 302.
49. Brigit Patmore, "Conversations with D. H. Lawrence."
50. Richard Aldington, "Introduction," in *Mornings in Mexico*, p. vi.
51. Mabel Luhan, *Lorenzo in Taos*, p. 339.
52. Edward Nehls, *D. H. Lawrence: A Composite Biography*, vol. 3, p. 427.
53. Vivian de Sola Pinto and Warren Roberts, eds., *The Complete Poems of D. H. Lawrence*, pp. 716–20.
54. Mabel Luhan, *Lorenzo in Taos*, p. 339.
55. D. H. Lawrence, "New Mexico."
56. D. H. Lawrence, "St. Mawr."

Chapter 6

1. Paul Shepard, "Introduction: Ecology and Man—A Viewpoint."
2. D. H. Lawrence, *Kangaroo*, ch. VIII.
3. Ibid.
4. Edith Cobb, *The Ecology of Imagination in Childhood*, p. 24.
5. D. H. Lawrence, "Aristocracy"; "The Crown"; and Gregory Bateson, "Form, Substance and Difference."
6. Frieda Lawrence, *Memoirs and Correspondence*, p. 273.
7. D. H. Lawrence, "Him with his Tail in his Mouth."
8. Del Ivan Janik, "D. H. Lawrence and Environmental Consciousness."
9. D. H. Lawrence, "Pan in America."
10. D. H. Lawrence, "New Mexico."
11. D. H. Lawrence, "Blessed Are the Powerful."
12. C. G. Jung, "The Phenomenology of the Spirit in Fairy Tales" in *Spirit and Nature*, pp. 438 and 444.
13. James Hillman and Michael Ventura, *We've Had a Hundred Years of Psychotherapy and the World's Getting Worse*, pp. 50 and 51.
14. D. H. Lawrence, "Morality and the Novel."
15. Fritjof Capra, quoted in Marilyn Ferguson, "In search of the 'real': holography, physics, imagination."
16. D. H. Lawrence, "Morality and the Novel."
17. Ibid.
18. D. H. Lawrence, "Him with his Tail in his Mouth."
19. Dorothy Brett, *Lawrence and Brett*, p. 238.
20. D. H. Lawrence, "Reflections on the Death of a Porcupine." Note: When Lawrence writes of the Holy Ghost crying, "I am lifted up! Lo! I am lifted up! I am here!", he is referring to what Jesus is supposed to have said on the cross. In fact, in his short essay, "We Need One Another," Lawrence actually quotes directly from the scripture: "And I, if I be lifted up, will draw all men unto me."
21. D. H. Lawrence, "The Crown."
22. Joseph Needham, *Science and Civilization in China*, vol. 2, p. 33.
23. Chuang Chou quoted in J. Legge, *The Texts of Taoism*, vol. 1, ch. 2.
24. Robert F. Heizer and Theodora Kroeber, eds., *Ishi, the Last Yahi*, p. 236.
25. Joseph Needham, *Science and Civilization in China*, vol. 2, p. 68.
26. Ludwig von Bertalanffy, "General Systems Theory—A Critical Review."
27. Ibid.
28. Ervin Laszlo, *The Systems View of the World*, p. 20.
29. Ibid., p. 25.
30. Ibid., p. 33.
31. Gary Snyder, "Coming in to the Watershed."

32. D. H. Lawrence, *The Rainbow*, ch. 6.
33. D. H. Lawrence, "We Need One Another."
34. D. H. Lawrence, *Psychology of the Unconscious*, p. 26 and "The Crown."
35. Stanley Diamond, *In Search of the Primitive*, pp. 160, 166 and 167.
36. James G. Cowan, "Aboriginal Solitude."
37. Arne Naess. In 1972, Naess first used the words *Deep Ecology* in a lecture at the Third World Future Research Conference in Bucharest. He used the concept of "blossoming" in an unpublished lecture at Pitzer College in Claremont, California in May of 1977. "The universal right to live and blossom" is one of the key concepts in his book, *Ecology, Community and Lifestyle* , pp. 166–67.
38. D. H. Lawrence, *Women in Love*.
39. D. H. Lawrence, "Why the Novel Matters."
40. D. H. Lawrence, *Apocalypse*, p. 45.
41. Ervin Laszlo, *The Systems View of the World*, p. 79.
42. Joseph Needham, *Science and Civilization in China*, vol. 2, p. 488.
43. Martin Heidegger, "The Thing."
44. Vincent Vycinas, *Earth and Gods: An Introduction to the Philosophy of Martin Heidegger*, p. 15.
45. Ibid., p. 235.
46. M. Scott Momaday, "Native American Attitudes to the Environment."
47. For a greater depth of treatment of this subject see Dolores LaChapelle, "Systemic Thinking and Deep Ecology: An Historical Overview."
48. D. H. Lawrence, "Apropos of *Lady Chatterley's Lover*."
49. D. H. Lawrence, "The Individual Consciousness vs. the Social Consciousness."
50. D. H. Lawrence, "Dana's *Two Years Before the Mast*."
51. Earl Brewster, *D. H. Lawrence: Reminiscences and Correspondence*, p. 288.
52. D. H. Lawrence, "The Flying Fish."

Chapter 7

1. Aldous Huxley, *The Letters of D. H. Lawrence*, p. 192.
2. Gertrude Levy, *The Gate of Horn*, p. 35.
3. Ibid., footnote on p. 35.
4. Jacquetta Hawkes, *A Land*, p. 159.
5. Quoted in John Holland Smith, *The Death of Classical Paganism*, p. 17.
6. Ibid., p. 3.
7. Ibid., p. 166.
8. Ibid., p. 242.
9. Ibid., p. 293.

10. George Santayana, quoted in William Everson, *Archetype West*, p. 57.
11. William Edward Hopkin, quoted in Edward Nehls, *D. H. Lawrence: A Composite Biography*, vol. 1, pp. 73 and 75.
12. D. H. Lawrence, *The White Peacock*, ch. 6.
13. D. H. Lawrence, *The Rainbow*, ch. 7.
14. Paul Shepard, *Man in the Landscape*, p. 172.
15. D. H. Lawrence, *Movements in European History*, pp. 32–33.
16. D. H. Lawrence, "Him With His Tail in His Mouth."
17. D. H. Lawrence, *Kangaroo*, ch. XI.
18. Ibid., ch. XII.
19. Ralph Metzner, *The Well of Remembrance*, p. 53.
20. Ibid., p. 13.
21. D. H. Lawrence, *Kangaroo*. ch. 8.
22. D. H. Lawrence, "New Mexico."
23. Frieda Lawrence, *Memoirs and Correspondence*, p. 170.
24. Mabel Luhan, *Lorenzo in Taos*, p. 70.
25. Harry T. Moore, *The Collected Letters of D. H. Lawrence*, vol. 2, p. 757.
26. Catherine Carswell, *Savage Pilgrimage*, pp. 132–33.
27. D. H. Lawrence, "St. Mawr."
28. D. H. Lawrence, "The Woman Who Rode Away."
29. Mabel Luhan, *Lorenzo in Taos*, p. 157.
30. D. H. Lawrence, *The Plumed Serpent*, pp. 251 and 252.
31. Witter Bynner, *Journey with Genius*, p. 22.
32. D. H. Lawrence, *The Plumed Serpent*, p. 51.
33. Ibid., p. 105.
34. Ibid., pp. 120 and 122.
35. L. D. Clark, *Dark Night of the Body*, Plate IV.
36. The name Malintzi, for Kate, which Cipriano suddenly cries out at a crucial time in the story, appears for the first time in the book on page 370. Various critics have remarked that Lawrence arbitrarily changed the name of the goddess which Kate was to become, having given her another name earlier in the book. The other criticism is that the name, Malintzi, does not appear in the Aztec pantheon.

   The name Malintzi, probably comes from the diminutive for la Malinche, a type of the "wailing woman," *la llorona*. A. Bullock says that wailing woman legends are found in Spain as well as Mexico. Forty-two different versions of the legend have been collected in the southwestern United States according to M. Simmons. One of the oldest versions of the legend concerns an Indian woman who was the mistress of Cortez and bore him a child. She killed it to prevent it from being raised as a Spaniard. She wanders to this day searching and wailing for her dead child. In other legends she is crying for her child which was killed by a jealous lover or husband, and in still other legends she has killed the child herself to prevent the wrath of jealousy.

These legends persist to this day as far north as Durango, Colorado. According to A. Bullock, the version in Taos is that she wanders along a waterway, carrying a decapitated child and a bloody axe. Kathleen Summit, a storyteller in Taos, told me that *la llorona* is often seen along the San Cristobal River. This river is near Lawrence's Kiowa ranch.

There are three *la llorona* types: *la llorona*, la Malinche, and la Infeliz Maria, according to E. Miller. The wailing sound is supposed to be felt through the entire body, not just heard in the ear. Some stories say that the cry becomes louder and louder and then fades away.

Although there is no record that Lawrence heard these stories, it seems likely that he did hear something of them while he was in Taos. The fear and awe surrounding the legend of the "wailing woman" would certainly mean more to him as a symbol than some little-known Aztec goddess. In fact it is a very appropriate name for Kate. Just as the original la Malinche seemed to betray her people by bearing a child to Cortez, so this new *la llorona*, Maltinzi, would be the reconciler of the two ways— the Indian and the white. She would be truly the Lady of the Two Ways— just as Ramon was called the Lord of the Two Ways in *The Plumed Serpent*. Sources for *la llorona* legends: Alice Bullock, *The Squaw Tree: Ghosts, Mysteries and Miracles of New Mexico*, (Santa Fe: The Lightning Tree, 1978), Marc Simmons, *Witchcraft in the Southwest: Spanish and Indian Supernaturalism in the Rio Grande*, (Flagstaff: Northland Press, 1974), Elaine K. Miller, *Mexican Folk Narrative from the Los Angeles Area*, (Austin: Univ. of Texas Press, 1973).

37. D. H. Lawrence, *The Plumed Serpent*, p. 415.
38. Harry T. Moore, ed., *The Collected Letters of D. H. Lawrence*, vol. 2, p. 859.
39. Dorothy Brett, *Lawrence and Brett*, p. 71.
40. D. H. Lawrence, *The Trespasser*, ch. XVI.
41. D. H. Lawrence, "Witch a la Mode."
42. D. H. Lawrence, "Sea and Sardinia."
43. D. H. Lawrence, *The Plumed Serpent*, p. 90.
44. John G. Neihardt, *Black Elk Speaks*, p. 180.
45. Alice G. Fletcher, "The Hako: A Pawnee Ceremony."
46. D. H. Lawrence, *The Plumed Serpent*. p. 178.
47. Ibid., ch. XXVI.
48. Vivian de Sola Pinto and Warren Roberts, eds., *The Complete Poems of D. H. Lawrence*, p. 764.
49. Paul Shepard, "A Post-Historic Primitivism."
50. Gary Snyder, *The Old Ways*, pp. 57, 60 and 63.
51. Harry T. Moore, ed., *The Collected Letters of D. H. Lawrence*, vol. 2, p. 833.

52. D. H. Lawrence, *The Plumed Serpent,* p. 388.
53. Vine Deloria, Jr., *God Is Red,* pp. 299, 298 and 294.
54. D. H. Lawrence, *The Plumed Serpent,* pp. 246–47.
55. Ralph Metzner, *The Well of Remembrance,* p. 57.
56. Vine Deloria, Jr., *God Is Red,* pp. 88, 91, 102 and 296.
57. George Barta, quoted in Peter Warshall, ed., "The Voices of Black Lake."
58. Harry T. Moore, ed., *The Collected Letters of D. H. Lawrence,* vol. 2, pp. 796–97.
59. D. H. Lawrence, *The Plumed Serpent,* pp. 389–92.
60. Damiéville, quoted in Joseph Needham, *Science and Civilization in China,* vol. 2, p. 473.
61. Chu Hsi, *The Philosophy of Human Nature,* pp. 269–70.
62. Herbert Fingarette, *Confucius: The Secular as Sacred,* pp. 7 and 8.
63. Ibid., p. 8.
64. Yen Yuan (1635–1704), quoted in William Theodore de Bary, *The Unfolding of Neo-Confucianism,* no paging.
65. William Gerhardi, "Literary Vignettes II."
66. D. H. Lawrence, [Autobiographical Fragment].
67. Katherine Mansfield, *Journal,* p. 141.
68. Frieda Lawrence, *Not I But the Wind,* p. 35.
69. D. H. Lawrence, *The Plumed Serpent,* pp. 357–58.
70. Ibid., pp. 359 and 360.
71. Ibid., p. 332.
72. D. H. Lawrence, "The Individual Consciousness vs. the Social Consciousness."
73. Gerry Gorsline and Linn House, "Future Primitive."
74. John Lame Deer and Richard Erdoes, *Lame Deer, Seeker of Visions,* pp. 243, 244.
75. Stanley Diamond, *In Search of the Primitive,* p. 167.
76. Aldous Huxley, ed., *The Letters of D. H. Lawrence,* p. 679.
77. D. H. Lawrence, "New Mexico."
78. D. H. Lawrence, "The Flying Fish."
79. Catherine Carswell, *Savage Pilgrimage,* p. 82.
80. D. H. Lawrence, "Apropos of *Lady Chatterley's Lover.*"
81. Dolores LaChapelle, *Earth Wisdom,* pp. 168–70.
82. Richard Aldington, *D. H. Lawrence,* p. 373.
83. Richard Aldington, *Life for Life's Sake,* p. 302.
84. Mark Schorer, "Two Houses, Two Ways."
85. Harry T. Moore, ed., *The Collected Letters of D. H. Lawrence,* vol. 2, p. 720.
86. Martin Green, *The Von Richthofen Sisters,* pp. 73 and 343. Note: Another early source of information for Klages and the Cosmic Circle is the scholar, Jane Ellen Harrison. Her book, *Themis: A Study of the Social*

Origins of Greek Religion, was published by Cambridge University Press in 1912 and her *Mythology* was published in 1924. She wrote of the Mother Goddess figures she found in ancient Greek and Cretan sculptures. She explains that "this supremacy of the mother marks a contrast with the Olympian system where Zeus the Father reigns supreme. It stands for the Earth Worship. The Cretan Great Mother was never admitted to Mt. Olympus but many of her sacred animals and attributes were lent to such Olympian goddesses as Artemis, Hera, and others."

Lawrence read Harrison's early book, thus he was familiar with the concepts, which later became the Magna Mater of Otto Gross in connection with Frieda before he ever met her. (See Chapter 3).

Marija Gimbutas's book, *The Goddesses and Gods of Old Europe*, published in 1982, also refers to goddesses which Harrison wrote about. Many recent books on the goddess use Gimbutas as a source, but not as many refer to Harrison's very early work on the goddess. Donna Wilshire's book, *Virgin, Mother, Crone: Myths and Mysteries of the Triple Goddess* (1994), does make use of Harrison's work as well as Gimbutas's and is an excellent basic resource book for the goddess.

87. Ibid., p. 356.
88. Vivian de Sola Pinto and Warren Roberts, eds., *The Complete Poems of D. H. Lawrence*, pp. 296–98.
89. Van Wyck Brooks, "Charles Godfrey Leland."
90. Earl Brewster, *D. H. Lawrence: Reminiscences and Correspondence*, p. 124.
91. Ibid., pp. 127–28.
92. Ibid., p. 277.
93. D. H. Lawrence, *The Man Who Died*.
94. Earl Brewster, *D. H. Lawrence: Reminiscences and Correspondence*, p. 149.
95. George J. Zytaruk, "The Phallic Vision: D. H. Lawrence and V. V. Rozanov."
96. Harry T. Moore, ed., *The Collected Letters of D. H. Lawrence*, vol. 2, p. 973.
97. D. H. Lawrence, "*Solitaria* by V. V. Rozanov."
98. Harry T. Moore, ed., *The Collected Letters of D. H. Lawrence*, vol. 2, p. 966–67.
99. D. H. Lawrence, *Etruscan Places*, p. 55.
100. Ibid., p. 75.
101. Ashley Montagu, "Introduction" in Richard Payne Knight, *Discourse on the Worship of Priapus*, p. vi and vii.
102. Richard Payne Knight, *Discourse on the Worship of Priapus*, pp. 18, 22 and 53.
103. Ibid., pp. 98 and 99.
104. Ibid., p. 69.

105. Thomas Wright, *The Worship of the Generative Powers*, pp. 7 and 8.
106. Ibid., pp. 18 and 28.
107. Ibid., pp. 49 and 50.
108. Ibid., p. 87 and 88.
109. Ibid., p. 42.
110. Ashley Montague, "Introduction" in Richard Payne Knight, *Discourse on the Worship of Priapus*, p. vi.
111. Charles Godfrey Leland, *Etruscan Roman Remains*, no paging.
112. D. H. Lawrence, *Lady Chatterley's Lover*.
113. G. Orioli, *Adventures of a Book Seller*, p. 233.
114. D. H. Lawrence, *Lady Chatterley's Lover*, Ch. XVII.
115. D. H. Lawrence, "If Women Were Supreme."
116. Frederick Carter, *D. H. Lawrence and the Body Mystical*, pp. 34 and 35.
117. Ibid. p. 38.
118. Ibid., p. 60.
119. Harry T. Moore, ed., *The Collected Letters of D. H. Lawrence*, vol. 2, p. 1222.
120. D. H. Lawrence, *Apocalypse*, pp. 41 and 46.
121. Ibid., pp. 195 and 45.
122. Frederick Carter, *D. H. Lawrence and the Body Mystical*, p. 380.
123. Mabel Luhan, *Lorenzo in Taos*, p. 350.
124. Achsah Brewster, *D. H. Lawrence: Reminiscences and Correspondence*, p. 309.
125. William Irwin Thompson, "Notes on an Emerging Planet."
126. D. H. Lawrence, *Apocalypse*, pp. 199 and 200.

Epilogue

1. Frieda Lawrence, *Not I But the Wind*, p. 35.
2. Dorothy Brett, *Lawrence and Brett*, p. 151.
3. Frieda Lawrence, *Not I But the Wind*, p. 200.
4. Vivian de Sola Pinto and Warren Roberts, ed., *The Complete Poems of D. H. Lawrence*, p. 697.

Bibliography

Aldington, Richard. *D. H. Lawrence: Portrait of a Genius But . . . .* New York: Duell, Sloan & Pearce, 1950.

_____. *Life for Life's Sake.* New York: Viking, 1941.

Allen, Paula Gunn. "The Sacred Hoop: A Contemporary Indian Perspective on American Indian Literature." Unpublished handout given to class in the Intercultural Program, Ft. Lewis College, Durango, Colorado, 1979.

Asquith, Cynthia. *Remember and Be Glad.* London: James Barrie, 1952.

Asquith, Herbert. *Moments of Memory: Recollections and Impressions.* New York: Scribner, 1938.

Bateson, Gregory. "Form, Substance, and Difference." *General Semantics Bulletin,* No. 37, 1970.

_____. "The Logical Categories of Learning and Communication." In *Steps To An Ecology of Mind,* Gregory Bateson. New York: Ballantine Books, 1972.

_____. *Mind and Nature: A Necessary Unity.* New York: E. P. Dutton, 1979.

_____. "Style, Grace, and Information in Primitive Art." In *Primitive Art and Society,* edited by Anthony Forge. Oxford: Oxford University Press, 1974.

Bedford, Sybille. *Aldous Huxley.* New York: Harper & Row, 1974.

Blair, Lawrence. *Rhythms of Vision.* New York: Warner Books, 1977.

Bodine, John B. *Taos Pueblo.* Santa Fe: Lightning Tree Press, n.d.

Bogen, Joseph E. "Educating Both Halves of the Brain." Symposium, May 1, 1977, School of Education and College of Continuing Education, The University of Southern California, in cooperation with The Institute for the Study of Human Knowledge, Los Angeles. Unpublished.

_____. "The Other Side of the Brain IV. The A/P Ratio." With Dezure, Tenhouten, and Marsh. *Bulletin of the Los Angeles Neurological Societies,* vol. 37, April 1972.

Bonewits, P. E. I. *Real Magic.* Berkeley: Creative Arts Book Co., 1979.

Bowers, C. A. *Critical Essays on Education, Modernity, and the Recovery of the Ecological Imperative.* New York: Teachers College, Columbia University, 1993.

Brand, Stewart. "Native American Church." *Psychedelic Review*, no. 9 (1967).

Brett, Dorothy. *Lawrence and Brett: A Friendship*. Santa Fe: The Sunstone Press, 1974. Original edition, Philadelphia: Lippincott, 1933.

Brewster, Earl, and Achsah Brewster. *D. H. Lawrence: Reminiscences and Correspondence*. London: Martin Secker, 1934.

Brooks, Van Wyck. "Charles Godfrey Leland." In *Fenollosa and His Circle*. New York: E. P. Dutton, 1962.

Bynner, Witter. *Journey with Genius: Recollections and Reflections Concerning the D. H. Lawrences*. New York: Day, 1951.

Callahan, Bob, ed. *A Jaime de Angulo Reader*. Berkeley: Turtle Island Foundation, 1979.

_____. "The World of Jaime de Angulo." Interview with Robert Duncan in *The Netzahualcoyotl News* 1 (Summer 1979): 1–5, 14–16.

Carswell, Catherine. *The Savage Pilgrimage: A Narrative of D. H. Lawrence*. London: Secker & Warburg, 1951. Original edition, London: Martin Secker, 1932.

Carter, Frederick. *D. H. Lawrence and the Body Mystical*. New York: Haskell House Publishers Ltd., 1972. Reprint of original edition, London: Denis Archer, 1932.

Cavitch, David. *D. H. Lawrence and the New World*. New York: Oxford University Press, 1969.

Chambers, Jessie (E. T.). *D. H. Lawrence: A Personal Record*, ed. J. D. Chambers. 2nd edition. London: Frank Cass & Co. Ltd., 1965. Original edition, London: Jonathan Cape Ltd., 1935.

Chizhevskii, A. L. "Atmospheric Electricity and Life." In *The Earth in the Universe*, edited by V. V. Fedynskii, translated from the Russian. Jerusalem: Israel Program for Scientific Translations, 1968. (Available from the U.S. Dept. of Commerce, Clearinghouse for Federal Scientific and Technical Information, Springfield, VA 22151).

Christie, Walter. "Embracing Biophilia." *Ecopsychology Newsletter*, no. 2 (1994).

Clark, L. D. *Dark Night of the Body: D. H. Lawrence's "The Plumed Serpent."* Austin: University of Texas Press, 1964.

Cobb, Edith. *The Ecology of Imagination in Childhood*. Dallas: Spring Publications, 1993.

_____. "The Ecology of Imagination in Childhood." *Daedalus*, 88 (Summer,

1959): 537–48.

Coon, Carleton S. *The Hunting Peoples*. Boston: Little Brown & Co., 1971.

Corke, Helen. *D. H. Lawrence: The Croydon Years*. Austin: University of Texas Press, 1965.

_____. *Lawrence and Apocalypse*. London: Heinemann, 1933.

Cowan, James G. "Aboriginal Solitude." *Parabola* (February 1992).

Cowen, Ron. "Receptor Encounters: Untangling the Threads of the Serotonin System." *Science News* (October 14, 1989): 248–50.

Dasmann, Ray. "Future Primitive." *CoEvolution Quarterly* (Fall 1976).

Davies, Rhys. "D. H. Lawrence in Bandol." *Horizon II* (October 1940), pp. 191–208.

de Bary, William Theodore. *The Unfolding of Neo-Confucianism*. New York: Columbia University Press, 1975.

Delany, Paul. *D. H. Lawrence's Nightmare*. New York: Basic Books Inc., 1978.

Deloria, Vine, Jr. *God Is Red*. Golden, CO: Fulcrum Publishing, 1973.

Diamond, Stanley. *In Search of the Primitive*. New Brunswick: Transaction Books, Rutgers, 1974.

_____, ed. *Primitive Vision of the World*. New York: Columbia University Press, 1969.

Douglas, Norman. *Looking Back*. New York: Harcourt Brace Jovanovich, 1933.

Ebbatson, Roger. *Lawrence and the Nature Tradition: A Theme in English Fiction*. Atlantic Highlands: Humanities Press Inc., 1980.

Erikson, Erik. *Childhood and Society*. New York: W. W. Norton Inc., 1950.

Everson, William. *Archetype West: The Pacific Coast as a Literary Region*. Berkeley: Oyez, 1976.

Farrington, G. *Francis Bacon: Philosopher of Industrial Science*. New York: Schuman, 1949.

Ferguson, Marilyn. "In search of the 'real': holography, physics, imagination." Report on the conference, "On the Nature of Reality," University of California at Santa Cruz (March 25–27, 1977). In *Brain Mind Bulletin*, February 10, 1977.

_____. "MacLean's 'triune' theory describes brain hierarchy." *Brain Mind Bulletin*. January 12, 1977.

Fingarette, Herbert. *Confucius:The Secular as Sacred*. New York: Harper and Row, 1972.

Fletcher, Alice C. "The Hako: A Pawnee Ceremony." Bureau of American Ethnology, *Twenty-second Annual Report*, Part 2 (1904).

Ford, Ford Madox. *Portraits from Life*. Boston: Houghton Mifflin Co., 1937.

Foster, Joseph. *D. H. Lawrence in Taos*. Albuquerque: University of New Mexico Press, 1972.

Foucault, Michel. *The History of Sexuality*. Vol. 1: An Introduction. New York: Pantheon Books, 1978.

Fowles, John. *The Tree*. Boston: Little Brown and Co., 1979.

Gahusha, T. and John Blick. "Stratigraphy of the Santa Fe Group, New Mexico." *Bulletin of the American Museum of Natural History*, vol. 144 (1971).

Gardiner, Rolf. *England Herself*. London: Faber & Faber, 1943.

Garnett, David. *The Golden Echo*. New York: Harcourt Brace Jovanovich, 1954.

Gauquelin, Michel. *The Cosmic Clocks*. New York: Avon Books, 1969.

Gazzaniga, Michael S. "The Split Brain in Man." *Scientific American* 217 (August, 1967): 24–29.

Gerhardi, William. "Literary Vignettes II." *The Saturday Review*. London, June 20, 1931, pp. 893–94.

Ghiselin, Brewster. "D. H. Lawrence in Bandol." *Western Humanities Review*, XII (Autumn, 1958).

Gimbutas, Marija. *The Goddesses and Gods of Old Europe 6500–3500 B.C.: Myths and Cult Images*. Berkeley: University of California Press, 1982.

Goodheart, Eugene. *The Utopian Vision of D. H. Lawrence*. Chicago: University of Chicago Press, 1963.

Gorsline, Jeremiah and Freeman House. "Future Primitive." In *Bundle #3*, "North Pacific Rim Alive," published in 1974 by Planet Drum Foundation, PO Box 31251, San Francisco CA 94131. Reprinted in *Home! A Bioregional Reader*. Edited by Van Andruss, Christopher Plant, Judith Plant and Eleanor Wright. Gabriola Island, B.C. Canada: New Society Publishers, 1990.

Gray, Cecil. *Musical Chairs, or Between Two Stools*. London: Home and Van Thal, 1948.

Green, Martin. *The Von Richthofen Sisters: The Triumphant and the Tragic Modes of Love*. New York: Basic Books Inc., 1974.

Halifax, Joan. *Shamanic Voices*. New York: E. P. Dutton, 1979.

Harrison, Jane. *Ancient Art and Ritual*. New York: Henry Holt, 1913.

_____. *Mythology*. London: Marshall Jones Co., 1924.

_____. *Themis: A Study of the Social Origins of Greek Religion*. Cambridge: Cambridge University Press, 1912.

Hart, Mickey. *Drumming at the Edge of Magic: A Journey into the Spirit of Percussion*. New York: Harper San Francisco, 1990.

Hawkes, Jacquetta. *A Land*. Boston: Beacon Press, 1994.

Heidegger, Martin. "The Thing." In *Poetry, Language, Thought*, translated by Albert Hofstadter. New York: Harper and Row, 1971.

Heinz, Ruth-Inge. *Shamans of the 20th Century*. New York: Irvington Publishers Inc., 1991.

Heizer, Robert F., and Theodora Kroeber, editors. *Ishi, the Last Yahi: A Documentary History*. Berkeley: University of California Press, 1979.

Hillman, James and Michael Ventura. *We've Had a Hundred Years of Psychotherapy and the World's Getting Worse*. New York: Harper San Francisco, 1992.

Hoffman, Frederick J. and Harry T. Moore, editors. *The Achievement of D. H. Lawrence*. Norman: University of Oklahoma Press, 1953.

Holbrook, May Chambers. "The Chambers Papers." In *D. H. Lawrence: A Composite Biography*, vol. 3, edited by Edward Nehls. Madison: University of Wisconsin Press, 1959.

Holt, John, editor. *Growing Without Schooling*, vol. 1, no. 1 (1977).

Hopkin, William E. "D. H. Lawrence: A Personal Memoir." A talk sponsored by the BBC and recorded by the Birmingham studios of the BBC on August 17, 1949. In *D. H. Lawrence: A Composite Biography*, vol. 1, edited by Edward Nehls. Madison: University of Wisconsin Press, 1957.

Hough, Graham. *The Dark Sun: A Study of D. H. Lawrence*. New York: Macmillan, 1957.

Hsi, Chu. *The Philosophy of Human Nature*, translated by J. Percy Bruce. London: Probsthain & Co., 1932.

Hunt, Valerie V. "A Study of Structural Integration from Neuromuscular, Energy Field, and Emotional Approaches." Rolf Institute, Box 1868, Boulder, Colorado, 1977.

Huxley, Aldous, editor. *The Letters of D. H. Lawrence*. New York: The Viking Press, 1936.

Illich, Ivan. "Needs." In *The Development Dictionary*, edited by Wolfgang

Sachs. London: Zed Books Ltd., 1992.

"The Jaime de Angulo Library," brochure of the Turtle Island Foundation, 2845 Buena Vista Way, Berkeley, California 94708.

Janik, Del Ivan. "D. H. Lawrence and Environmental Consciousness." *Environmental Review* (Winter 1983): 359–71.

Jastrab, Joseph and Ron Schaumburg. *Sacred Manhood, Sacred Earth*. New York: Harper Collins Publishers, 1994.

Jeffers, Robinson. Foreword. In D. H. Lawrence, *Fire and Other Poems*. San Francisco: Grabhorn Press, 1940.

Jung, C. G. "Letter to Miguel Serrano, September 14, 1960." In *C. G. Jung: Letters*, vol. 2, 1951–1961, edited by Gerhard Adler and Aniela Jaffé. Princeton: Princeton University Press, 1973.

_____. *Memories, Dreams, Reflections*, edited by Aniela Jaffé. New York: Vintage, 1963.

_____. "The Phenomenology of the Spirit in Fairy Tales." In *Spirit and Nature, Papers from the Eranos Yearbooks*, vol. 1, edited by Joseph Campbell. Princeton: Princeton University Press, 1954.

Jung, Hwa Yol and Petee Jung. "Towards a New Humanism: The Politics of Civility in a No Growth Society." *Man and World: An International Philosophical Review*, 9 (1976): 283–306.

Keynes, John Maynard. *Two Memoirs: Dr. Melchior: A Defeated Enemy* and *My Early Beliefs*. New York: Augustus M. Kelley, 1949.

King, Emily Lawrence. Contributions to the BBC Third Programme's "Son and Lover," (8 May 1955). In *D. H. Lawrence: A Composite Biography*, vol. 1, edited by Edward Nehls. Madison: University of Wisconsin Press, 1957.

Knight, Richard Payne. *A Discourse on the Worship of Priapus and its Connection with the Mystic Theology of the Ancients*. New York: Julian Press, 1969. Reprint of 1786 edition. (This book also contains the text of Thomas Wright's *The Worship of the Generative Powers*.)

Koestler, Arthur. *The Ghost in the Machine*. New York: Macmillan Co., 1967.

Kramer, Joel. *The Passionate Mind*. Millbrae, California: Celestial Arts, 1974.

Krishnamurti, J. *Freedom from the Known*. New York: Harper and Row, 1975.

LaChapelle, Dolores. *Earth Wisdom*. Los Angeles: Guild of Tutors Press, 1978.

_____. "Systemic Thinking and Deep Ecology: An Historical Overview." *Earthday X Colloquium: On the Humanities and Ecological Consciousness*,

April 21–24, 1980. University of Denver, Denver, Colorado.

_____. and Janet Bourque. *Earth Festivals*. Silverton, CO: Finn Hill Arts, 1985.

Lame Deer, John, and Richard Erdoes. *Lame Deer, Seeker of Visions*. New York: Simon and Schuster, 1972.

Laszlo, Ervin. *The Systems View of the World*. New York: George Braziller, 1972.

Latouche, Serge. "Standard of Living." In *The Development Dictionary*, edited by Wolfgang Sachs. London: Zed Books Ltd., 1992.

Lawrence, Ada, and G. Stuart Gelder. *Young Lorenzo: Early Life of D. H. Lawrence*. New York: Russell & Russell, 1966. Reprint of 1931 edition.

Lawrence, David Herbert. "America, Listen to Your Own." *New Republic* (December 15, 1920). Reprinted in *Phoenix: The Posthumous Papers of D. H. Lawrence*, edited by Edward D. MacDonald. New York: The Viking Press, 1968 pp. 87–91.

_____. *Apocalypse*. New York: The Viking Press, 1966. Paging from Viking Compass edition.

_____. "Apropos of *Lady Chatterley's Lover*." London: Mandrake Press, 1930. Reprinted in *Phoenix II: Uncollected, Unpublished, and Other Prose Works by D. H Lawrence*, edited by Warren Roberts and Harry T. Moore. New York: The Viking Press, 1968, pp. 487–515.

_____. "Aritisocracy." In *Reflections on the Death of a Porcupine and Other Essays*, Michael Herbert, ed. Cambridge: Cambridge University Press, 1988, pp. 365–76.

_____. [Autobiographical Fragment]. In *Phoenix*. New York: The Viking Press, 1968, pp. 817–38.

_____. "Autobiographical Sketch." In *D. H. Lawrence: A Composite Biography*, vol. 3, edited by Edward Nehls. Madison: University of Wisconsin Press, 1959. Reprinted in *Phoenix II*. New York: The Viking Press, 1968, pp. 300–02.

_____. "Blessed Are the Powerful." In *Reflections on the Death of a Porcupine*. Philadelphia, 1925. *Reprinted in Phoenix II*. New York: The Viking Press, 1968, pp. 436–43.

_____. "Certain Americans and an Englishman." *New York Times* (December 1922).

_____. "The Crown." *The Signature* (October 8, October 18, and November 4, 1915). Reprinted in *Phoenix II*. New York: The Viking Press, 1968, pp.

365–415.

_____. "Dana's *Two Years Before the Mast*." In *Studies in Classic American Literature*. New York: Albert & Charles Boni, 1930.

_____. "Education of the People." In *Phoenix*. New York: The Viking Press, 1968, pp. 587–668.

_____. "Enslaved by Civilization." In *Phoenix II*. New York: The Viking Press, 1968.

_____. *Etruscan Places*. In *Twilight in Italy*, introduction by Anthony Burgess. New York: The Viking Press, 1972. (Several short books collected in this volume.)

_____. *Fantasia of the Unconscious*. New York: The Viking Press, 1960.

_____. "Flowery Tuscany." *New Criterion* (October, November, December, 1927). Reprinted in *Phoenix*. New York: The Viking Press, 1968.

_____. "The Flying Fish." In *Phoenix*. New York: The Viking Press, 1968.

_____. "Gifts of Fortune, by H. M. Tomlinson." In *Phoenix*. New York: The Viking Press, 1968.

_____. "Hawthorne and *The Scarlet Letter*." In *Studies in Classic American Literature*. New York: Albert & Charles Boni, 1930.

_____. "A Hay Hut Among the Mountains." In *Love Among the Haystacks and Other Pieces*. London, 1930. Reprinted in *Phoenix II*. New York: The Viking Press, 1968, pp. 37–43.

_____. "Herman Melville's *Moby Dick*." In *Studies in Classic American Literature*. New York: Albert & Charles Boni, 1930.

_____. "Him with his Tail in his Mouth." In *Reflections on the Death of a Porcupine*. Philadelphia, 1925. Reprinted in *Phoenix II*, pp. 426–35.

_____. "The Hopi Snake Dance." In *Mornings in Mexico*. London: William Heinemann Ltd., no date, pp. 61–79.

_____. "If Women Were Supreme." *Evening News* (October 5, 1928). Reprinted under the title, "Matriarchy," in *Phoenix II*. New York: The Viking Press, 1968, pp. 549–52.

_____. "Indians and Entertainment." In *Mornings in Mexico*. London: William Heinemann Ltd., n.d., pp. 45–53.

_____. "The Individual Consciousness vs. the Social Consciousness." In *Phoenix*. New York: The Viking Press, 1968, pp. 761–64.

_____. "Introduction to These Paintings." In *The Paintings of D. H. Lawrence*. London: Mandrake Press, 1929. Reprinted in *Phoenix*. New York: The

Viking Press, 1968, pp. 551–86.

_____. *Kangaroo*. New York: The Viking Press, 1960. Paging from Compass Books Edition.

_____. *Lady Chatterley's Lover*. New York: The New American Library Inc., 1959.

_____. "A Little Moonshine with Lemon." In *Mornings in Mexico*. London: William Heinemann Ltd., n.d., pp. 80–82.

_____. *The Lost Girl*. London: William Heinemann Ltd., 1955.

_____. *Love Among the Haystacks*. In *Four Short Novels*. New York: The Viking Press, 1965. Paging from the Compass Books Edition.

_____. ". . . Love Was Once a Little Boy." In *Reflections on the Death of a Porcupine*. Philadelphia, 1925. Reprinted in *Phoenix II*. New York: The Viking Press, 1968, pp. 444–59.

_____. *The Man Who Died*. In *St. Mawr and The Man Who Died*. New York: Random House, Vintage Books Edition, n.d.

_____. "The Manufacture of Good Little Boys." *Vanity Fair* (September 1929). Reprinted in *Phoenix II*. New York: The Viking Press, 1968, pp. 578–81.

_____. "Mercury." *Atlantic Monthly* (February 1927). Reprinted in *Phoenix*. New York: The Viking Press, 1968, pp. 35-39.

_____. "Morality and the Novel." *Calendar of Modern Letters* (December 1925). Reprinted in *Phoenix*. New York: The Viking Press, 1968, pp. 527–32.

_____. *Mornings in Mexico*, Introduction by Richard Aldington. London: William Heinemann Ltd., n.d.

_____. *Movements in European History*. London: Oxford University Press, 1921. (Originally printed under the pseudonym, Lawrence H. Davison.) Reissued by Oxford University Press, 1971 under D. H. Lawrence's own name.

_____. "New Mexico." *Survey Graphic* (January, 1918). Reprinted in *Phoenix*. New York: The Viking Press, 1968, pp. 141–50.

_____. "Nottingham and the Mining Countryside." *Adelphi* (June–August 1930). Reprinted in *Phoenix*. New York: The Viking Press, 1968, pp. 133–40.

_____. "Pan in America." In *Phoenix*. New York: The Viking Press, 1968, pp. 22–31.

_____. *The Plumed Serpent*. New York: Alfred A. Knopf, 1951.

_____. *Psychoanalysis and the Unconscious* and *Fantasia of the Unconscious*.

New York: The Viking Press, 1960.

_____. *The Rainbow*. New York: Viking Press, 1961. Paging from Penguin Books Edition, 1977.

_____. "Reflections on the Death of a Porcupine." In *Reflections on the Death of a Porcupine and Other Essays*, Michael Herbert, ed. Cambridge: Cambridge University Press, 1988, pp. 347–64.

_____. "Review of *Gifts of Fortune* by H. M. Tomlinson." Reprinted in *Phoenix*. New York: The Viking Press, 1968, p. 343.

_____. *Sea and Sardinia*. New York: The Viking Press, 1961.

_____. "*Solitaria*, by V. V. Rozanov." *Calendar of Modern Letters* (July 1927). Reprinted in *Phoenix*. New York: The Viking Press, 1968, pp. 367-371.

_____. *Sons and Lovers*. New York: The Viking Press, 1958. Paging from Viking Compass Edition.

_____. "The Spirit of Place." In *Studies in Classic American Literature*. New York: Albert & Charles Boni, 1930.

_____. *St. Mawr* and *The Man Who Died*. New York: Random House, Vintage Books Edition. n.d.

_____. *Studies in Classic American Literature*. New York: Viking, 1961.

_____. "Study of Thomas Hardy." In *Phoenix*. New York: The Viking Press, 1968, pp. 398–516.

_____. "Sun." In *The Complete Short Stories of D. H. Lawrence*, vol. II. New York: The Viking Press, 1961. Viking Compass Edition, pp. 528–45.

_____. *The Trespasser*. London: William Heinemann Ltd., 1955.

_____. *Twilight in Italy*. London: Heinemann, 1950.

_____. "We Need One Another." *Scribner's Magazine* (May 1930). Reprinted in *Phoenix*. New York: The Viking Press, 1968, pp. 188–95.

_____. *The White Peacock*. Carbondale: Southern Illinois University Press, 1966.

_____. "Whitman." In *Studies in Classic American Literature*. New York: Albert & Charles Boni, 1930.

_____. "Why the Novel Matters." In *Phoenix*. New York: The Viking Press, 1968, pp. 533–38.

_____. "The Witch A La Mode." In *The Complete Short Stories of D. H. Lawrence*, vol. I. New York: The Viking Press, 1961. Viking Compass Edition, pp. 54–70.

_____. "The Woman Who Rode Away." In *The Complete Short Stories of D. H.*

Lawrence, vol. II. New York: The Viking Press, 1961. Viking Compass Edition, pp. 546–81.

_____. *Women in Love*. New York: The Viking Press, 1960.

Lawrence, Frieda. *Frieda Lawrence: The Memoirs and Correspondence*, ed. E. W. Tedlock, Jr. London: William Heinemann Ltd., 1961.

_____. *Not I But the Wind*. New York: The Viking Press, 1934. Paging from reprint. St. Clair Shores, Michigan: Scholarly Press Inc., 1972.

Leavis, F. R. *D. H. Lawrence, Novelist*. New York: Alfred A. Knopf, 1965.

Lee, R. B., and I. Devore, editors. *Man the Hunter*. Chicago: Aldine Press, 1968.

Legge, James, translator. *The Texts of Taoism*, vol. 1. Oxford: Oxford University Press, 1891.

Leland, Charles Godfrey. *Etruscan Roman Remains*. London: T. Fisher Unwin, 1892.

Lesemann, Maurice. "D. H. Lawrence in New Mexico." *The Bookman*, LIX (March 1924): 29–32.

Leviton, Richard. "How the Weather Affects Your Health." *East West* (September 1989): 64–67, 112–13.

Levy, Gertrude. *The Gate of Horn: A Study of the Religious Conceptions of the Stone Age and their Influence upon European Thought*. London: Faber & Faber, n.d.

Lewis, C. S. *Surprised by Joy: The Shape of My Early Life*. London: Collins, 1965.

Luhan, Mabel Dodge. *Lorenzo in Taos*. New York: Alfred Knopf, 1932.

Lutyens, Mary. *Krishnamurti: Years of Awakening*. New York: Farrar, Strauss & Giroux, 1975.

Mansfield, Katherine. *Journal*. J. Middleton Murry, ed. London: Constable, 1954.

Marshack, Alexander. "The Compleat Calendar." *The Sciences* IV No. (1965).

Meeker, Joseph W., ed. *New Natural Philosophy Reader*. Los Angeles: Guild of Tutors Press (forthcoming).

Merrild, Knud. *With D. H. Lawrence in New Mexico: A Memoir of D. H. Lawrence*. New York: Barnes and Noble, Inc., 1965.

Metzner, Ralph. *The Well of Remembrance: Rediscovering the Earth Wisdom Myths of Northern Europe*. Boston: Shambhala, 1994.

Meyerhoff, Barbara G. "Balancing Between Worlds: The Shaman's Calling."

Parabola 1 (Spring 1976): 6–13.

Meyers, Jeffrey. *D. H. Lawrence: A Biography*. New York: Alfred A. Knopf, 1990.

Miles, Josephine. *Eras and Modes in English Poetry*. Berkeley: University of California Press, 1964.

Momaday, M. Scott. "Native American Attitudes to the Environment." In *Seeing with a Native Eye*, edited by Walter Holden Capps. New York: Harper & Row, 1976, pp. 80–82.

Moore, Harry T., ed. *The Collected Letters of D. H. Lawrence*. 2 vols. New York: The Viking Press, 1962.

_____. *The Priest of Love: A Life of D. H. Lawrence*. New York: Farrar, Strauss and Giroux, 1974.

Mori, Haruhide, ed. "A Conversation on D. H. Lawrence." Transcription of a panel discussion, March 7, 1952, the twenty-second anniversary of Lawrence's death. The panel consisted of Aldous Huxley, Frieda Lawrence Ravagli, Majl Ewing, Lawrence Clark Powell and Dorothy Mitchell Conway. Los Angeles: Friends of the UCLA Library, 1974.

Murry, John Middleton. *Son of Woman: The Story of D. H. Lawrence*. Jonathan Cape, 1954. Reissue of the 1931 edition, paging the same.

Naess, Arne. *Ecology, Community and Lifestyle: Outline of an Ecosophy*. Cambridge: Cambridge University Press, 1989.

Needham, Joseph. *Science and Civilization in China*, vol. 2. Cambridge: Cambridge University Press, 1956.

Neff, John C. "A Visit to Kiowa Ranch." *The New Mexico Quarterly* VII (May 1937): 116–20.

Nehls, Edward. *D. H. Lawrence: A Composite Biography*. 3 vols. Madison: University of Wisconsin Press, 1957–1959.

Neihardt, John G. *Black Elk Speaks*. Lincoln: University of Nebraska Press, 1961.

Nelson, Melissa. "Reclaiming an Indigenous Mind." *Ecopsychology Newsletter*, No. 2, 1994.

The Netzahualcoyotl News 1 (Summer 1979). Berkeley, Turtle Island Foundation, 1979.

Neville, George H. "The Early Days of D. H. Lawrence." *The London Mercury* XXIII (March 1931): 477–80.

Nichols, John. *If Mountains Die: A New Mexico Memoir*. New York: Alfred A.

Knopf, 1979.

Nin, Anais. *D. H. Lawrence: An Unprofessional Study*. London: E. W. Titmus, 1932. Reissued Denver: A. Swallow, 1964.

Olmsted, D. L. *Achumawi Dictionary* (University of California Publication in Linguistics) Vol. 45. Berkeley: University of California Press, 1966.

Ong, Walter J. *The Presence of the Word: Some Prolegomena for Cultural and Religious History*. New Haven: Yale University Press, 1967.

Orioli, G. *Adventures of a Bookseller*. New York: McBride, 1938.

Ornstein, Robert E. *The Psychology of Consciousness*. San Francisco: W. H. Freeman & Co., 1972.

Parkinson, Thomas. "The Poetry of Gary Snyder." In *The Southern Review* (July 1968): 616–32.

Parsons, Elsie. *Taos Pueblo*. Reno: Sage Books, 1963.

Partridge, Ernest "Environmental Ethics: Obstacles and Opportunities." Paper presented at *Earthday X Colloquium: On the Humanities and Ecological Consciousness*, April 21–24, 1980. University of Denver, Denver, Colorado.

Patmore, Brigit. "Conversations with D. H. Lawrence." *The London Magazine* IV (June 1957): 31–45.

Pearce, Joseph Chilton. *Magical Child*. New York: E. P. Dutton, 1977.

Pelletier, Wilfred, and Ted Poole. *No Foreign Land*. New York: Pantheon Books, 1973.

Petersen, William. *Man, Weather, Sun*. Springfield: Charles C. Thomas, 1947.

Pinto, Vivian de Sola, and Warren Roberts, eds. *The Complete Poems of D. H. Lawrence*. London: William Heinemann, 1957.

Poggioli, Renato. *The Phoenix and the Spider*. Cambridge: Harvard University Press, 1957.

Prichard, Katharine Susannah. "Lawrence in Australia." *Meanjin: A Literary Magazine*, 15 (1954): 2–7.

Rappaport, Roy A. "Energy and the Structure of Adaptation." *CoEvolution Quarterly* (spring, 1974), pp. 20-28.

Rexroth, Kenneth. *An Autobiographical Novel*. New York: New Directions, 1969.

Rifkin, Jeremy. *Time Wars*. New York: A Touchstone Book, 1989.

Robert, Jean. "Production." In *The Development Dictionary*, edited by Wolfgang Sachs. London: Zed Books Ltd., 1992.

Rowse, A. L. *The English Past: Evocations of Persons and Places*. New York: Macmillan, 1952.

Russell, Bertrand. "Portraits from Memory—III: D. H. Lawrence." *Harper's Magazine* CCVI (February 1953): 93–95.

Sachs, Wolfgang, ed. *The Development Dictionary*. London: Zed Books, 1992.

Sagar, Keith. *The Life of D. H. Lawrence*. New York: Pantheon Books, 1980.

Sahlins, Marshall. *Stone Age Economics*. Chicago: Aldine-Atherton Inc., 1972.

Schoenberner, Franz. *Confessions of a European Intellectual*. New York: Macmillan, 1946.

Schorer, Mark. "Two Houses, Two Ways." *New World Writing*. New York: The New American Library of World Literature Inc., 1953.

Schweickart, Russell. "No Frames, No Boundaries." In *Earth's Answer*, edited by Michael Katz, William P. Marsh, and G. G. Thompson. New York: Lindisfarne Books/Harper & Row, 1977.

Scully, Vincent. *The Earth, the Temple, and the Gods: Greek Sacred Architecture*. New Haven: Yale University Press, 1962.

_____. *Pueblo/Mountain, Village, Dance*. New York: The Viking Press, 1975.

Shepard, Paul. "Introduction: Ecology and Man—A Viewpoint." In *The Subversive Science: Essays Toward An Ecology of Man*, edited by Paul Shepard and Daniel McKinley. Boston: Houghton Mifflin Co., 1969.

_____. *Man in the Landscape: A Historic View of the Esthetics of Nature*. New York: Alfred A. Knopf, 1967.

_____. "A Post-Historic Primitivism." In *the Wilderness Condition: Essays on Environment and Civilization*, Max Oelschlaeger, ed. San Francisco: Sierra Club, 1992, pp. 40–89.

_____. *The Tender Carnivore and the Sacred Game*. New York: Charles Scribner's Sons, 1973.

Shrapnel, Norman. "Eastwood Turns the Immortal Memory to Account." *Manchester Guardian*. March 18, 1955, p. 7.

Smith, John Holland. *The Death of Classical Paganism*. New York: Charles Scribner's Sons, 1976.

Snyder, Gary. "Coming into the Watershed." Speech given at the Conference for the Center of California Studies on February 6, 1992.

_____. *The Old Ways*. San Francisco: City Lights Books, 1977.

Spilka, Mark. *The Love Ethic of D. H. Lawrence*. Bloomington: Indiana University Press, 1955.

Steiner, Stan. "The Sun Is Becoming Darker: The Ultimate Energy Crisis." *Akwesasne Notes* (Autumn 1974).

Stevens, Henry Bailey. *The Recovery of Culture.* New York: Harper & Row, 1949.

Taimni, I. K. *The Science of Yoga; A Commentary on the Yoga-Sutras of Patanjali in the Light of Modern Thought.* Wheaton: The Theosophical Publishing House, 1967.

Tedlock, Ernest W., Jr. *D. H. Lawrence, Artist and Rebel.* Albuquerque: University of New Mexico Press, 1963.

Thompson, William Irwin. "Notes on an Emerging Planet." In *Earth's Answer,* edited by Michael Katz, William P. Marsh and G. G. Thompson. New York: Lindisfarne Books/Harper & Row, 1977, pp. 206–29.

Tindall, William York. *D. H. Lawrence and Susan His Cow.* New York: Columbia University Press, 1939.

Tucci, Giuseppi. *The Theory and Practice of the Mandala.* New York: Samuel Weiser, 1973.

von Bertalanffy, Ludwig. "General Systems Theory—A Critical Review." In *General Systems Yearbook of the Society for General Systems Research,* 7 (1962): 1–20.

Vycinas, Vincent. *Earth and Gods: An Introduction to the Philosophy of Martin Heidegger.* The Hague: Martinus Nijhoff, 1961.

Waller, Robert. "Out of the Garden of Eden." *New Scientist and Science Journal* 49 (September 2, 1971): 528.

Warshall, Peter, ed. "The Voices of Black Lake." *CoEvolution Quarterly* 39 (winter 1976–77): 64–69.

Waters, Frank. *Pumpkin Seed Point.* Chicago: Sage Books, 1969.

Watson, Lyall. *Heaven's Breath: A Natural History of the Wind.* New York: William Morrow & Co., 1984.

White, Jonathan. *Talking on the Water: Conversations about Nature and Creativity.* San Francisco: Sierra Club Books, 1994.

Whyte, David. *The Heart Aroused.* New York: Doubleday, 1994.

Wickramasinghe, Martin. *The Mysticism of Lawrence.* Colombo, Ceylon: M. D. Gunasena and Company, 1951.

Wilshire, Donna. *Virgin Mother Crone: Myths and Mysteries of the Triple Goddess.* Rochester: Inner Traditions, 1994.

Wilson Edward O. *Biophilia.* Cambridge: Harvard University Press, 1984.

_____. *The Diversity of Life*. Cambridge: Harvard University Press, 1992.

Wright, Thomas. *The Worship of the Generative Powers During the Middle Ages of Western Europe*. New York: Julian Press, 1969. Reprint of the 1866 edition. (This book also contains the text of Richard Knight's *A Discourse on the Worship of Priapus*.)

Zytaruk, George. "The Phallic Vision: D. H. Lawrence and V. V. Rozanov." *Comparative Literature Studies* IV (1967): 283–97.

_____, ed. *The Quest for Rananim: D. H. Lawrence's Letters to S. S. Kotelianky, 1914 to 1930*. Montreal: McGill-Queen's University Press, 1970.

Index